IN
DEFENSE
OF
HISTORY

Also by Richard J. Evans

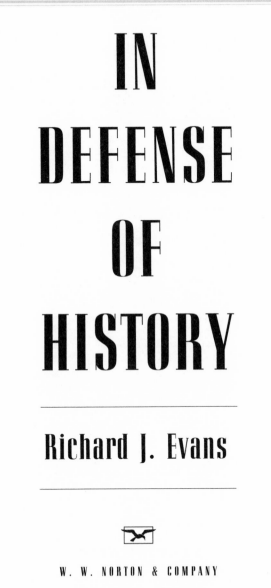

IN DEFENSE OF HISTORY

Richard J. Evans

W. W. NORTON & COMPANY

NEW YORK · LONDON

For information about permission to reproduce selections from this book, write to Permissions,
W. W. Norton & Company, Inc., 500 Fifth Avenue, New York, NY 10110.

The text of this book is composed in Bembo
with the display set in Corvinus Skyline
Desktop composition by Lane Kimball Trubey
Manufacturing by The Maple-Vail Book Manufacturing Group
Book design by JAM Design

Library of Congress Cataloging-in-Publication Data

Evans, Richard J.
In defense of history / Richard J. Evans. —1st American ed.
p.   cm.
Rev. ed. of: In defense of history.
Includes Bibliographical references and index.
ISBN 0-393-04687-7
I. Evans, Richard J. In defense of history. II. Title.
D16.8.E847   1999
907—dc21   98-24422
CIP

W. W. Norton & Company, Inc., 500 Fifth Avenue, New York, N.Y. 10110
http://www.wwnorton.com

W. W. Norton & Company Ltd., 10 Coptic Street, London CW1A 1PU

1 2 3 4 5 6 7 8 9 0

For Christine, with love

CONTENTS

ACKNOWLEDGMENTS

My first debt is to the students at Birkbeck College, University of London, with whom I have spent many fruitful evenings discussing historical knowledge, truth, and objectivity and to the colleagues in the History Department at Birkbeck who encouraged me to turn my rough ideas on history and its current predicament into a book. During the many rewritings and reworkings of the text since then I have had the benefit of constructive criticism from many people, but I would especially like to thank David Cannadine for his wise criticisms and Neil Belton, at Granta Books, for his detailed and helpful comments. Ros Tatham helped me find out what happened at the Stalybridge Wakes. Christine Corton, as always, has provided support and encouragement and read the proofs with a trained eye. My thanks to all of them.

RICHARD J. EVANS
London, March 1997

PREFACE TO THE AMERICAN EDITION

FOR this American edition I have included consideration of major work that has been published in this field since March 1997, added or amended a few historical examples to make them more relevant to an American readership, and altered a few passages where it seemed to me that the critics of the British edition had succeeded in finding obscurities or errors in the text. The essence of my arguments, however, remains unchanged. I am grateful to Steve Forman, of W. W. Norton & Company, for his help and advice. A comprehensive and periodically updated reply to my critics can be found at the following Web site: http://ihr.sas.ac.uk/ihr/reviews.mnu.html.

RICHARD J. EVANS
London, February 1998

IN
DEFENSE
OF
HISTORY

INTRODUCTION

I

THIS book is not about history, but about how we study it, how we research and write about it, and how we read it. In the postmodern age, historians are being compelled to address these questions afresh. Of course, there have been many attempts to tackle them in the past. But they need to be confronted by every new generation of historians in turn. Currently the field is held by two books published thirty or more years ago by the British historians Edward Hallett Carr and Sir Geoffrey Elton. E. H. Carr's *What Is History?* has been widely used as an introduction to historical study by teachers and students since its first publication in 1961, and it is easy to see why. Carr was a practicing historian of vast experience, who had the ability to think clearly about difficult philosophical issues and to communicate his thought in a concise, witty, and thoroughly readable manner. *What Is History?* does not talk down to the student in the manner of conventional history primers or introductions to the study of history. It addresses itself to the reader as an equal. Carr engages in lively arguments with many other historians about the nature of history. He challenges and undermines the belief, brought to university study by too many students on leaving high school, that history is simply a matter of objective fact. He introduces them to the idea that history books, like the people who write them, are products of their own times, bringing particular ideas and ideologies to bear on the past.

Against Carr's relativistic approach to historical study, it is common practice to pit G. R. Elton's *The Practice of History,* published in 1967. Elton's book mounts a trenchant defense of the belief that history is a search for the objective truth about the past. It concludes optimistically that historians' efforts in this enterprise more often than not meet with success. Elton, too, was a practicing historian of enormous experience, and in the course of dispensing a good deal of sensible advice on how history should be studied, written, and taught, his book also had a lot to say about particular historians and the ways in which they either lived up to or (more commonly) failed to live up to the ideals he proclaimed. While Carr championed a sociological approach to the past, Elton declared that any serious historical work should have a narrative of political events at its core. Those which did not, he dismissed as not really being proper history at all. And while Carr enjoined his readers to study the historian before they studied his "facts," Elton told his readers to focus above all on the documentary record left by the past, the ultimate arbiter of historical accuracy and truth, and to leave historians and their motives to themselves.

While both Elton and Carr are still very much worth reading, there is, however, as critics have remarked, something rather strange about two books written more than thirty years ago still serving as basic introductions to a scholarly discipline.[1] Yet in many colleges and universities in Britain, the United States, and other countries they undoubtedly do.[2] Although some historians seem to think that Elton continues to represent "conventional wisdom in the historical profession,"[3] or (more pretentiously) the "*doxa* amongst professional academic historians,"[4] in practice this has long ceased to be the case. Few historians would now defend the hard-line concept of historical objectivity espoused by Elton. The prevalence of historical controversy, endemic in the profession for decades, has long since disabused historians of the idea that the truth lies buried in the documents and that once the historian has unearthed it, no one ever need perform the same operation again. It is more true to say that there has been a "merging of the mainstreams around the E. H. Carr position," insofar as there is any general agreement among historians at all.[5]

Nothing has outdated the views not only of Elton, but even of Carr, more obviously than the arrival in the 1980s of postmodernist theory, which has called into question many, if not most, of the arguments put forward by both of them.[6] Instead of causes, which Carr regarded as central to historical scholarship, the "linguistic turn" has given us discourses. History is widely argued to be only one discourse among many. The notion of scientific history, based on the rigorous investigation of primary sources, has been widely attacked. Increasing numbers of writers on the subject deny that there is any such thing as historical truth or objectivity—both concepts defended, in different ways, by Carr as well as Elton. The question is now not so much "What Is History?" as "Is It Possible to Do History at All?" The result has been that in place of the optimistic belief in the progress of the discipline held in different ways by both Carr, who saw it in the expansion of historical scholarship, and Elton, who saw it in the accumulation of historical knowledge, historians at the end of the twentieth century are haunted by a growing, fin-de-siècle sense of gloom. "A time of uncertainty and of epistemological crisis; a critical turning point: such," observed the French historian Roger Chartier in 1994, "are the diagnoses, mostly apprehensive, given of history in recent years."[7] The intellectual historian David Harlan, writing in 1989, thought that historical studies were indeed undergoing "an extended epistemological crisis."[8] In the mid-1990s, American historians Joyce Appleby, Lynn Hunt, and Margaret Jacob echoed this view: "History has been shaken right down to its scientific and cultural foundations."[9] The postmodernist view that language could not relate to anything except itself must, as another alarmed historian observed, "entail the dissolution of history" and "necessarily jeopardises historical study as normally understood."[10] The postmodernist challenge, warned distinguished Princeton historian Lawrence Stone, had plunged the historical profession "into a crisis of self-confidence about what it is doing and how it is doing it."[11] The sense of crisis is widespread.[12] "Historians," declared another writer on the subject, "have suffered a major theoretical challenge to the validity of their subject."[13] Some indeed see this challenge as more than merely theoretical: "Poststructuralism," in one historian's opinion, even "threatens to throw historians out of work" by robbing their discipline of its traditional legitimacy and raison d'être.[14] Thus, according to one outraged Australian academic, what we are witnessing is the "killing of history," in which the traditional practice of the discipline "is a visibly deteriorating path to research grants, publication, conferences and academic employment."[15] Such has been the power and influence of the postmodernist critique of history that growing numbers of historians themselves are abandoning the search for truth, the belief in objectivity, and the quest for a scientific approach to the past. David Harlan has even gone so far as to remark that "by the end of the 1980s most historians—even most working historians—had all but given up on the possibility of acquiring reliable, objective knowledge about the past."[16] If this is indeed the case, no wonder so many historians are worried about the future of their discipline.

I I

YET far from this sense of crisis being universal among practicing historians, many commentators have discerned a widespread sense of complacency among historians in the mid-1980s. While American intellectual historian Allan Megill indicted the historical profession in 1989 for what he called its "sclerotic self-satisfaction"[17] in the face of the postmodernist challenge, the medievalist Nancy F. Partner, writing in 1995, thought this same attitude was "entirely commendable," adding:

> The theoretical destabilizing of history achieved by language-based modes of criticism has had no practical effect on academic practice because academics have had nothing to gain and everything to lose by dismantling their special visible code of evidence-grounded reasoning and opening themselves to the inevitable charges of fraud, dishonesty and shoddiness.[18]

British historian James Vernon similarly complained in 1994 about his colleagues' "general air of complacency" about postmodernism. "While elsewhere," he noted, "historians are at least discussing the problems of writing social history in the 1990s, indeed the possibility of writing 'history' at all in these post-modern times, the editorial of *Social History*'s fiftieth issue boldly declared that 'social history is emphatically not in crisis.' "[19] "Far from the historian being beleaguered," another British historian, Patrick Joyce, observed in 1991, "the commanding heights of academy history seem secure against the skirmishing bands outside, though some notable walls have fallen, chiefly in the United States." In Britain, Joyce's view is that "rank indifference rather than outright hostility" is the "dominant response."[20] Much of "the historical profession at large," he has complained, has tended to "fail to register the intellectual history of their own time, above all the now decades-long challenge to received ways of historical thinking represented by what may loosely be termed post-modernism."[21] In 1995 he repeated his charge in an article published as a contribution to a controversy on history and postmodernism in the British journal *Social History*. "The *Social History* journal he commented, somewhat ungratefully abusing the publication which has formerly acted as a vehicle for his arguments, "is a good example . . . of the poacher turned gamekeeper. The elders of social history remain in station still, supported by a younger generation of scholars largely immune to the intellectual history of our own times."[22]

Of course, by "the intellectual history of our own times," what Joyce really meant was his own ideas. The fact that they were being debated in the journal itself amounted to an implicit rebuttal of his complaint. Thanks not least to Joyce's own interventions, the debate in Britain has become steadily more heated and has been gathering pace in an increasing number of scholarly journals. Already by 1993 two American specialists in British history could describe it as "a now all-pervasive academic discourse."[23] In 1995 even the much-maligned editor of *Social History* was forced to admit that as a result of the emergence of postmodernism, the optimism with which he had founded the journal in the late 1970s was now "in shreds."[24] By the late 1990s, therefore, there can be little doubt that the debate about history, truth, and objectivity unleashed by postmodernism has become too widespread for all but the most obscurantist to ignore. The critics' complaints of complacency and self-satisfaction among the historical profession now seem to be little more than a rhetorical means of goading those whom they are criticizing into making a reply.

No less a traditionalist than Sir Geoffrey Elton himself charged into the lists not long before he died, to underline the growing sense among historians that the enterprise in which they were engaged was under severe and unprecedented attack. Elton roundly denounced postmodernist ideas on history as "menacing," "destructive," "absurd," and "meaningless." "Total relativism," he declared, was "the ultimate heresy," a "virus" of "frivolous nihilism" that was infecting a disturbing number of young historians, above all in the United States. "In battling against people who would subject historical studies to the dictates of literary critics," he pronounced, "we historians are, in a way, fighting for our lives. Certainly, we are fighting for the lives of innocent young people beset by devilish tempters who claim to offer higher forms of thought and deeper truths and insights—the intellectual equivalent of crack."[25] It is not only among conservatives like Elton that alarm bells of this sort have been ringing. The left-liberal historian Lawrence Stone has called upon historians to arm themselves to repel the new intellectual barbarians at the disciplinary gates. If postmodernists gained any more influence, he warned, "history might be on the way to becoming an endangered species."[26] On the socialist left, the radical historian Raphael Samuel, progenitor of *History Workshop*, warned in one of his last publications that "the deconstructive turn in contemporary thought" invited everyone to "see history not as a record of the past, more or less faithful to the facts," but "as an invention, or fiction, of historians themselves."[27] He made it clear that this was something which he found completely unacceptable. Arthur Marwick, founding professor of history at Britain's Open University, voiced his fears that history students would find the postmodernists' "presumptuous and ill-informed criticisms" of history "disorienting" and might "even be persuaded that the history of the historians is worthless."[28] Postmodernist ideas, he declared, were a "menace to serious historical study."[29] Theories which "suggest that historians are in the business of creating—not discovering or interpreting—historical meaning," added two historians from the University of Pennsylvania, "undermine our authority, the mystique of our enterprise, the very purpose of our work."[30]

Where so many historians are issuing such dire warnings couched in such colorful and alarmist language, something important is clearly going on. No one should doubt that the postmodernist challenge to historical study as conceived in different ways by Carr and Elton is a serious one. Some of the intellectual barbarians at the disciplinary gates are loitering there with distinctly hostile intent. "Autumn," declared the Dutch postmodernist Frank Ankersmit triumphantly in 1990, "has come to Western historiography."[31] Similarly, Keith Jenkins, author of two recent postmodernist critiques of history, announced approvingly in a reconsideration of Carr's work published in 1995: "We have reached the end of modernist versions of what history is."[32] Patrick Joyce has declared that "contemporary history," meaning history as practiced today, "is itself in fact the offspring of modernity" and therefore part of the intellectual world which postmodernity is now displacing.[33] As Geoff Eley and Keith Nield, two British historians who have tried to moderate in the controversy, have remarked of the two opposing sides, "A theoretical *hauteur* instructs a redoubt of methodological conservatism, and the latter shouts defiantly back. Between the two lies a silence, a barrier that in these tones cannot be crossed."[34]

"For progress in understanding the truth and objectivity of history," a cool Australian observer of the debate has advised, "each side must attend more closely to what the other is saying."[35] Drawing up the disciplinary drawbridge has never been a good idea for historians. For centuries they have profited immeasurably from the invasions of neighboring disciplines, starting with philology, the foundation of the methods of source criticism associated with the name of the great German historian Leopold von Ranke in the nineteenth century, and moving on through economics, sociology, anthropology, statistics, geography, psychology, and other alien forces as time has gone on. Lawrence Stone himself has in the past been one of the main advocates—and practitioners—of the opening up of history to influences from the social sciences. Why not influences from literary criticism and linguistic analysis as well? Historians should approach the invading hordes of semioticians, poststructuralists, New Historicists, Foucauldians, Lacanians, and the rest with more discrimination. Some of them might prove more friendly, or more useful, than they seem at first sight.

Moreover, the questions they raise—about the possibility or impossibility of attaining objective knowledge, the elusive and relative nature of truth, the difficulties involved in distinguishing between fact and fiction—do not merely challenge historians to reexamine the theory and practice of their own discipline but also have wider implications that go far beyond the boundaries of academic and university life. In this sense, the problem of how historians approach the acquisition of knowledge about the past, and whether they can ever wholly succeed in this enterprise, can stand for the much bigger problem of how far society at large can ever attain the kind of objective certainty about the great issues of our time that can serve as a reliable basis for taking vital decisions on our future in the twenty-first century.

III

IN many ways it makes sense to approach such wider questions by looking at how we acquire knowledge about the past. Many of the problems involved in finding out about contemporary society and politics are very similar. Yet the past presents more difficulties because it is no longer with us. Moreover, the theory and history of history have become a separate branch of learning in itself since Carr and Elton wrote, and in the process it has developed its own concepts and its own jargon, which have made it often rather impenetrable to outsiders. Some have indeed argued that the nature of historical explanation is a topic best left to the philosophers. How we know about the past, what historical causation is, how we define a historical fact, whether there is such a thing as historical truth or objectivity—these are questions that most historians have happily left to one side as unnecessary distractions from their essential work in the archives.[36] "Many historians," one observer has correctly noted, "are by instinctive inclination hostile to philosophical and methodological criticism of their work, often wishing to rely instead on 'common sense.' "[37] Nor have the few historians who have actually ventured to write about their discipline necessarily earned the plaudits of their colleagues. "Historians," the Oxford specialist on French history Theodore Zeldin has observed, ". . . are probably no more reliable as guides to their own work than politicians are to their policies."[38] Or, to change the analogy, as his former Oxford colleague Norman Stone has remarked, "it is probably as much a mistake to ask a working historian to discuss this theme as to ask a painter to give his views on aesthetics."[39]

Of course, very few historians in practice have possessed the necessary expertise to discuss the theory of history at a level that a trained philosopher would consider acceptable. On the other hand, the level of abstraction at which most studies of historical epistemology operate is so theoretical, so far removed from actual problems experienced by working historians, that the subject in general is of little practical relevance to what historians actually do.[40] One of the few twentieth-century scholars who were equally at home in the two fields of history and philosophy, R. G. Collingwood, was the author of both the *Oxford History of Roman Britain* and a celebrated philosophical treatise on *The Idea of History*. But there is no indication at all that the two books stood in any relation to each other; they might have been written by two different people. Indeed, one philosopher of history has remarked rather loftily that "philosophers interest themselves in history for their own purposes: the instrumental value, or disvalue, of their investigations to history is wholly accidental."[41] Thus we have what has often seemed to be a dialogue of the deaf.

Some historians have even disputed the right of nonhistorians to write about the nature of historical knowledge and explanation at all. It should come as no surprise that Sir Geoffrey Elton was among them. Drawing up the disciplinary drawbridge again, he declared roundly: "There is no reason why great historians (or indeed lesser ones) should not have their manner of thinking and operating investigated, but such studies are pointless unless the investigator can demonstrate that he knows at first hand what working on the materials left to us by the past actually means."[42] In other words, only historians are qualified to talk about history, a view echoed in only slightly less stentorian tones by others, such as Arthur Marwick. Even the great French historian Fernand Braudel once pronounced that history as a discipline "cannot be understood without practicing it."[43] Yet the influential American writer on the theory of history Hayden White has made the obvious retort that the "insistence that only historians know what historians really do is similar to modern scientists' objections to being studied by sociologists, ethnographers, philosophers and *historians*" themselves.[44] Historians are therefore denying to other disciplines the right they claim for their own.

White is surely correct to insist that historians—teachers as well as students—have a lot to learn from what others outside the discipline tell them. Moreover, as Raymond Martin, another commentator on these issues, has remarked, "When it comes to understanding *the past*, historians are the acknowledged experts. But when it comes to understanding *how we understand the past*, there are no experts."[45] Historians, the American apostle of quantitative history Robert Fogel has declared somewhat gloomily in the light of all this, have a choice: "Either they ignore the philosophers and get on with what they are doing, but that might mean that they will continue to work without understanding how they are doing it. Or they down tools to listen to the philosophers, but this will most likely mean that tools will stay permanently downed."[46] But this counsel of despair is belied by the numerous examples of practicing historians who have managed to do both. Increasing numbers of historians, provoked perhaps by the challenge of postmodernism, are finding it necessary to reflect on the nature of the project they are engaged in. The more this happens, the better. As three American historians have remarked in their recent, jointly authored book on this subject, "It is time we historians took responsibility for explaining what we do, how we do it, and why it is worth doing."[47]

To be sure, postmodernist critics of history and the historical profession have sometimes dismissed the views of practicing historians
as not worth listening to anyway (unless of course they simply accept
without criticism the ideas the postmodernists themselves are pro-
pounding). "Those who announce the advent of postmodernism," as
Perez Zagorin, an eminent American specialist on seventeenth-century England, has observed, frequently claim that it "cannot be with-
stood."[48] This is true. "Times have moved on," Patrick Joyce has
declared, "and historians simply have to learn to keep up with
them."[49] Similarly, Keith Jenkins has asserted roundly that "today we
live within the general condition of *postmodernity*. We do not have a
choice about this. For postmodernity is not an 'ideology' or a position we can choose to subscribe to or not; postmodernity is precisely our condition: it is our fate."[50] Thus debating whether or not we
should accept it is a futile exercise. But of course, "postmodernity" is
only a word we use to describe something whose presence in the
human condition some have diagnosed but others still dispute. Given
the stress laid upon the shifting nature of concepts by postmodernists, and the emphasis given to the indirect, contingent, or even
arbitrary or nonexistent correspondence of words to reality, the dogmatic and apodictic tone of Jenkins's declaration that postmodernity
is an indisputable fact of life seems strangely out of place, coming as
it does from an exponent of such ideas.

Moreover, just because an intellectual trend seems irresistible is no
reason for not resisting it. Lest this seem a legacy of my own education in Oxford, that proverbial home of lost causes, let me refer to a
case of an intellectual trend that swept all before it rather farther
afield. In the 1920s and 1930s German historians overwhelmingly
believed in the primacy of foreign policy in shaping a nation's history and linked this to a political drive to provide historical arguments
for revising the Treaty of Versailles and recovering the territories lost
by their country at the end of the First World War. The German historical profession blocked the careers of those who thought otherwise and, except for a small handful of its members, collaborated
willingly in the Nazi seizure of power and the Nazification of university education. Was this, however, any reason for not resisting

them? And did this irresistible trend not damage the quality and reputation of German historical scholarship for a generation? It would
of course be going too far to draw a parallel between postmodernism
and fascist ideology. The real conclusion to be drawn from this example is surely that arguments and theories, however dominant in the
intellectual life of their day, have to be assessed on their own merits,
not accepted uncritically simply because they are espoused by the
majority. In similar vein, some apologists for postmodernism have a
tendency to proclaim that they have already won the argument and
that there is no point any longer in historians' trying to refute them.[51]
But the fact is that historians' replies to at least some postmodernist
critiques of history have caused some postmodernist theorists to shift
their ground in crucial respects, just as historians themselves have
been forced to shift their ground by postmodernist critiques. What
we have, in other words, is no longer a dialogue of the deaf but a
genuine debate. Historians themselves have an important contribution to make to this debate. The theory of history is too important a
matter to be left to the theoreticians. Practicing historians may not
have a God-given monopoly of pronouncing sensibly on such matters, but they surely have as much right to try to think and write
about them as anybody else, and the experience of actually having
done historical research ought to mean that they have something to
contribute which those who have not shared this experience do not.

CHAPTER ONE

THE HISTORY OF HISTORY

I

HOWEVER much they might have agreed on the need for accuracy and truthfulness, historians down the ages have held widely differing views on the purposes to which these things were to be put and the way in which the facts they presented were to be explained. In medieval and early modern times, many historians saw their function as chronicling the working out of God's purposes in the world. Things happened, ultimately, because God willed them to happen; human history was the playground of supernatural forces of good and evil. The rationalist historians of the Enlightenment substituted for this a mode of historical explanation which rested on human forces, but they still thought of their work as a species of moral illustration. In the greatest of the Enlightenment histories, for example, Edward Gibbon's *Decline and Fall of the Roman Empire*, the actors are moral qualities rather than human beings, and the ultimate lesson is that superstition, fanaticism, and religious belief, all of which were of course anathema to Enlightenment rationalists, were dangerous forces that had brought down one great and benign empire and could well wreak further havoc in the future if they were not eradicated. History was "philosophy teaching by example"; human nature was universal, unchanging, and unhistorical.[1]

In the Romantic era, historians came to repudiate this kind of thinking. Under the influence of writers like Sir Walter Scott, they came to see the past as exciting because it was different. Under the influence of political theorists like Edmund Burke, they began to argue that it provided the only possible basis for the kind of political stability that had been so rudely shattered by the great French Revolution of 1789. The purpose of history came to be seen not as providing examples for some abstract philosophical doctrine or principle but simply as finding out about the past as something to cherish and preserve, as the only proper foundation for a true understanding and appreciation of the institutions of state and society in the present. The lead in this change of direction was provided by the German historian Leopold von Ranke, a scholar whose exceptionally long life and extraordinary productivity made him into something of a legend. The author of over sixty volumes, including multivolume histories of the popes, of Germany in the time of the Reformation, of the Latin and Germanic nations, he began a history of the world when he was eighty-three years of age and had completed seventeen volumes by the time of his death in 1886 at the age of ninety-one. He was converted to history by the shock of discovering that Scott's novel *Quentin Durward* was historically inaccurate. He determined therefore that he would apply the methods he had learned as a philologist to the study of historical texts in order to make such inaccuracy impossible in the future.

Ranke's contribution to historical scholarship was threefold. First, he helped establish history as a separate discipline, independent from philosophy or literature. "To history," he wrote in the preface to one of his works, "has been assigned the office of judging the past, of instructing the present for the benefit of future ages. To such high offices this work does not aspire: it wants only to show what actually happened."[2] This last phrase is perhaps Ranke's most famous, and it has been widely misunderstood. The German phrase which Ranke used—"*wie es eigentlich gewesen*"—is better translated as "how it essentially was." By it, Ranke meant that he wanted to penetrate by a kind of intuitive understanding to the inner being of the past.[3]

In pursuit of this task, said Ranke, the historian had to recognize that "every epoch is immediate to God"[4]—that is, God in His eternity made no distinction between periods of history; all were the same in His eyes. In other words, the past could not be judged by the standards of the present. It had to be seen in its own terms. This was the second major contribution which Ranke made to historical scholarship: the determination to strip away the veneer of posthumous condescension applied to the past by philosophizing historians such as Voltaire and to reveal it in its original colors; to try to understand the past as the people who lived in it understood it, even while deciphering patterns and interconnections of which they had been largely unaware. One conclusion that followed from this doctrine was that at any given time, including the present, whatever existed had to be accepted as divinely ordained. Ranke was a profoundly conservative figure, who equated the actual and the ideal and regarded the European states of his day as "spiritual substances . . . thoughts of God."[5] This distanced him from the Prussian school of German historians, from nationalists such as Treitschke, who condemned his impartiality and regretted his universalism. The fact that he regarded all states, not just Prussia, as supreme examples of God's purposes working themselves out on earth gave him, on the other hand, a reputation for impartiality that greatly helped the spread of his influence abroad.[6]

Third, and perhaps most important, Ranke introduced into the study of modern history the methods that had recently been developed by philologists in the study of ancient and medieval literature to determine whether a text, say, of a Shakespeare play or of a medieval legend like the *Nibelungenlied* was true or corrupted by later interpolations, whether it was written by the author it was supposed to have been written by, and which of the available versions was the most reliable. Historians, argued Ranke, had to root out forgeries and falsifications from the record. They had to test documents on the basis of their internal consistency and their consistency with other documents originating at the same period. They had to stick to "primary sources," eyewitness reports and what Ranke called the "purest, most immediate documents" which could be shown to have originated at the time under investigation, and avoid reliance on "secondary sources," such as memoirs or later histories generated after the event. Moreover, they had to investigate and subject to the critical method *all* the sources relating to the events in which they were interested. They should not be content, as, for example, Gibbon had been, to rely on printed documents and chronicles generally available in libraries. They had instead to sally forth, as Ranke did, into the archives, to work their way through the vast unpublished hoards of original manuscripts stored up by the state chancelleries of Europe. Only then, by gathering, criticizing, and verifying all the available sources, could they put themselves in a position to reconstruct the past accurately.

The application of philological techniques to historical sources was a major breakthrough. Ranke's principles still form the basis for much historical research and teaching today. Advanced, document-based seminars in many contemporary universities, for example, offer a basic training in source criticism; students are examined on extracts from set documents and are expected to comment on them in terms of their internal consistency, their relationship to other documents on the same subject, their reliability, and their usefulness as a source. Questions of authenticity and attribution continue to be vitally important in historical research. Forgeries, as the lamentable case of the "Hitler Diaries" showed more than a decade ago, are still regrettably common; outright falsification and doctoring of the evidence abound in printed collections of documents and other publications relating to subjects such as the origins of the First World War and the Third Reich. They are even more common in medieval history. Technological innovation has added substantially to the Rankean armory; the "Hitler Diaries" were easily exposed as forgeries by simple testing of the age of the paper on which they were written, which dated from the 1950s; perhaps Hugh Trevor-Roper (Lord Dacre), who originally "authenticated" them for the London *Times* newspaper, should not have rested content with the fact that the name Adolf Hitler was signed at the bottom of every page.[7] Whatever the means they use, historians still have to engage in the basic Rankean spadework of investigating the provenance of documents, of inquiring about the motives of those who wrote them, the circumstances in which they were written, and the ways in which they relate to other documents on the same subject. The perils which await them should they fail to do this are only too obvious.

All these things have belonged to the basic training of historians since the nineteenth century, and rightly so. However many forgeries and falsifications there have been, they seldom escape undetected for long. Skeptics who point to the fact that all sources are "biased" and conclude from this that historians are bound to be misled by them are as wide of the mark as politicians who imagine that future historians will take their memoirs on trust. Nor is there anything unusual in the fact that a modern discipline places such heavy reliance on principles developed more than a century and a half before: Chemistry, for example, still uses the periodic table of elements, while medical research continues to employ the mid-nineteenth-century device of "Koch's postulates" to prove that a microorganism is the carrier of a particular disease. These analogies with scientific method point up the fact that when source criticism was introduced into historical study, it, too, was regarded as a "scientific" technique. Its use legitimated history as an independent profession, and those historians in other countries who wanted to establish themselves on a professional basis soon began to flock to Germany to undergo training at the feet of its leading exponents in Göttingen or Berlin.

In the course of this Rankean revolution, the university-based historical seminar in which future members of the profession were trained, wrote Herbert Baxter Adams, had "evolved from a nursery of dogma into a laboratory of scientific truth."[8] The French historian Fustel de Coulanges, teaching at Strasbourg University, roundly declared in 1862 that "History is, and should be, a science."[9] The understanding of science which these claims implied was basically inductive. Out there, in the documents, lay the facts, waiting to be discovered by historians, just as the stars shone out there in the heavens, waiting to be discovered by astronomers; all historians had to do was apply the proper scientific method, eliminate their own personality from the investigation, and the facts would come to light. The object of research was thus to "fill in the gaps" in knowledge—a rationale that is still given as the basis for the vast majority of Ph.D. theses in history today. As the most widely used primer in historical method at the time, by the French historians Claude Langlois and Charles Seignobos, remarked, "When all the documents are known, and have gone through the operations which fit them for use, the work of critical scholarship will be finished. In the case of some ancient periods, for which documents are rare, we can now see that in a generation or two it will be time to stop." Similar beliefs were indeed common in the natural sciences. When the German physicist Max Planck took up his studies in the 1870s, for example, he was warned by his professor that it would be a waste of time, since there was nothing left to discover in the field.[10]

But these views rested on a series of misapprehensions. The belief that all the evidence left to posterity by the past *could* actually be surveyed and evaluated was already beginning to look less plausible even before the end of the nineteenth century, as new techniques and discoveries in archaeology began to open up whole new areas of knowledge even about the most distant periods in time. From early on in the twentieth century, too, historians began to look away from the narrow confines of the history and antecedents of the nation-state toward economic history, social history, cultural history, and, subsequently, other new branches of historical inquiry as well. New questions, it seemed, could render previously neglected areas of evidence freshly meaningful. As the passing of time continued to consign new ages to history, historians also began to realize the almost exponential growth that was taking place in the quantity of source material available to them. Late-nineteenth-century American and European society was not only vastly more populous than before, not only produced many more documents, reflecting both the increase of literacy and the rapidly increasing functions of the state, but also produced new kinds of sources, from mass newspapers to photographs and films. "The history of the Victorian Age will never be written," declared Lytton Strachey in a fit of ironic despair: "We know too much about it."[11]

Not only the idea of the final discovery of all the facts that could be known, but also the notion of a truly scientific history, began to seem more than a little shaky by the turn of the century, too. Many of the advocates of a scientific approach to history failed to practice what they preached. A. F. Pollard, founder of the Institute of

Historical Research at London University, established to introduce professional scientific training for history postgraduates, made little use of manuscript sources in his own work on Tudor history, preferring instead to use the transcripts and summaries provided in the *Calendars of State Papers*, which of course were shot through with inevitable mistakes and lacunae, seriously reducing the reliability of his writings.[12] Even the great Ranke was open to criticism according to the criteria which he himself did so much to establish. His writing, far from being "colorless," as some thought, was suffused with metaphor.[13] His belief that he was writing objective history derived to a great extent from the fact that he based a great deal of his work on the dispatches of Venetian ambassadors to various European states, documents which themselves gave a deliberate impression of neutrality and value-free reporting. As John Pemble has pointed out, "to the next generation Ranke was not Rankean enough." His Venetian sources were partial, selective, and narrow, and he made too little use of other archival material; only in this way, indeed, was he able to write so much. "Flaubert once commented," as Pemble remarks, "that writing history was like drinking an ocean and pissing a cupful. Ranke it seemed was doing the opposite."[14]

The realization that the founders of scientific history had all too often failed to follow their own precepts did not stop historians before the First World War from proclaiming the virtues of the scientific approach; on the contrary, it merely spurred them to greater efforts. In 1903, in a famous inaugural lecture as Regius Professor of Modern History in Cambridge, J. B. Bury declared that

> History is a science, no less and no more. . . . History is not a branch of literature. The facts of history, like the facts of geology or astronomy, can supply material for literary art . . . but to clothe the story of human society in a literary dress is no more the part of a historian as a historian, than it is the part of an astronomer to present in an artistic shape the story of the stars.

Bury pointed up the contrast between history as literature and history as science by referring to the example of the man he called the "greatest living historian," the German Theodor Mommsen. Mommsen's stature as a historian lay, Bury declared, not in his authorship of a widely read Roman history, which merely gave him a reputation as a "man of letters" (indeed, it won him the Nobel Prize for literature), but in his detailed critical compilation of Roman inscriptions and his specialized studies on Roman law. Here was the realm in which he had applied the scientific method; here was his true claim, therefore, to greatness as a historian. It was this example, Bury implied, that others should follow.[15]

II

ONE member of the audience at that lecture in Cambridge in 1903 was the twenty-six-year-old George Macaulay Trevelyan, who was to be appointed to the Regius chair when Bury died in 1927. Trevelyan took the lecture as a deliberate personal insult to his great-uncle the Whig historian Lord Macaulay, whose *History of England* had been one of the greatest literary sensations of the early Victorian era. He rushed into print with an uncharacteristically savage denunciation, in his essay "Clio: A Muse," referring in this title to the muse of history in ancient Greek mythology.[16] The "crusade" which Bury and others were waging against the "artistic and emotional treatment of the whole past of mankind," said Trevelyan, had become so successful that it now threatened "the complete annihilation of the few remaining individuals" who still thought history was an art. If history was merely a "chronicle of bare facts arranged on scientific principles," then "literature, emotion and speculative thought" would be "banished" from the human race's contemplation of its own past.[17] In his long career Trevelyan did much to bridge the gap between the historian and the public in such widely popular works as his *English Social History*. Contrary to what many of his detractors have alleged, he was thoroughly professional both in his university career and in his research, which he based, especially in the case of his magnum opus, a magnificent three-volume history of *England under Queen Anne*, on scholarship that was as rigorous as it was extensive.[18] But although he paid due regard to the "scientific" aspects of his subject, he thought that "the idea that the facts of history are of value as part of an exact science confined to specialists is due to a misapplication of the analogy of physical science." The natural sciences, he thought, were valuable in terms of practical utility and in the deduction of laws of cause and effect, whether or not the general public understood them. But history had no practical value unless it was widely disseminated among the public, and nobody had ever succeeded in deriving general laws of cause and effect from history in such a way that they stood the essential test of such laws in the physical sciences—namely, by enabling people to predict the future. Trevelyan conceded that "the collection of facts, the weighing of evidence as to what events happened, are in some sense scientific; but not so the discovery of the causes and effects of these events."

In reaching this judgment, of course, he was echoing the original principles of Ranke, who had distinguished in his day between the rigorous principles of source-criticism needed for an accurate representation of events in the past and the intuitive method needed to establish the "interconnectedness" of these events and penetrate to the "essence" of an epoch. It was this latter operation, which Ranke conceived of in Romantic and religious terms, and Trevelyan in literary and aesthetic terms, that made the difference, in the view of both of them, between the chronicler and the historian. History, said Trevelyan, was a mixture of the scientific (research), the imaginative or speculative (interpretation), and the literary (presentation). What the historian required was not "more knowledge of facts," which in any case would always be incomplete. Nobody was ever going to unravel scientifically the mental processes of twenty million Frenchmen during the Revolution of 1789. Nor could interpretations of this event be arrived at by a mere process of induction. The causes and effects of the Revolution could never be known scientifically like the causes and effects of some chemical reaction, nor could they be grounded on discoverable laws like the law of gravity or the second law of thermodynamics. The historian who would give the best interpretation of the Revolution was the one who, "having discovered and weighed all the important evidence available, has the largest grasp of intellect, the warmest human sympathy, the highest imaginative power."

Trevelyan was essentially a *nationalist* historian; his major works were histories of England, and his objection to the "scientific" conception of history was grounded not least on the fact that it was German. "Who is the Mother Country to Anglo-Saxon historians?" he asked in his essay. "Some reply 'Germany,' but others of us prefer to answer 'England.' The methods and limitations of German learning presumably suit the Germans, but are certain to prove a strait waistcoat to English limbs and faculties. We ought," he declared, "to look to the free, popular, literary traditions of history in our own land." He also lamented the fact that "the historians of to-day were trained by the Germanising hierarchy to regard history not as . . . a 'story,' but as a 'science.' " The Germanizing tendencies of the period, he thought, were authoritarian and hierarchical, and unsuited to the liberal intellectual traditions of his own country.[19]

Just as Trevelyan looked to English traditions and circumstances as the source of historical inspiration, so in other European countries, too, historians rejected the universalizing tendencies of both Enlightenment writers such as Voltaire and Gibbon and Romantics such as Ranke. Popular, nationalist history had reached its apogee in Britain with Macaulay, in France with Michelet, in Germany with Treitschke, and it was not without its influence even on the most "scientific" of scholars in the late nineteenth century. Virtually all historians, for example, assumed that the nation-state was the primary object of historical study. The emerging historical profession was dominated by the view that the historian's task lay principally in the study of the origins and development of states and in their relations with one another. Even the most narrow and rigorous of learned articles were usually written within this framework, while huge resources of scientific scholarship were lavished on the publication of vast documentary collections designed to provide the basic materials for national histories, such as the *Monumenta Germaniae Historica* and the *Calendars of State Papers*.

The Prussian school of historians, led by such figures as J. G. Droysen, was happy to proclaim that "the German nation has outstripped all others" in its application of the critical method to historical sources, but it was just as critical as Trevelyan was of the notion that this was sufficient to constitute history in itself. "History," declared Droysen, "is the only science enjoying the ambiguous fortune of being required to be at the same time an art." He complained that because the German middle classes had for so long considered "the German method in history pedantic, exclusive, unenjoyable," they all read Macaulay instead, or turned to the great French historian and statesman Thiers, so that "German historical judgment" and even "German political judgment" were "formed and guided . . . by the rhetorical superiority of other nations." The German middle classes did indeed look to the examples of English liberalism and the principles of the French Revolution for much of the nineteenth century. The Prussian school of historians set themselves the task of demonstrating through a mixture of scientific method, historical intuition, and literary skill the superiority of Prussian values and their inevitable triumph in the unification of Germany in 1871. They could claim at least some credit for the drift of middle-class opinion in Germany from a liberal to a more authoritarian form of nationalism in the last three decades leading up to the First World War.[20]

In the United States the scientific conception of history was challenged from a number of different angles. Some, following the example of the turn to cultural history pioneered by Karl Lamprecht in Germany—and, after a major controversy, decisively rejected by the historical profession in that country—proclaimed a "new history" which would ally itself with the social sciences and look beyond politics and the nation-state to broader aspects of economy, culture, and society. Others, such as Charles Beard and Carl Becker, took this further and turned this methodological radicalism to the explicit political purposes of the Progressive movement, arguing that history's fundamental task was to clear away the encrusted myths and dogmas which prevented America, in their view, from reforming and adapting to the modern industrial age. Beard's famous book *An Economic Interpretation of the Constitution of the United States* created a major scandal by arguing that the Constitution reflected not the enduring democratic values which so many Americans thought it did, but the narrow and outdated economic interests of a small, propertied eighteenth-century elite. Both at the time and subsequently, many more conservative historians charged Beard and his allies with a fateful departure from scholarly standards in the interests of present-day politics, an abandonment of the disinterested search for truth and the study of the past for its own sake which should be the primary purpose of every serious historian. Yet no one could deny that the Progressive historians conformed to the basic scholarly canons of the post-Rankean age.[21]

Already before 1914, therefore, the ability of the scientific method to deliver a neutral and value-free history was under some doubt. Its credibility was even more severely shaken by the events of 1914–18 and their aftermath. Professional historians in every country rushed into print with elaborate defenses of the war aims of their own governments and denunciations of other Great Powers for having begun the conflict. Substantial collections of documents on the origins of the war were produced with all the usual scholarly paraphernalia and edited by reputable professionals, but on principles of selection that seemed manifestly biased to colleagues in other countries. The rigorous scientific training which they had undergone seemed to have had no effect at all in inculcating a properly neutral and "objective" attitude to the recent past, a view that was underlined as the 1920s progressed by the continuing violent controversies between extremely learned and scholarly historians about the origins of the war.[22] Moreover, among British, French, and American historians, the support for the war of the overwhelming majority of the "scientific" German colleagues whose work they so admired came as a further blow.[23] Many historians who had studied in Germany now rushed to denounce German scholarship as pedantic and antidemocratic. "The age of German footnotes," as one of them declared in 1915, "is on the wane."[24] And for G. M. Trevelyan, the defeat of the Germans also represented the defeat of "German 'scientific history,' " a mirage which had "led the nation that looked to it for political prophesy and guidance" about as far astray as it was possible to go.[25]

The war also revealed previous, apparently neutral scholarly histories of, for example, Germany or nineteenth-century Europe to have been deeply flawed in their interpretations. Events such as the

Russian Revolution, the Treaty of Versailles, the triumph of modernism in art, music, and literature increased this sense of disorientation among historians. Reflective historians of the older generation realized that their faith in objectivity had accompanied their sense of living in an ordered and predictable world. One senior American historian, Clarence Alvord, confessed after the war that he had always "conformed to the canons of my science . . . walked along the straight and narrow road of approved scholarship . . . learned to babble the words of von Ranke . . . prided [myself] on telling the story *wie es eigentlich gewesen. . . ."* This had all been very fine, he said, while the world was a safe place to live in and people had been able to believe in ordered, rational, and inevitable progress. But now, he wrote, "all the spawn of hell roamed at will over the world and made of it a shambles. . . . The pretty edifice of . . . history which had been designed and built by my contemporaries was rent asunder. . . . The meaning we historians had read into events was false, cruelly false." If unpredictable and uncontrollable forces were shaping the present, it seemed, then the previous belief of historians that they could understand by a simple process of induction the forces that shaped the past now seemed dangerously naive.[26]

Some historians now despaired of finding any pattern or meaning in the past at all. As the English liberal historian H. A. L. Fisher remarked in the preface to his widely read *History of Europe*, published in 1934,

> Men wiser and more learned than I have discerned in history a plot, a rhythm, a predetermined pattern. These harmonies are concealed from me. I can see only one emergency following upon another as wave follows upon wave, only one great fact with respect to which, since it is unique, there can be no generalizations, only one safe rule for the historian: that he should recognize in the development of human destinies the play of the contingent and the unforeseen. . . . The ground gained by one generation may be lost by the next.[27]

History, in this bewildered view, was just "one damned thing after another," devoid of meaning, and not capable of interpretation in any wider sense at all.

Such views were reinforced at a more theoretical level by the changing nature of the natural sciences in this period. Einstein's general theory of relativity (1913), widely popularized after it was confirmed by astronomical observation in 1919, helped create an intellectual climate in which it was thought that the "aspect of things" changed with the position of the observer. The idea of the relativity of observer and fact was applied to history by a number of interwar philosophers as well, in particular by the liberal Italian thinker Benedetto Croce and his English counterpart R. G. Collingwood. In doing so, they were echoing prewar German philosophers such as Wilhelm Dilthey, who had begun to take a skeptical view of the possibility of objective knowledge about the past. They also paralleled the much more far-reaching doubts of cultural pessimists in Germany under the Weimar Republic, for whom Germany's defeat in the First World War had rendered history largely meaningless. Croce argued that historians were guided in their judgment as to what documents and events were important in the past, and what were unimportant, by their present concerns. All history was thus written, consciously or unconsciously, from the perspective of the present; "all history," in Croce's famous phrase, "is contemporary history."[28] Collingwood went even further by arguing that "all history is the history of thought" because the documents left to the historian by the past were meaningless unless the historian reconstituted the thought that they expressed. "History," Collingwood concluded, "is the re-enactment in the historian's mind of the thought whose history he is studying."[29]

If we leave aside for the moment the merits and defects of such arguments, what all this did in broad terms was to blur the distinction commonly made by prewar historians, even those of a literary bent such as G. M. Trevelyan, between fact and interpretation. It was not a case, in their view, of the historian observing, collecting, and verifying the facts and then "interpreting" them. The very act of observing and collecting them was itself governed by the historian's *a priori* beliefs about the past. Such views gained currency not least because, as E. H. Carr wrote, "after the First World War, the facts seemed to smile on us less propitiously than in the years before 1914, and we were therefore more accessible to a philosophy which sought to diminish their prestige."[30] The crisis-ridden decades of the 1920s, 1930s, and 1940s, with their economic privations, international conflicts, revolutionary upheavals, and, perhaps above all, their revelations, in Italy, Spain, Russia, and Germany, of violence and inhumanity on a scale, and to a degree, previously thought barely possible severely undermined the belief in progress that had sustained the historians of the prewar era. The new scientific discoveries and concepts destroyed the belief that history writing would one day come to an end when everything had been discovered. If "discovery" depended not least on the intentions and assumptions of the historian influenced by the context of his own age, then it became clear that every fresh age would have to research and write the history of all past ages from scratch, all over again.

III

ALL these developments reflected the fact that the chaotic and disturbed interwar period was not, on the whole, a great age of historical scholarship. Economic dislocation in Europe and America meant that historians' income declined, relatively few new historians were trained, and in the many European countries—the majority, in fact—which fell victim to dictatorships, free historical inquiry ceased. It was only after the Second World War, as economic recovery began, and the mass armies of the 1930s and 1940s were finally demobilized, that a new generation of historians entered the profession. They were immediately confronted with the task of overcoming the skepticism and disorientation of their predecessors in the interwar years. Many historians tried to reassert what they regarded as the traditional values of historical scholarship, which they thought had been perverted by the political and intellectual pressures and upheavals of the previous few decades. Their mentor and example in England was the Polish-born historian Sir Lewis Namier, whose scholarship was famously painstaking and exact. As one of his pupils noted, he thought that "if history was not to be a catalogue of suppositions, . . . it had to be solidly based on minute facts." Namier thought that Freud rather than Ranke had established the scientific principles on which the study of the past could be more solidly based than before, and to this extent he was prepared to update the notion of "scientific" history. But the consequences he drew from this belief were far removed from those of the speculative American psychohistorians of recent decades. Namier always eschewed speculation, so he never thought that he could find out enough about an individual in the past to subject his character to psychoanalysis. However, he did think, as a result of his Freudian views, that what drove people to do the things they did were essentially personal motives and forces rather than ideologies or beliefs.

Namier used this approach, combined with formidably thorough and exhaustive research, to devastating effect in his most famous book, *The Structure of Politics at the Accession of George III*. The book was launched as a frontal assault on the "Whig interpretation" of British history, which saw eighteenth-century politics in terms of a struggle between the forces of liberty and constitutionalism, led by the Whigs, and absolutism and royal power, represented by the Tories. In the Whig view, the latter cause was eventually taken up by George III and his pet minister, Lord Bute. The new king's tendencies toward absolutism lost England the American colonies under the premiership of Lord North. Namier looked beyond these ideologies to the personal relationships of the politicians involved. By a minute investigation of these, he suggested that "party" was irrelevant, ideology unimportant; what mattered was the struggle of individuals through patronage and kinship networks for power, money, and influence. Seen in these terms, what led to the political crisis was the disruption to these networks caused by the accession of a new king, not any particular beliefs which he might have held or political principles with which he might have clashed. In this way, Namier's rapierlike scholarship deflated and destroyed the Whig interpretation of British history by puncturing it at its most vulnerable point.

There was no doubting that this was a major and significant scholarly achievement. When I was an undergraduate in the 1960s, Namier's *Structure of Politics* was considered by history tutors to have been the greatest work ever penned about English history, and

Namier was a god. "Namier," one historian said, "perhaps, has found the ultimate way of doing history." "If Namier had his way," another remarked, "all controversies would cease, and we would know as much historical truth as is humanly possible." "Fifty years from now," one of his disciples declared at the beginning of the 1960s, "*all* history will be done as Sir Lewis does it." Namier, as even E. H. Carr admitted, was "the greatest British historian to emerge on the academic scene since the First World War."[31] Seen from the perspective of the late 1990s, however, these claims appear ludicrously inflated.[32] Typically, what British empiricists admired in Namier was the thoroughness of his scholarship; they more or less ignored his Freudianism as an embarrassing but excusable Continental heresy. Many historians since Namier have matched his painstakingly high standards of archival scholarship. They have long since reestablished the centrality of party labels and party ideology to the politics of the majority of the eighteenth century and made the 1760s, Namier's chosen decade, seem rather exceptional by comparison. Nobody would nowadays maintain that George III's constitutional practice was the same as that of his predecessors, and assiduous historians have made the inevitable discovery that Namier, in his anxiety to exculpate the king, was highly selective in his use of evidence and not above "pruning" his quotations from the sources to serve his argument.[33] The belief that Namier had found a new method of writing history was misplaced. Already in the 1950s there were those who complained that he had "taken the mind out of history" in his reduction of political action to the operation of individual self-interest.[34] In the hands of his pupils and emulators, and indeed eventually in his own, his method degenerated into mindless prosopography, ending up with a series of narrow and arid studies of eighteenth-century cabinets and producing that great white elephant of twentieth-century British historical scholarship, the huge (and hugely expensive) multivolume *History of Parliament*, a compilation which amounts in the end to little more than a minutely researched biographical dictionary of MPs through the ages, flattering to MPs, which is no doubt why they subsidize it, but of little influence in advancing historical understanding in a larger sense.[35]

Like H. A. L. Fisher, Namier saw no pattern in history and distrusted ideas and ideologies, an approach which was reassuring to the pragmatism of British intellectuals. He despised and distrusted the masses whose emergence onto the social and political scene in the wake of the postwar Labour government was so threatening to conservative university dons. Insofar as he raised the standards of English historical scholarship with his meticulous, indeed obsessive pursuit of unpublished manuscript materials, he undoubtedly performed a useful service. But English historians were excessively intimidated by this and thought that Namier had replaced Whig myth with true objectivity. He had not. Namier's work did not attract much attention when it first appeared in 1927. He really came into his own after the war. His views held sway among British historians in the 1950s and 1960s not least because they were well suited to the atmosphere of the Cold War, in which the Communist advocacy of the interests of the masses, belief in the "laws" of history and progress, and enthronement of ideology and belief at the center of the historical process and historical interpretation were thought of by liberals and conservatives as principles to be combated in the interests of the freedom of the individual.[36] Soviet historians, it was believed, had betrayed the ideals of factual accuracy, neutrality, and detachment in the same way as Nazi historians had. History had become a means of indoctrination, pressed into the service of the state, and of the spread of Communism. Western history, on the contrary, was now held to represent the virtues of accuracy, objectivity, and truthfulness.

The Cold War reassertion of objectivity which underpinned Namier's overwhelming influence in Britain in the 1950s and early 1960s also took place in the philosophy of science, where Sir Karl Popper, a philosopher of Viennese origin who dedicated his life to combating the claims of Marxism to be a scientific doctrine, reasserted the objective nature of scientific knowledge in two highly influential works, *The Poverty of Historicism* and *The Open Society and Its Enemies*. Popper argued that objective knowledge could best be approached through propositions for which one could specify the conditions under which they might be falsified. Theories, such as Marxism, which accounted for everything, and could be adapted to any circumstances, were merely metaphysical; only theories which did not claim to explain everything, yet which resisted attempts to prove them false, were truly scientific. Popper excoriated the Marxist view that history had a discernible direction and was subject to laws; objective knowledge of history, he said, could only be obtained in respect of short- or medium-term developments, where it was clear what evidence was needed to falsify the interpretations put forward. No historical evidence could "disprove" the idea that history was moving through stages toward the goal of a Communist society because every conceivable kind of evidence could be adapted to fit the theory if so desired. On the other hand, the idea that, for example, the First World War was caused by German aggression *could* be falsified (in theory at least) because it was possible to specify the kind of evidence that would be needed to prove or disprove it.[37]

I V

THIS reassertion of historical objectivity came at a time in the 1950s and 1960s when the historical profession was reestablishing itself, undergoing slow but steady growth, and recapturing the social and financial position it had enjoyed in the late nineteenth century. Not only Britain and the United States, but other countries, too, experienced similar developments. In West Germany the growing prosperity brought about by the postwar "economic miracle" allowed historians, like other university professors, to regain much of the power and status they had had before the upheavals of Weimar and the anti-intellectual assaults of Nazism. A determination to distance themselves from the outrageous lies and distortions of Nazi historiography gave them a belief in the value of an "objective" approach to history that has never entirely deserted them since. The German historians of the post-1968 generation, the first to have reached professional maturity in the postwar era, eagerly imported the theories and methods of American and, above all, neo-Weberian sociology into their work, in an attempt to escape from the perils of subjectivity which had engulfed the old tradition of liberal nationalist historiography in their country in the 1930s and 1940s. So pervasive was the influence of the social sciences on German historiography that there were proposals to dissolve history as a separate subject in the secondary school curriculum and incorporate it into social studies, citizenship education, political science, and the like, while university undergraduates were now taught, as indeed they still are in Germany, to present their work not in the traditional form of literary essays but after the manner of social scientific research reports instead. The rhetorical style of the social sciences still pervades the work of professional historians in Germany, too, with a passive, anonymous written style dominant, all reference to the author as an individual eliminated, and the word "I" banished even from the preface and acknowledgments of the typical German research monograph or work of historical synthesis. The cult of the individual under Nazism provoked a similar negative reaction among German historians, who on the whole avoided biography and concentrated on writing the history of people in the past as a history of averages, groups, and global trends instead.[38]

The same decade saw the invasion of the social sciences into history in Britain as well, launched by a famous issue of the *Times Literary Supplement* in 1966, in which a series of young historians heralded the transformation of their discipline by imported theories and methods from anthropology, social theory, and statistics. Beginning with E. H. Carr himself, historians queued up to urge history and the social sciences to move closer together.[39] Writing in 1976, Lawrence Stone claimed that the influence of the social sciences was refining the historian's conceptual apparatus and research strategies, while rigorous quantification was destroying many cherished historical myths. The social sciences were posing new questions for the historian to answer, new hypotheses to test, and transforming the discipline beyond recognition as a result.[40] In France, too, a "scientific" and "objective" approach to the past gained in prestige and influence in the postwar years. It was exemplified above all with the group of historians associated with the journal *Annales*, who had begun their work before the war but only really gained significant influence after it. By incorporating the methods of economics, sociology, and especially geography and statistics into their approach to the past, the *Annales* historians thought that it would be possible to make history far more objective and scientific than ever before. The traditional methods and objects of inquiry no longer sufficed. History should be the central, synthesizing discipline of the social sciences. It had to quantify. "History that is not quantifiable," remarked Emmanuel Le Roy Ladurie, one of the school's leading exponents, in 1979, "cannot claim to be scientific." "Tomorrow's historian," he added, "will have to be able to programme a computer in order to survive."[41] Even when the journal changed its subtitle in 1994 to readmit political history, after a good deal of soul-searching, it still defiantly declared itself to represent *Histoire: sciences sociales*.

These beliefs reached their most extreme form, perhaps, in the United States in the late 1960s and 1970s with the rise of "social science history." One of its principal exponents, the econometric historian Robert Fogel, drew a sharp distinction between "scientific" and "traditional" history.[42] Scientific history, made possible above all by the computer, rested not on vague, incomplete, implicit, and inconsistent sets of assumptions about human behavior in the way that traditional history did, but on explicitly elaborated, sometimes mathematical models that could be rigorously tested by quantitative means. It applied not to individuals but to groups, and sought to develop not particular explanations but general hypotheses which could be statistically tested. It assumed that there were systematic relationships among events, structures, and processes in history. It was, he argued, neutral and nonideological. It tended to be carried out by teams of scholars, just as experimental programs in the natural sciences did, rather than by the individual scholars who were the norm for the researcher in traditional history. It also addressed itself not to a wider public but to a specialist readership of fellow scientists, just as the natural sciences did.

Scientific methods used in this way, argued Fogel, were overturning the received wisdom of traditional history on many points and thus proving their superiority. Peter Laslett and the Cambridge Group of demographic historians, for instance, had demonstrated the statistical prevalence of the nuclear family in preindustrial society and established a relatively high age at marriage, confounding traditional historians' belief in the dominance of extended family forms and the normality of marriage at a very early age. Similar, major advances in knowledge had come in many branches of economic history through the application of scientific, statistical methods.[43] Convinced that not only demographic and economic history, but also social and political history, indeed all forms of history, had to be put onto this new scientific basis, the "cliometricians" of the 1970s unrolled a vastly ambitious program of disciplinary transformation which was intended to spell the end of traditional history altogether.[44] There was a widespread feeling in the 1970s that "traditional" history had proved vulnerable to the criticisms of relativists like Carr because it had not been scientific enough. By the end of the decade, there was a general consensus among observers of the historical profession that, as Georg G. Iggers put it, historical scholarship over the decades had become "scientifically ever more rigorous." "Historians have become more committed than ever to the scientific ideal of history."[45]

But were the differences between "scientific" and "traditional" history in fact so very great? Not surprisingly, Sir Geoffrey Elton did not think so. He pointed to the fact that what he had described as "traditional" history was itself widely regarded by its defenders as "scientific" well into the second half of the twentieth century. Teamwork was common in some areas in "traditional" history, too, from the editing of documents to the compilation of propographies. Cliometrics had delivered only on a very limited number of generally rather narrow questions. When it came to the really big issues in history, it had to remain silent because they could not be solved by quantitative methods.[46] A glance at *Social Science History*, the flagship journal of the cliometricians, will easily support Elton's claim. Moreover, it quickly became clear that the ability of Fogel's scientific methods to settle beyond dispute even the questions they did address was highly questionable. In 1974 Fogel and his collaborator Stanley L. Engerman published a formidable two-volume study of slavery in the old American South. Full of elaborate statistical charts, tables, and equations, it claimed to represent a new level of scientific rigor in testing well-worn hypotheses. The result was a set of con-

clusions which overturned existing, "traditional" historical orthodoxy. Slavery was not, as had previously been thought, unprofitable,
economically inefficient, and bad for the slaves. Fogel and Engerman
argued that the economic efficiency of slavery was so high that slaves
benefited from standards of living at least as high as those of free
workers at the time. In defending themselves against accusations of
political incorrectness for espousing such a view, the two authors
suggested that this showed how proud the slaves could be of their
achievements and how dubious, even racist, were claims that their
labor had been unproductive.[47]

Fogel and Engerman were immediately attacked by their fellow
historians for flawed statistical procedures, misuse and overinterpre-
tation of sources, vague hypotheses, and plain inaccuracy. One group
of critics concluded at the end of a lengthy reexamination of the data

> that *Time on the Cross* is full of errors. The book embraces errors of
> mathematics, disregards standard principles of statistical inference,
> mis-cites sources, takes quotations out of context, distorts the views
> and findings of other historians and economists, and relies upon dubi-
> ous and largely unexplained models of market behavior, economic
> dynamics, socialization, sexual behavior, fertility determination, and
> genetics (to name some).

Moreover, all the errors apparently had a "consistent tendency" to
work in favor of Fogel and Engerman's overall argument. When the
faults were corrected and the evidence was reexamined, the two
authors' entire argument simply fell apart. Quantification and statistics had thus signally failed to deliver the "scientific" certainties their
advocates had proclaimed.[48]

Moreover, the cliometricians' claim to be achieving a higher,
indeed virtually unassailable level of objectivity and certainty
through the use of properly scientific methods was also being undermined by new developments in the philosophy of science. After the
broadly empiricist position of Popper had held sway in the 1950s,
Thomas Kuhn's postempiricist view of science, expounded in 1962
in his enormously influential book *The Structure of Scientific*

Revolutions, took over as the dominant explanatory model. In place of the existing view of science as continuous progress, Kuhn argued that most scientists worked, often unconsciously, within a "paradigm" or set of theories, assumptions, research agendas, and so on, which guided their experiments and ensured that their observations matched the theories they held. Paradigms could thus not be falsified, and anomalies, where the data did not fit the paradigm, were usually ignored or worked around. Only when the anomalies had accumulated to a point where they caused a general sense of unease in the scientific community did the search for a new paradigm begin. The disadvantage of a new paradigm was often, however, that it failed to account for some phenomena that the old one succeeded in explaining. Moreover, different paradigms constituted different mental worlds, which were not comparable with one another. Thus science was not necessarily progressive, and falsifiable scientific theories were not established by experimental confirmation but were maintained by intellectual consensus. This view was widely attacked by scientists as irrationalist and relativist, portraying their disciplines as guided by "mob rule." But by the 1970s it had become the dominant view among philosophers of science and was being applied to other forms of knowledge as well. To be sure, Kuhn believed that the natural sciences progressed entirely free of any external influences and insisted that his ideas were not applicable to other fields. Nor is the Kuhnian notion of a paradigm really applicable to history; historians in general do not work within rigid and constricting paradigms.[49] But substitute the words "historical interpretation" for "scientific paradigm," and one can see that those historians who did take Kuhn's ideas on board found their implications to be strongly relativist as well as corrosive of the idea that the "scientific" credentials of history could be established by methods that guaranteed the production of "objective" knowledge about the past.

By the 1980s, therefore, the long search for a scientific method of history had failed to yield any definitive results. The period in which the social sciences, encouraged by historians like E. H. Carr, had been exerting their influence over the practice of historical research and in the most extreme cases, such as that of Fogel, threatening to displace "traditional" methods of history altogether seemed to be coming to an end.[50] The argument that history is, or should be, a science, in principle no different from quantum mechanics or crystallography, began to come under renewed and sustained attack, more radical than ever before. In the next chapter, we turn to see to what extent the belief that history is a science has managed to weather the storm.

CHAPTER TWO

HISTORY, SCIENCE, AND MORALITY

I

ATTEMPTS to turn history into a science have been going on for the best part of two centuries now, and show no signs of letting up. Yet as E. H. Carr correctly observed, the question of whether or not history is a science has been discussed in Anglo-American circles largely because of "an eccentricity of the English language".[1] The trouble originated with the German term *Wissenschaft*, which simply means a discipline or body of organized knowledge. Germans have never had any difficulty in applying it to a whole range of subjects, including not only *Naturwissenschaft* but also *Sozialwissenschaft*, *Geschichtswissenschaft*, and *Literaturwissenschaft*. Yet the mere attempt to translate these terms into English indicates the problem. "Natural science" and even "social science" sound fine,[2] but "historical science" and "literary science" do not. We can use the term "sociology" or "geology," but "historiology" somehow has never become general usage. In German the discipline of history, *Geschichtswissenschaft*, has been classified from the outset as a *Geisteswissenschaft*, an aspect of the organized study of the human spirit, and so the debate about the scientific or nonscientific nature of history has never arisen.[3]

Modern philosophies of science, said Carr, argued plausibly that the natural scientist was anything but a neutral observer of autonomous processes in the laboratory. In history and the social sciences, moreover, human beings were studying other human beings, or in other words, humanity was studying itself, while in the natural sciences the object of study in most cases was not human but something else. But even this distinction breaks down in fact in disciplines such as medicine, biology, biochemistry, experimental psychology, and the like.[4] Carr would have been more correct in concluding that in no subject could there be an entirely clear separation between the researcher and the object of research. As Sir Geoffrey Elton observed, "the post-Newtonian view of the physical world, denying the absolute, allowing for the unpredictably contingent, and accepting the effect of the observer upon the matter observed, might not be a bad analogy for good history."[5] In this sense, the difference between the views of Carr and Elton on this matter did not seem so great, though Elton thought that history in the end was neither an art nor a science. "History," he declared proudly, "is a study different from any other and governed by rules peculiar to itself."[6] However, far from being irrelevant or unimportant or based on a mere terminological misunderstanding, the debate over whether history is an art or science has been central to historians' self-understanding for more than a century. Even in Germany there has been intensive discussion over whether or not the methods and approaches of natural science can be applied to history in its guise as a "human science" or whether it can or should be classified as a "social science"; so the debate in effect goes beyond the Anglo-Saxon linguistic boundary after all.

Many writers have argued that history is not a science because while scientific knowledge is cumulative, historical knowledge is not. Clearly, our knowledge of physics or chemistry today rests on the foundations built by the scientific discoveries of the past, from Newton and Faraday to Einstein and Rutherford, even if some of the theories propounded by those who laid those foundations have now been superseded. But because each historian by and large advances a different interpretation from that of previous historians studying the same subject, many commentators have concluded that historical knowledge does not accumulate in the way that scientific knowledge does; historians are usually more concerned to dispute the findings of their predecessors than to build on them. Such conclusions were vigorously disputed by Sir Geoffrey Elton, who declared optimistically that through the steady accumulation of empirical knowledge, professional historians were advancing "ever nearer to the fortress of truth," even if they would never be able to capture it completely. The limitations of practicality meant that any one historian could only establish "new footholds in the territory of truth," but as historians gathered particular truths about aspects of a subject, they would be able to put them together to form a picture that was ever more complete.[7] Of course, he conceded, historical research was subject to review and revision, but if it were good, its reconstruction of the past would mostly stand up to future tests.[8] Writing a definitive history of something, so definitive that it would never need to be written again, was an ambition that was not only laudable in his eyes but also eminently achievable. Predictably enough, perhaps, such views have not gone unchallenged in their turn. Thus, according to Keith Jenkins, for example, Elton's claim that historical knowledge did grow over time and that we know in the present vastly more about, for example, the Tudor age than we did twenty or thirty years ago, means that he "sees himself as standing at the end of a process" of the accumulation of historical knowledge, in which the historians of the past are judged according to what they have contributed to this Eltonian teleology. This smacks of an arrogance that historians would do better to avoid.[9]

Anyone who has carried out historical research quickly becomes aware that his knowledge is more complete than that of others; this is an experience common even to the humblest of Ph.D. students within a few months of starting on their project. The reason for this is that the materials left to us by the past are so extensive that all the historians who have ever worked have done little more than scratch the surface of the deposits which have accumulated, and continue to accumulate, over time. Of course, the farther back we go in time, the less evidence there is, and the more thoroughly what there is has been worked over by previous generations of historians. Even in medieval or ancient history, however, there are still many new things to discover, which do not necessarily depend on a reworking of old

material. Indeed, despite the emphasis of university teaching on controversy, debate, and interpretation, the majority of working historians probably consider that adding to our knowledge of the past—
"filling in a gap"—is just as important as transforming our understanding of what is already known, if not more so. It is in this sense,
to begin with, that historical knowledge is cumulative. The
researcher identifies gaps in knowledge with reference to what is
already known. Far from this meaning that we rate previous historians according to what they have contributed to our own work, we
are usually concerned above all to escape from them by doing something different. Moreover, distance not only adds to our knowledge,
but also adds to our understanding. Even E. H. Carr conceded that
the farther in time historians got from, say, Bismarck, the closer they
were likely to get to an objective judgment of his work.[10] Moreover,
the fact that historical knowledge is constantly being added to often
enables historians to advance new interpretations in the fields they
are studying, whatever the theoretical impulses behind these interpretations might be.

Another reason for distinguishing between history and science is
the argument that the former must necessarily involve an element of
moral judgment, while the latter does not. E. H. Carr met this assertion with a flat denial. Historians, according to Carr, should not
judge the past in moral terms; their purpose was rather to understand
how the past had contributed to human progress. It was pointless, for
example, to condemn slavery in the ancient world as immoral; the
point was to understand how it came about, how it functioned, and
why it declined, opening the way to another form of social organization. This view was put most trenchantly by Professor David
Knowles, the great British medievalist, who rejected moral judgment
as an aspect of history, observing that "the historian is not a judge,
still less a hanging judge."[11] Since Knowles was not only an eminent
historian but also a Benedictine monk of saintly character and ascetic
appearance, his views on this matter are certainly deserving of
respect. It is, moreover, easy to discover moral judgments by historians that reveal themselves in retrospect to be little more than articu-
lations of the prejudices of their own day. The Victorians were par-

ticularly apt to condemn figures in the past for sexual behavior that would scarcely raise an eyebrow in the present, a tendency whose relentless lampooning in that classic satire on history textbooks Sellar and Yeatman's *1066 and All That* should by now have laid to rest forever.[12] But while historians would scarcely judge a medieval monarch as "a bad man, but a good king" or "a good man, but a bad king" anymore, the issue is rather different when it comes to twentieth-century dictators such as Hitler and Stalin. Carr suggested that moral denunciations of such figures often served to deflect attention from the responsibility of the wider society that produced them, and considered that moral judgment was perfectly acceptable when applied to the latter.[13] But this, too, was problematical since he went on to suggest that moral standards were relative and that historians should judge past societies not in relation to some absolute standard but in relation to one another.[14] Since Carr ridiculed the application of Victorian moral standards to the Middle Ages, however, the validity of this principle would seem in practice to be rather doubtful.

No doubt Knowles was right to argue that historians should not engage in explicit moral judgments on the past, an argument which was convenient indeed for him as a Catholic monk dealing with English monasticism in the fifteenth and early sixteenth centuries, when monks and nuns alike had been widely condemned by Protestant historians for all kinds of supposedly immoral behavior. In practice, however, Knowles certainly did engage in moral judgment, relating the behavior of all the subjects of his work to the eternal and divinely commanded rule of St. Benedict, the founder of monasticism. No human historian, he implied, but God Himself had the role of passing judgment here. The lesson of the story he told, Knowles wrote on the final page of his vast work, was that "when once a religious house or a religious order ceases to direct its sons to the abandonment of all that is not God . . . it sinks to the level of a purely human institution."[15] Hence his comments on William More, prior of Worcester, whose "life was in great part that of a country squire," that "he followed . . . the way of the world" has to be read as moral criticism.[16] In Knowles's view, the decline of the monasteries in the late Middle Ages was real, and indeed, judged by such high religious standards, it certainly was. Measuring medieval monks and nuns against these standards—a task which he carried out with great subtlety and scrupulosity—was what Knowles's four-volume history was principally about, and this rather simplistic approach arguably prevented him from gaining the kind of sophisticated and differentiated interpretative perspective on the behavior of the regular clergy that might have been possible had he, for example, approached their belief systems and their changing social roles and mores in secular terms, using the kinds of anthropological theories employed by subsequent historians of other belief systems such as witchcraft.

Yet despite his failure to follow it in practice, the principle Knowles laid down—of avoiding explicit moral judgments on the past and the people who lived in it—is surely a good one for the historian to follow. A historian who uses terms like "wicked" and "evil" about a person or persons in the past will only succeed in looking ridiculous. While this is to be avoided, however, it is perfectly legitimate to point out in factual terms when people in the past, such as monks and nuns, behaved in private in a manner quite different from that which they advocated for other people, and boasted of themselves, in public. Readers will then be able to draw their own conclusions about the morality of it all.

To be sure, moral judgments are unavoidable when one deals with a whole range of historical issues. But what is achieved by the use of moral invective? If a historian wishes to demonstrate that slavery in the American South was morally wrong, for example, the way to do it is to employ not moral or philosophical arguments but historical ones: to show, for instance, that it oppressed the slaves, that it involved cruelty and brutality, that it caused deprivation, disease, and death. If the historian simply says it was evil, no one will take that seriously. Overloading the historian's text with expressions of moral outrage will add little to the argument. Moreover, *explaining* how the system of slaveownership came into being, how it worked, what attitude the slaves and slaveowners had toward it and why, and what were the larger historical forces behind its rise and fall is the real task of the historian. These things in no way affect the moral aspects of the question because in the end whatever the larger forces at work, human beings still have the possibility of moral choice open to them in any given situation. "To explain everything," a French historian once remarked, "is to excuse everything," but this is simply not true. We may, for instance, explain the horrific tortures and executions of the Salem witches by reference to a whole range of factors from the nature of Puritan religious doctrine to the social structure and social conflicts that divided the local community at the time; none of this, however, lessens the moral repugnance that most of us feel when reading about the terrible fate that overtook those who were arrested and condemned.

In making moral judgments on the past, historians have far more powerful rhetorical and stylistic weapons at their disposal than mere denunciation: sarcasm, irony, the juxtaposition of rhetoric and reality, the factual exposure of hypocrisy, self-interest, and greed, the uncommented recounting of courageous acts of rebellion and defiance, the description of terrible acts of hatred and violence. All this can be achieved without the direct application of the transient moral vocabulary of the society the historian is living in. Particularly in periods of mass destruction, such as the years 1914–45, it is difficult for the historian not to take a moral stance, but that moral stance is still best articulated historically. In a similar way, there is surely a moral element involved in all kinds of research in the natural sciences, from embryology to nuclear physics. Moral concerns may drive scientific research, or they may emerge from it; the key point surely is that just as in history, the element of moral judgment, insofar as it is exercised at all, is in the end extraneous to the research rather than being embedded in the theory or methodology of it.

If some have adduced the moral dimension as an argument against the scientific nature of history, another reason often given for supposing that history is not a science is the fact that historians' conclusions cannot be experimentally replicated. But of course, important aspects of a number of sciences are based, like history, on observation rather than on experimentation, such as, for example, astronomy. Such observation may not be directly visual; it may be indirect, for instance, as when the existence of the planet Pluto was postulated through the observation of irregularities in the orbital path of the next outermost planet in the solar system, Neptune, which could have been caused only by the exertion of a gravitational pull from a large but as yet unseen object farther out. We can return to this evidence, or to other forms of traces, such as radio waves, from which the existence of certain objects in outer space can be inferred, just as we can return to historical documents, but we cannot somehow create them in experiments, as we can a chemical reaction. Yet nobody has ventured to claim that astronomy is not a science. It is not necessary, therefore, to engage in elaborate defenses of the scientific nature of history of the sort Sir Geoffrey Elton engaged in when he claimed that historical fact, because it could not be manufactured by the historian, was actually more independent of the observer than scientific fact was.[17] In nonexperimental sciences the distinction simply breaks down.

II

PERHAPS the most serious challenge to history's claim to be scientific rests on the belief that a true science can exist only if it is able to posit general laws. This argument has a long pedigree, going back at least as far as a notorious remark made by the English Rankean James Anthony Froude in 1864: "It often seems to me as if history is like a child's box of letters, with which we can spell any word we please. We have only to pick out such letters as we want, arrange them as we like, and say nothing about those which do not suit our purpose."[18] Froude's enemies seized on this statement as an admission that the procedures he himself adopted were arbitrary and unscientific. But he meant it in fact as a criticism of philosophies of history such as that of his contemporary Henry Thomas Buckle, who believed that the movement of history could be scientifically reduced to a series of mathematical formulae. In Froude's view, history had to confine itself to a presentation of the facts and not be used to "spell out" theories of a "scientific" nature. Indeed, in every case where historians have tried to prove generally applicable laws of history, they have been easily refuted by critics who have demonstrated instances in which they do not apply—most notoriously, perhaps, in the case of Arnold Toynbee's once-popular *A Study of History*. Published in thirteen volumes between 1934 and 1947, this vast work ranged across twenty-one human "civilizations" and six thousand years of human history, drawing from them a series of general laws according to which civilizations rise, develop, and collapse.

Toynbee's laws are detailed and exact. He posits, for example, four methods by which great men appear in history to save civilizations in danger of imminent collapse, and he presents the stages in which new institutions emerge from the body of a disintegrating civilization in the form of a table. The work was hailed by the press as "an immortal masterpiece" and "the greatest work of our time." Yet professional historians, foremost among them Pieter Geyl, a thoughtful writer on modern historiography as well as a leading specialist on the history of the Netherlands, were deeply skeptical. Geyl charged that Toynbee simply selected the evidence he wanted and picked out a few arbitrary strands from the tangled skein of historical fact. In arguing that "ease" was inimical to the growth of civilization, Toynbee, for example, pointed to the triumph of the hardy New Englanders in seventeenth- and eighteenth-century North America over the effete French in Louisiana or the idle Spaniards in Florida. "The greater the difficulty, the greater the stimulus"; thus American civilization was born, and triumphed, out of hardship and adversity in combating the challenge of a hostile environment. Yet Toynbee ignored the fact that the conquest of New Amsterdam which turned it into New England was carried out in 1664 by the luxurious court of Charles II, and he suppressed other explanations for the eventual hegemony of the New Englanders, from the decline of Spain as an imperial power to the superiority of British sea power at a time when the French were embroiled in wars on the European continent. The explanation in other words had to be sought in the relative positions of the colonial powers, not in the relationship of the settlers of New England to their environment. "Challenge and response" was completely irrelevant here.

Geyl charged that this example was typical of the "innumerable fallacious arguments and spurious demonstrations of which the whole book is made up." Toynbee was a prophet, not a historian:

> It is not only—not even in the first place—the looking for laws, the generalizations, even the faulty reasonings, that offend; it is the vision itself in which every age and every civilization is judged by a standard foreign to it and its importance restricted to what it contributed to the progress of an arbitrarily chosen principle. The historian believes that history can enrich the civilization of his own age especially by trying to enter into the habits of thought and the relationships of past generations and that only thus can these be understood. . . . To see a self-styled historian reducing the whole of the wonderful and mysterious movement of history to one single motif, rejecting whole centuries as uninteresting, forcing it all into the scheme of a presumptuous construction, strikes him as going against all that history stands for.

Geyl also lambasted the "spate of moral judgments" which gushed from Toynbee's pen, above all in the final volume of *A Study of History*, in which the author launched a violent attack on "neo-paganism" and defended Christianity as the only defense of civilization against barbarity of the sort that had overwhelmed Germany and Europe during the Second World War. All this was deeply unhistorical, utterly alien to the spirit of the historian's enterprise.[19]

Toynbee's huge and pretentious work enjoyed only a brief vogue before disappearing into the obscurity in which it has languished, along with similar tracts such as Buckle's *History of Civilization*, ever since.[20] Most historians have always believed the establishment of general laws to be alien to the enterprise in which they are engaged. This clearly differentiates them very sharply from natural scientists. Yet there have been some exceptions, most notably in recent times E. H. Carr. In trying to refute the argument that history was not a science because it posited no general laws, Carr pointed out that while no two historical events were identical, no two atoms were either, no two stars, no two living organisms, nor any other two things that any scientist studied. Yet this did not stop scientists from framing their laws. Similarly, "the very use of language," he said, "commits the historian, like the scientist, to generalization."[21] He pointed out that history was as concerned with generalization as any science was; it was not merely confined to the establishment of particular, isolated facts. It taught lessons, as, for example, the constant reference made by delegates at the Versailles Conference in 1919 to the Vienna Congress of 1815, and countless other examples showed; in this sense, it could be used to predict the future, on the basis of a knowledge of given conditions, and thus to shape it. Carr poured scorn on the argument that history was not a science because it could not predict the future. The law of gravity, he observed, could not predict that a particular apple would fall at some particular time and in some particular place. Scientific laws operated only under certain specific conditions, and Carr sought to rescue the predictive capabilities of history by making the claim that historians could, for instance, say that a revolution was going to occur in some country or other if conditions there were the same as in similar countries where revolutions had already taken place.[22] Thus, he concluded, history was just like any other science in its generation of laws and its predictive capacities.

Those who have attempted to assimilate history to the social sciences have often tried to take account of this point. Social scientific history concerns itself overwhelmingly with averages and means, not with discrete individuals. The *Annales* school interested itself in collective behavior and mentalities, not in individuals, while the cliometricians worked only on statistically significant numbers of people, if they worked on people at all. Yet history clearly includes the study of individual people, events, and structures as well as groups and collectivities. The differences that exist between two human beings, even when they live in the same time and place, are vastly more complex than the differences between two atoms or two molecules. Human individuality is far greater than microbial individuality. This makes the framing of general laws to cover it correspondingly far more difficult.

Carr was blurring important distinctions in his discussion of the matter. For laws are not the same as generalizations. As the English historian John Vincent puts it, "where science asserts, say, the Second Law of Thermodynamics, it is asserting something more than a pattern with inevitable exceptions."[23] The latter, however, is all that history, even Marxist history, can hope to aspire to. Moreover, even the most inexperienced history student can dispute interpretations put forward by even the grandest of professors, while no chemistry or biology student is going to dispute the scientific laws taught in the classroom by the most junior instructor. The American intellectual historian Allan Megill has made the distinction between laws and generalizations particularly clear:

> In historians' language, the following invented statement counts as a generalization . . . : "As a result of the growth of towns and trade, feudalism gave way to incipient capitalism in late medieval and early modern Europe." The "problem of generalization[,]" as historians conceive of it, is usually the problem of how to get from fragmentary and confusing data to such larger assertions. But such assertions are not what the logical positivists, or Windelband before them, had in mind when they spoke of general laws. In "nomothetic" science, the desired generalizations *transcend* particular times and places, as in, for instance, this invented statement: "*Whenever*, within a feudal system, towns and trade begin to grow, . . . *then* feudalism gives way to capitalism."[24]

In this latter case, a single exception would be enough to invalidate the law. In the former case, it would not undermine the generalization but, on the contrary, prove an interesting exception to it that would itself require explanation.

While many people, especially politicians, try to learn lessons from history, history itself shows that very few of these lessons have been the right ones in retrospect. Time and again, history has proved a very bad predictor of future events. This is because history never repeats itself; nothing in human society, the main concern of the historian, ever happens twice under exactly the same conditions or in exactly the same way. And when people try to use history, they often do so not in order to accommodate themselves to the inevitable, but in order to avoid it. For example, British politicians in the postwar era based much of their conduct of foreign policy on the belief that the "appeasement" of dictators, such as was carried out by Prime Minister Neville Chamberlain in his relations with Hitler in 1938 and 1939, could only lead to disaster. In practice, however, this very belief only too often led to disaster itself, most notoriously in 1956, when the British prime minister, Sir Anthony Eden, obsessed with the desire to avoid the "appeasement" of dictators which he had himself criticized in the later 1930s, launched an ill-advised and unsuccessful military strike against the Egyptian government under President Nasser when it nationalized the Anglo-French–owned Suez Canal.

Again, many of the Russian Bolsheviks thought that because the events of 1917 constituted Russia's bourgeois revolution, they would have to wait a long time before they were followed by the proletarian revolution that was their ultimate goal. It was Lenin and Trotsky who argued that unlike previous bourgeois revolutions, in England in 1640, for example, or France in 1789, the Russian Revolution could be given a permanency which would enable it to lead on immediately to the dictatorship of the proletariat. Having surmounted this problem, however, they were then faced with the fact that the two historical revolutions to which they looked back, in seventeenth-century England and eighteenth-century France, had both ended in military dictatorships, run respectively by Oliver Cromwell and Napoleon Bonaparte. After Lenin's death in 1924, fear of this happening again was a material influence in causing the leading Bolsheviks to gang up on Trotsky, the head of the Red Army and the man who everyone thought was most likely to become the Russian Bonaparte. Thus in practice the historical law of revolutions broke down because people in one revolution used the memory of previous ones to change the way they occurred.

Nor does history enable one to predict revolutions, however they are defined. Historians notoriously failed to predict, for example, the fall of the Berlin Wall and the collapse of the Soviet Union in 1989-91.[25] In any case, although Carr argued repeatedly that the historian's role was to use an understanding of the past in order to gain control of the future, very few historians indeed have shared this concept of their function in the sense of using the past as the basis for concrete predictions. The fact is that while a chemist, for instance, knows in advance the result of mixing two elements in a crucible, the historian has no such advance knowledge of anything, nor is trying to gain such knowledge really central to the business in which historians are engaged.

History, then, can produce generalizations, although the broader they are, the more exceptions there are likely to be and the farther removed they will become from hard evidence which can be cited in their support. Its objects of study are in no sense confined to discrete individuals or events. It can identify, or posit with a high degree of plausibility, patterns, trends, and structures in the human past. In these respects it can legitimately be regarded as scientific. But history cannot create laws with predictive power. An understanding of the past might help in the present insofar as it broadens our knowledge of human nature, provide us with an inspiration—or a warning—or suggest plausible, though always fallible, arguments about the likely possibilities of certain things happening under certain conditions. None of this, however, comes anywhere near the immutable predictive certainty of a scientific law. All those who thought, or claimed, that they had discovered laws in history, from Marx and Engels to Toynbee and Buckle, were wrong; indeed, as we have seen, as soon as Marxists in Russia thought they recognized a historical law, they proceeded to do their level best to break it.

An instructive recent example has been that of the Yale historian Paul M. Kennedy, whose profoundly researched and carefully argued study of *The Rise and Fall of the Great Powers* argued that there was a pattern in modern history according to which wealthy states created empires but eventually overstretched their resources and declined. Illustrated with wealth of historical detail, the book attracted attention not because of its learned demonstration of the reasons for the failure of the Habsburg Empire to achieve European domination in the sixteenth and seventeenth centuries, but because of its conclusion that the United States would be unable to sustain its global hegemony far into the twenty-first century. At a time when U.S. President Ronald Reagan was about to ride off into the sunset, this gloomy prophecy struck a deep vein of anxiety in the American people. The book became a best seller overnight. Written in 1987, the book also made a point of arguing that the Soviet Union was not close to collapse, so that the situation seemed to many American readers to be ominous indeed.[26] Within a few years these prophecies had been confounded. The Soviet Union had indeed collapsed, not in the international war which Kennedy had argued was the invariable and inevitable trigger for such processes, but in a process of internal transformation and disintegration. The world hegemony of the United States seemed more assured than ever and in the economic boom of the 1990s showed few signs of suffering from the "imperial overstretch" which Kennedy had prophesied. In the first seven chapters of his book, in other words, Kennedy, writing as a historian, had produced some instructive and workable generalizations about the rise and fall of international superpowers and the relationship of economic and military strength. These chapters also incidentally demonstrated the continuing vitality and viability of "grand narrative" in history. Had Kennedy stopped here, his book would not have attracted the attention it did and would not have sold so many copies. But it would also have been better history. As soon as he turned his generalizations into laws and used them, in his final chapter, to prophesy the future, he ran into trouble. It is always a mistake for a historian to try to predict the future. Life, unlike science, is simply too full of surprises.

III

IF history is not a science, then are historians any different in essence from novelists or poets? Historians have often attempted to distinguish what they do from what artists do by arguing that their discipline does indeed require a rigorous professional or scientific training, while if art and music also need a technical expertise which can be acquired only through education, writing novels or poems, despite the proliferation of creative writing courses in recent years, demonstrably does not. Sir Geoffrey Elton was particularly insistent on this point. The series of examples of readings of source material with which Elton illustrated his claim suggest that by "training" he meant that historians had to learn about the technical details of the documents they used, or in other words, the meaning for contemporaries of the language they employed, and the nature and customs of the institutions in which the documents were produced. Thus it was necessary to know, for instance, that when a medieval English king differentiated in his correspondence between recipients he addressed as "trusty and well-beloved" and "right trusty and well-beloved," this did not indicate the difference between a distant political ally and a close one, but rather reflected the social status of the addressee. Or that when noble families in early modern Europe had pictures painted in which their children were dressed in adult clothes, this did not mean, as the amateur historian Philippe Ariès had supposed, they had no notion of childhood as a separate stage of human existence. Other sources indicate that in everyday life children were indeed dressed differently from adults; they were put in grown-up clothes just to have their portraits painted.[27]

All this may be both admirable and true, but what does it have to do with scientific training? The basic point Elton seems to want to make is that in order to understand a source, historians have to ask how it came into existence, what purposes it served those who created it, and how they proceeded to bring it into being. But how much training do they need for this, and in what does it consist? Traditionally, historians have been trained by being put through an undergraduate degree, culminating in the documentary-based special subject, and then by doing a Ph.D. This has involved a kind of trial and error technique, with the student handing the tutor or supervisor essays, drafts, or chapters of a thesis and getting them back with critical comments. This has been backed up by the research seminar, in which the professor and others have led critical discussions of students' work, but this, too, essentially operates by the same principle. Even so rigorous a historian as the English medievalist T. F. Tout, a champion of the importation of German research methods into British universities in the early part of the twentieth century, observed that students were trained to be professional historians "by observation, osmosis and occasional words of advice."[28] In saying this, he was echoing the great German historian of ancient Rome, Theodor Mommsen, who declared in 1874 that it was a "dangerous and harmful illusion for the professor of history to believe that his-

torians can be trained at the University in the same way as philologists or mathematicians most assuredly can be." The true historian, he
said, was "not trained but born."[29] Modern historians frequently
agree with this point. While there is plenty of training, and there are
plenty of rules for assessing the factual reliability of the traces left by
the past, as two American historians have observed, "there is no training and there are no rules for the process of constructing a story out
of the disparate pieces of evidence. . . . When it comes to creating a
coherent account out of these evidential fragments, the historical
method consists only of appealing to the muse."[30]

Mommsen's skepticism about the necessity of even a very modest
degree of training in the making of a good historian was echoed a
century later by the Oxford specialist in modern French history,
Theodore Zeldin, who argued in 1976 that "the ideals or models that
historians have set before their pupils have always been rapidly forgotten." "Personally," he went on,

> I have no wish to urge anyone to write history in any particular way.
> I believe that the history you write is the expression of your individ-
> uality; I agree with Mommsen that one cannot teach people to write
> history; I believe that much more can be gained by encouraging young
> historians to develop their own personality, their own vision, their own
> eccentricities, than by setting them examples to follow. Original histo-
> ry is the reflection of an original mind, and there is no prescription
> which will produce that.[31]

There was something very English, perhaps, in the view of this particular Oxford don that the best way to become a good historian was
to become a good eccentric. Eccentric people, one might argue, produce eccentric history. Certainly—if we assume he has obeyed his
own maxim—that has been the case with Zeldin himself, whose most
recent books, *Happiness* and the best-selling *An Intimate History of
Humanity,* have concentrated, respectively, on the imaginary adven-
tures of a girl called "Sumdy" and on the real personal life histories of
a handful of individuals, mainly French, in the present, as the starting
point for a series of ruminations on the possible ways individuals in
the West might shape their personal lives in the coming century.

Most historians, in practice, would agree that at least some degree of training and supervision is necessary to equip young scholars for a career in the profession and that the Ph.D. is probably the best way of doing this. The historian's training through the Ph.D. is necessarily mostly training on the job, learning through practice. But historians do also have to learn theories and techniques before they are let loose on their materials; they must absorb not only the Rankean principles of source criticism and citation but also ancillary skills, such as languages, paleography, statistics, and so on. Moreover, they have to read and digest a large amount of contextual material and master the secondary literature relating to their subject. This kind of training, it has been argued, is more characteristic of a craft than a science. History, the American historical theorist Hayden White has observed, is not a "science that utilizes technical languages, hypothetico-deductive arguments controlled by experimental methods, and laboratory procedures relatively well canonized and agreed on by practitioners of the discipline in question," but "rather a craftlike discipline, which means that it tends to be governed by convention and custom rather than by methodology and theory and to utilize ordinary or natural language."[32] But is science actually defined by any of the things which White says history is not? We have already seen that experimental methods and laboratory procedures are not necessary to constitute a basically observational science such as astronomy. Much, if not most, training in many of the sciences consists of learning the material (properties of elements and the like) and mastering ancillary techniques, such as mathematics, spectroscopy, computer imaging, and so on. Much the same could be said of history. Moreover, historical research has its agreed procedures. The differences in the end are not as great as one might initially suppose.

IV

AS White suggests, history per se does not have a specialized technical language of its own in the way that, say, microbiology or climatology does. Like many historians, Sir Geoffrey Elton, for example, argued that all historians should try to write clearly and comprehensibly, and there is nothing wrong with that; but he also declared that no historical problem was "incapable of being explained with full clarity to any person of reasonable intelligence," and that in practice is a very debatable claim.[33] There are many historical works, for example, in econometric history or demographic history, which clearly do require a good deal of technical knowledge to understand. Technical language is also used by many historians in specialized areas of research. Discussions of such topics as the medieval manorial economy, the structure of landholding and serfdom in eighteenth-century central Europe, the legal basis of the slaveholding system in the old American South, and the debate on stamp duty and other aspects of taxation policy in prerevolutionary America can be highly technical and comprehensible only to the initiated. But does this make it scientific, and historical work written in nontechnical language nonscientific? The distinction seems entirely artificial. Of course, in practice, when we deal with an area of the past in which obsolete technical terms are involved, it is frequently impossible to avoid using specialized terminology. But this surely does not abrogate the historian's general responsibility to write as clearly and unpretentiously as is possible under the circumstances. Lamenting the tendency in recent years to move away from this habit, Lawrence Stone says that he was taught "that one should always try to write plain English, avoiding jargon and obfuscation, and making one's meaning as clear as possible to the reader."[34] It is hard to disagree with him. Clarity of presentation, after all, is a necessary part of intellectual precision. There is nothing necessarily "unscientific" or sloppy about it; quite the reverse.

Yet historians, as White points out, customarily use the medium of literary prose, involving all kinds of images and figures of speech which are not present in the sources they employ. This means that they are doing far more than merely reporting or reflecting the sources. Indeed, far from wanting them to expunge literary artifice from their work, White positively encourages historians to write in a colorful way, since telling the story plain and unvarnished in his view does not deliver anything more "scientific," merely an impoverished and unimaginative historical text.[35] Similarly, another American intellectual historian, Dominick LaCapra, also points to the way in which "the 'voice' of the historian . . . employs self-critical reflection about its own protocols of inquiry, and makes use of modes such as irony, parody, self-parody, and humor, that is, double- or multiple-voiced uses of language."[36] He goes on to call for historians to be still more self-conscious about their use of language. "The anti-rhetoric of plain style, or, more elaborately, of 'scientificity,' " he points out, implies a quest for a mathematically precise language that is illusory.[37] It would not be going too far to say that it was itself a form of rhetoric.

Some philosophers, like Hans Kellner, draw the conclusion from all this that metaphorical descriptions cannot be true; but if there is a resemblance between the central features of what the metaphor refers to as metaphor and what it refers to as fact, then a metaphorical description actually can be true. If we talk of a "revolution," for example, the metaphor of a wheel or piston turning around does resemble the fact of rapid historical change at times like 1789 in France and 1917 in Russia.[38] Provided we define our terms carefully and remain aware of the need for such correspondences in the use of metaphor, White's exhortation surely has a good deal to recommend it, as does LaCapra's. Metaphor and imagery can illuminate the past just as much as statistics and social theory. Yet this should add to rather than detract from the clarity and precision of the historian's arguments and interpretations. In unpracticed hands, the return of history to a literary mode can have unfortunate consequences. The American historian Marjorie Becker, author of a monograph on the Mexican Revolution of 1910, claims, for example, that she uses metaphors "with great liberality" in her book because "the separation between history and poetry is a false and dangerous one." The publisher's advertising copy for her book claims that this results in a "beautifully written work." Yet the reviewer for the Times Literary Supplement, a leading expert in the field, considered the book's style "rambling, opaque and affected."[39] In the end it is better for historians to stick to a plain style, unless they are very sure of what they are doing, and to make sure that literary artifice, when they employ it, is used consciously and in the service of clarification rather than obfuscation.

While most historians trundle on with a style that is either plain or literary, give or take a handful of quantifiers who prefer to express themselves in mathematical formulae, literary theorists who write about history adopt a very different tactic. Hayden White, as Russell Jacoby, one of his most acute critics, has noted, "assumes the idiom of the cool scientist scoffing at the emotionalism of the artist." An inspection of White's own rhetoric, Jacoby comments, reveals "the language—and cadence—of aggressive science." Similarly, Dominick LaCapra in his view shows a "palpable disdain" for "less than technical prose." The *ne plus ultra*, or perhaps the *reductio ad absurdum*, of this tendency, occurs in Sande Cohen's book *Historical Culture*, which is written in such technical language that it is supplied with a glossary so that the ordinary reader can understand the words it commonly uses, such as *actantial, psychologeme,* and *distransitivity*.[40] Now, of course, there is nothing wrong in itself with the invention of new terms to denote newly discovered or newly posited phenomena. But this goes far beyond such necessary technicality. As Jacoby notes, moreover, "the concentration on language and texts by the new intellectual historians ignores language and texts—their own."[41] He is puzzled that scholars who advocate history's return to literature should write so badly themselves, but he is missing the essential point here, which is that they do not think of themselves as historians anymore, least of all in the sense they are advocating, but as literary scientists.

As three American historians have recently pointed out in their reflections on the current state of the debate, "history is much more than a branch of letters to be judged only in terms of its literary merit."[42] If it were so judged, of course, it would generally found wanting. Few historians write competently; fewer still display any real mastery of the language in which they publish their work. Most history books are hopelessly unreadable. For this situation, the dominance in the past thirty years of social science models bears a lot of responsibility. Professional historians publish works that no sane person would attempt to read from beginning to end, works that are designed explicitly for reference rather than for reading. They usually lack the kind of literary ability that would make their work rival that of major poets or novelists. If they had it, no doubt most of them would be writing poems or novels. In the end, of course, there is no reason why historians' works should not be subjected to literary and linguistic analysis. It can often sharpen up our perceptions of their thought. Historical writings in truth are so diverse that the style in which they are written runs from the rebarbatively technical and formula-laden work of econometric or demographic historians at one extreme to the literary gems and masterpieces of practiced communicators at the other. Ultimately, however illuminating it may be in itself, the study of historians' writings as linguistic texts is almost bound to be of secondary importance to their critical scrutiny as pieces of historical scholarship in the long run. The historians who can be read for literary pleasure are few indeed, and most of them, such as Gibbon, Michelet, Tocqueville, and Carlyle, wrote in the eighteenth or nineteenth century, which is no doubt why literary analysts have concentrated their attentions on this period rather than applying their techniques to historians of the twentieth, when the desire to be scientific has increasingly driven literary qualities out of their texts. Thus we have a paradoxical situation in which arguments are overwhelmingly advanced—by Hayden White, Stephen Bann, Linda Orr, and many others—about the nature of the historian's enterprise as a whole on the basis of a reading of the subject's practitioners writing a century or more ago.[43] Given the extent to which historical research has moved on in purely empirical terms since then—we now know a lot more about the French Revolution than any nineteenth-century authors did—it is not surprising that such an approach feels justified in largely neglecting the empirical content of what Michelet, Tocqueville, and their contemporaries wrote. For modern and contemporary historians writing in the present, however, the critical scrutiny of their work as historical scholarship generally remains more important than their analysis as literary texts.

V

GIVEN the vast range of styles and modes in which history is written and researched today, defending it as necessarily or even preferably scientific can be a dangerous game. Yet many historians persist in claiming that their discipline as a whole, whenever and however it is practiced by university-based professionals, is characterized precisely by its superiority to vaguer and more literary forms of analysis. "The techniques of deconstruction or discourse analysis," declares Professor Arthur Marwick of Britain's Open University, for example, "have little value compared with the sophisticated methods historians have been developing over the years."[44] In view of his stout championing of the historian's superior sophistication, it seems legitimate to ask how Marwick has deployed these "sophisticated methods" in his own work. Here is one sample, taken from Marwick's discussion of the popular novels of Jeffrey Archer in his book *Culture in Britain since 1945*: "I have read only one of these novels: I found my attention firmly held while reading, but, the book finished, I had only the feeling of deepest nullity: no perceptions broadened, nothing to think about, just nothing—the classic outcome of empty entertainment, the opposite pole from serious art."[45] Does this kind of judgment really reflect the "sophisticated methods historians have been developing over the years"? In another book, on *Beauty in History*, Marwick waxes lyrical about "the most beautiful black woman I personally have ever seen, an absolutely beautifully proportioned and intensely appealing face, surmounted by close-cropped fuzzy hair." Further examples of his "sophisticated methods" can be found in the same work when he states that "most people tend to look better full face than in profile" and that "What we find most desirable is most beautiful, what is beautiful we wish to possess."[46] Such personal opinions and gems of homespun wisdom permeate a book which argues in the face of a mass of historical evidence that human beauty has never varied according to the eye of the age or the society in which it has been assessed. According to Marwick, it has always been judged throughout history by absolute and unvarying standards. These turn out of course to be Marwick's own: those of a middle-class white male living in late-twentieth-century Britain. Apart from indulging in such obvious arrogant and unreflective subjectivity, Marwick's "sophisticated methods" also include innumerable opaque and half-thought-out metaphors, as in: "Politicians liked to speak of the 'mosaic' of the Welfare State; in reality it was more of a crazy paving" or "These austerity years were a threshold to the whole first post-war era: rock-hard and grey, whitened maybe by dedication and labour, but opening on the warmer times within."[47] The main characteristic of the Marwickian metaphor is obviously its complete absence of identifiable meaning. This kind of thing would not have been easily accepted by the more austere exponents of the scientific view of history such as J. B. Bury, Herbert Baxter Adams, or Fustel de Coulanges.

As Isaiah Berlin observed many years ago, in history "there plainly exists a far greater variety of methods and procedures than is usually provided for in textbooks on logic or scientific method."[48] History, in the end, may for the most part be seen as a science in the weak sense of the German term *Wissenschaft*, an organized body of knowledge acquired through research carried out according to generally agreed methods, presented in published reports, and subject to peer review. It is not a science in the strong sense that it can frame general laws or predict the future. But there are sciences, such as geology, which cannot predict the future either. The fact seems to be that the differences between what in English are known as the sciences are at least as great as the differences between these disciplines taken together and a humane discipline such as history. "Science" here is only a convenient label, so no wonder its application varies from one language to another. To search for a truly "scientific" history is to pursue a mirage. Insofar as it has succeeded in generating new methods and techniques, this quest has of course been enormously beneficial. But every time a new wave of historians comes along and declares its method—whether it is philology, as in the nineteenth century, or economics, sociology, anthropology, psychology, statistics, linguistics, or literary theory, as in the twentieth—to be the one true "scientific" way of studying the past, rendering all previous historical methods outmoded at a stroke and consigning all previous historical writing to the realm of myth, anyone on the receiving end of this kind of rhetoric is entitled to a healthy degree of skepticism. For such claims have never been able to establish themselves for very long. History is not only a science in the weak sense of the word; it is, or can be, an art, in the sense that in skillful hands it can be presented in a literary form and language that achieve comparability with other literary works of art and are widely recognized as such. It is also a craft, as the great French historian Marc Bloch insisted, because its practitioners learn on the job how to handle their materials and wield the tools of their trade.[49] It is all of these things not least because it is a varied and protean discipline, and historians approach what they do in many different ways.

CHAPTER THREE

HISTORIANS AND THEIR FACTS

I

WHAT is a historical fact? Sir Geoffrey Elton, for one, had no doubts about the matter (there were indeed few things about which he had doubts). A historical fact was something that happened in the past, which had left traces in documents which could be used by the historian to reconstruct it in the present. In order to perform this operation successfully, the historian had in the first place to shed all prejudices and preconceptions and approach the documents with a completely open mind. "Ideological theory," Elton declared, "threatens the work of the historian by subjecting him to predetermined explanatory schemes and thus forcing him to tailor his evidence so that it fits the so-called paradigm imposed from outside." He argued instead that the material left to us the past must be read "in the context of the day that produced it. . . . The present must be kept out of the past if the search for the truth of that past is to move towards such success as in the circumstances is possible."[1] Thus the historian's questions should be formulated not by some present theory but from the historical sources themselves.[2]

In putting forward this view, Elton was disagreeing strongly with E. H. Carr's definition of a historical fact. Carr argued that a past event did not become a historical fact until it was accepted as such by historians. His example was the fact that a gingerbread seller was kicked to death by a crowd at Stalybridge Wakes in 1850; until mentioned by George Kitson Clark in a book on Victorian England, this was not, Carr says, a historical fact. Historical facts were therefore constituted by theory and interpretation. They did not exist independently.[3] There is a semantic confusion here which has caused endless trouble ever since Carr fell into it, and it needs clearing up before the discussion can proceed. A historical fact is something that happened in history and can be verified as such through the traces history has left behind. Whether or not a historian has actually carried out the act of verification is irrelevant to its factuality; it really is there entirely independently of the historian. This is why historians commonly speak of "discovering" facts about the past, for instance, in coming across a source which tells them of this previously unknown incident at the Stalybridge Wakes. Where theory and interpretation come in is where facts are converted into evidence (that is, facts used in support of an argument), and here theory and interpretation do indeed play a constitutive role. For historians are seldom, if ever, interested in discrete facts entirely for their own sake; they have almost always been concerned with what Ranke called the "interconnectedness" of these facts. Thus the fact of the gingerbread salesman's death can be used as evidence in a number of different ways, according to the historian's purpose: as an aspect of crowd behavior in this period, for example, as part of a study of food supplies, as an example of festivals and leisure pursuits, as an element in a history of the Manchester area, and so on. Nevertheless, while it is multifaceted as evidence, the gingerbread salesman's death is singular as fact. Facts thus precede interpretation conceptually, while interpretation precedes evidence.

The likelihood of the gingerbread salesman's unfortunate death being a historical fact in this sense is moderately but not overwhelmingly high because the reference Kitson Clark used for it was not a contemporary one, but a set of memoirs written long after the event, and memoirs are sometimes unreliable even where they are giving eyewitness accounts of happenings in the past. If I had been Kitson Clark, I should have looked for a contemporary document to verify my claim. It is for this reason, I think, not because it has not been widely quoted elsewhere (except in discussions of Carr's *What Is History?*)[4] that the status as a historical fact of the gingerbread salesman's murder in 1850 must be regarded as still provisional, to say the least. The seconder and sponsors for its membership of the (not very select) club of historical facts awaited by Carr must be not other historians but other, preferably contemporary documents, and these so far have not been found. Contemporary newspapers reported the fair very fully, but where Kitson Clark stressed the role of drink in leading to acts of violence, the papers noted that "very few drunken people were seen in the streets at any time during the wakes." There were descriptions of morris dancers and archery displays and accounts of an ascent in a balloon, but no mention of any violent incidents at all, though one paper did report the arrest of some petty thieves who had come over from Manchester. Kitson Clark cited Sanger's memory of the wakes as an example of the persistence of rough, brutal, and drunken behavior from the eighteenth century into the early Victorian era. The contemporary sources, which went out of their way to stress the "large audience" that "patiently listened" to the speeches of "a company of teetotallers" who had come over to the wakes on the Sunday, would seem rather to indicate the opposite.[5]

But even if we could find contemporary documents which established the fact of the gingerbread salesman's death, would the historian's account reflect reality in the same way as the contemporary sources did? The answer must be yes and no. When Kitson Clark mentions the incident, his text might theoretically at least be taken as a direct reflection of a real event. But when he uses this fact as evidence for an argument about violence in Victorian England, then the matter stands rather differently. Before we can accept his argument, we need a lot more evidence besides. In addition, the likelihood is that Kitson Clark wanted to put forward an argument about Victorian violence and went looking for the evidence rather than the other way around, and as we have seen, he did not look far enough, or he would have recognized that the evidence he selected was not very sound. It would be wrong, therefore, to suppose that the historian's work begins at the archive door. In reality, it begins long before. The historian formulates a thesis, goes looking for evidence, and discovers facts.[6]

Fact and evidence are therefore conceptually distinct and should not be confused with each other. Not only Carr but other writers on this subject get the two mixed up. The question of what is a fact, for instance, plunges the postmodernist writer Alan Munslow into terrible confusion. He puts the word "fact" into the quarantine of quotation marks, as if it were some loathsomely infectious concept it was dangerous to touch. "Can professional historians," he asks, "be relied upon to reconstruct and explain the past objectively by infer-ring the 'facts' from the evidence . . . ?" Obviously not, is the implied answer to this plainly rhetorical question. Here Munslow seems to use "evidence" in the sense of "sources." Elsewhere he cites a well-known history of America which states that President James Madison was "small of stature . . . light of weight . . . bald of head, and weak of voice."[7] The implication is that he was a weak president (though why this should be so is unclear; one can think of many men with bald heads who were not at all weak, such as Julius Caesar; many power-ful men who were light and small in physique, such as Napoleon; and many strong leaders who had feeble speaking voices, such as Bismarck). Munslow says this is translating evidence into facts; here he seems to have a different concept of evidence, though exactly what he means by it is not very clear. It is surely more helpful to say that in this example the writers (if that is what they are indeed doing) are translating *facts* (bald head, weak voice, etc.) into *evidence*, using undoubted facts about Madison's physical characteristics as evidence for a more interpretative point about his inner character and the nature of his presidency. When Munslow asserts that the historians in question present Madison's weakness as a fact, he is misusing the concept. It is only by reversing the normal senses of fact and inter-pretation, indeed, that he is able to argue that the latter generates the former and not the other way around.[8]

But the terminological confusion that has bedeviled the whole debate about historical facts does not stop here. A similar misunder-standing to that engendered by Carr can be found in the distinction drawn by White between facts and events. An event, he tells us, is something that happened, but a fact is something constructed by the historian or existing in the remains of the past, in documents.[9] In historical terms, I think it fair to say, a fact does not have to be an event; for example, it could be a building, now long since disappeared, in a certain place, or a boundary between two states, or a set of stocks and shares owned by a government minister, or a legal prohibition of some activity or other, or a liaison between a politician and a courtesan, or the thickness of armor plating on a battleship or tank, or any one of a vast range of things, none of which could be described as an "event," even if it was connected to an event. An event is a fact, but a fact is not necessarily an event. History is not just about events; it is about many other aspects of the past, too, and that applies not just to economic, social, cultural, or intellectual history but to much more "event-oriented" kinds of history, such as political or military history, as well.[10]

Thus White is wrong to imply that historiographical consensus about any event in the past is difficult to achieve and is always open to revision from another perspective, if he means that future historians will start to say that the Stalybridge Wakes did not take place in 1850, or that there were no gingerbread salesmen there (they were recorded in the newspapers already cited), or make some other factual assertion of this kind. Only if new evidence is found to amend or cast doubt on the historian's account of a fact—as in the case of the (now seemingly rather dubious) story of the gingerbread seller's death at the Stalybridge Wakes—does revision at this level take place. But it is doubtful whether White really does mean this. If he means, as I think he does, that there will always be argument about what the alleged death of the gingerbread salesman meant for the state of public order in Victorian England and how it is to be interpreted as evidence for larger arguments about the period, then surely he is right.[11]

II

WHAT is at issue, therefore, is how historians use documents not to establish discrete facts, but as evidence for establishing the larger patterns that connect them. Are these patterns, these connections already there waiting to be discovered by a neutral process of cognition, or do historians put them there themselves? Some writers on history have argued that historians are deceiving themselves if they imagine their documents to be a kind of transparent window through which larger truths about the past become visible. So great, they suggest, are the problems which the documents present that the "traditional confidence" of historians that they can get their facts "right," or reach through the sources to the "essential truth" beyond, is completely misplaced.[12] In this view, as the American medievalist Nancy F. Partner has observed, historical "facts" become "constructed artifacts no different in cognitive origin than any made thing or 'fiction.' "[13] "The basic claim of historians that their narratives rest on fact," two of her colleagues have confidently asserted, "can be, indeed has been, dismantled."[14] This is not least because "documents," as Dominick LaCapra has remarked, "are texts that supplement or rework 'reality' and not mere sources that divulge facts about 'reality.' "[15] Documents are always written from somebody's point of view, with a specific purpose and audience in mind, and unless we can find all that out, we may be misled. Too often, claims LaCapra, historians unwittingly carry the biases of such documents directly into their own writing (or, as he puts it, "All history, moreover, must more or less blindly encounter the problem of a transferential relation to the past whereby the processes at work in the object of study acquire their displaced analogues in the historian's account.")[16] Thus he concludes, "Historians often read texts as simple sources of information on the level of content analysis."[17] This amounts in his view to a "reductive use of texts and documents."[18]

In similar vein, another American historian, Catriona Kelly, has claimed as an achievement of postmodernist theory the fact that "antagonistic, combative and counter-intuitive strategies of textual reading" have all been "developed in the wake of deconstructionism." She urges historians to adopt an "aggressive attitude" to the sources, "concentrating not on the most obvious interpretation, but on secondary layers of meaning." But this injunction has had little measurable effect. "The impact of non-referential language theory, deconstruction and the exposure of hegemonic interests embedded in what used to pass for neutral description" has not, as Nancy F. Partner has noted, "left the ancient discipline shattered beyond recuperation."[19] This is perhaps because "reading against the grain," as Kelly tells historians they should now begin to do, has been the stock-in-trade of our profession for a very long time.[20] Historians, as Lawrence Stone has protested, were even in his youth ("forty or fifty years ago") taught "that documents—we did not call them texts in those days—were written by fallible human beings who made mistakes, asserted false claims, and had their own ideological agenda which guided their compilation; they should therefore be scrutinized with care, taking into account authorial intent, the nature of the document, and the context in which it was written." Since he also says in the same article, written in 1992, that he was taught "forty or fifty years ago" that "we should follow the advice of E. H. Carr and before we read the history, examine the background of the historian," and since Carr did not proffer such advice until the publication of *What Is History?* in 1961, or in other words only thirty years before, we may perhaps doubt whether Stone really was taught all these things in his youth. But he clearly believes them now, and indeed he is right to say that these are all assumptions on which historians conventionally operate. He also claims to have been taught "that perceptions and representations of reality are often very different from, and sometimes just as historically important as, reality itself," and this, too, is a fact of which any historian dealing with original source material is often only too painfully aware, since it makes the task of writing history a good deal more complicated than it would be if sources were indeed the kind of one-to-one reflection of the real world that postmodernists apparently believe historians think they are.[21]

"The whole art of historical research, in many cases," as Raphael Samuel pointed out in one of his last writings, "is to *detach* documents from the 'discourse' of which they formed a part and juxtapose them with qualitatively different others." This involves not ignoring or discounting the language in which they are written, but comparing it with the language of the other documents in question. Ever since the ancient Greek historian Thucydides, historians have grappled with the problem of "measuring words against deeds," as Samuel says, "and attempting to judge their representativity." It might be illuminating in some cases to juxtapose seemingly unrelated events, or to range freely through history, as the French philosopher-historian Michel Foucault does, ignoring questions of historical specificity unless they can be assimilated to free-floating discourses. But the general value of such an exercise is limited. "Instead of grubbing about in the archives," Samuel complains, "they [i.e., postmodernists] can take the higher ground where universes of meaning clash and craggy peaks dispel the clouds of unknowing. Instead of painstakingly documenting the past, they can imaginatively re-invent it."[22] Samuel's feeling that this kind of freedom can be achieved only by a measure of intellectual irresponsibility is palpable.

The real question at issue here is *what enables us* to read a source "against the grain," and here theory does indeed come in. Theory of whatever kind, whether it is a general set of theses about how human societies are structured and human beings behave or whether it is a limited proposition about, say, the carnivalesque in history, or the nature of human communication within a preindustrial village, derives from the historian's present, not from the historian's sources. It is vital for the historian to use it. Without anthropological theory developed in the study of African rural society in the twentieth century, for example, the history of witchcraft in the seventeenth century would not have made the huge leaps in understanding which it has achieved in the last twenty-five years, gains which have come about because only anthropological theory, for example, enabled Keith Thomas to read the sources in a new and original way.[23] Without Marxist theory, urban and labor history would be enormously impoverished, and a major, influential classic such as E. P. Thompson's *The Making of the English Working Class* would never have been written.[24] Without modern economic theory, historians would have no understanding of industrialization and would not have known how to read or use the quantitative and other evidence that it generated.

If ideas and theories in the historian's own time are what allow a reading of documentary material in a way that cuts across, or runs counter, to the purposes of the people who wrote it, then it follows that the same document can be legitimately used as evidence for a variety of purposes by different historians. It is manifestly not the case that there is always a one-to-one correspondence between the evidence provided in a source or a document and the fact to which it refers. Thus, for example, in his famous book *Montaillou*, the French historian Emmanuel Le Roy Ladurie read the inquisitorial reports for different evidence and in many cases different facts from those quarried from them by previous writers. While they had been interested in the Inquisition itself, and in the Cathar heresy it was attempting to extirpate, Le Roy Ladurie was interested in using the *incidental* details the heretics revealed about their everyday lives to construct an intimate portrait of human relationships and human existence in a medieval village.[25] Characteristically, Sir Geoffrey Elton criticized him for doing this, considering he should have stuck to the Inquisition, as his predecessors had done.[26] But it is difficult to see any justification for this argument. Elton is completely wrong in his view that there is only one legitimate way to read a given document. Documents can be read in a variety of ways, all of them, theoretically at least, equally valid. Moreover, it is obvious that our way of reading a source derives principally from our present-day concerns and from the questions that present-day theories and ideas lead us to formulate. Nor is there anything wrong in this.

Critics of "documentary fetishism" have homed in on this point and treated the Eltonian position as if it were a universally accepted orthodoxy. The intellectual historian H. Stuart Hughes has leveled the charge that historians in the United States "seem to have forgotten—if they ever properly learned—the simple truth that what one may call progress in their endeavors comes not merely through the discovery of new materials but at least as much through a *new reading* of materials already available."[27] Hughes of course has a strong vested interest in asserting this "simple truth," since he has never discovered any new material himself in any of his publications but has devoted his entire career to going over old ground. His view is shared by William H. McNeill, of the University of Chicago, who used the occasion of his presidential address to the American Historical

Association in 1986 to castigate his colleagues for practicing a "historiography that aspires to get closer and closer to the documents—
all the documents and nothing but the documents"—because this
meant "merely moving closer and closer to incoherence, chaos, and
meaninglessness."[28] Coming from a historian whose lifelong specialism had been in the history of the whole world from the beginnings
of humanity to the present, and whose acquaintance with original
documents was correspondingly limited, this view was perhaps
unsurprising, if somewhat tactlessly expressed.

In a slightly wider sense, perhaps Elton was right to note that criticisms of "documentary fetishism" and the advocacy of reinterpretation as the primary task of the historian have mainly emanated from
intellectual historians. After all, they use sources in a different way
from most historians: as interpretative vehicles for ideas, not as clues
to an exterior reality. Moreover, they work with a very limited number of classic texts, written by a handful of authors or, in other words,
in a field where new documentary discoveries have inevitably
become extremely rare. Reinterpretation is therefore often the only
option available to them. When an intellectual historian reads
Hobbes's *Leviathan* and Marx's *Das Kapital*, it is not in order to use
their writings to reconstruct something outside them, but in order to
construct an interpretation of what they mean or meant. There are
indeed many interpretations of these thinkers' ideas, not least because
the systems of thought Hobbes and Marx constructed were so wide-
ranging that they never became completely closed. But the possibility of reinterpreting them by means of new documentary discoveries has almost ceased (though one can never be completely sure that
no new documents by or about them will turn up, scholars have
been combing every conceivable archive for them for decades, and it
seems rather unlikely).[29]

The impatience of intellectual historians with their colleagues'
concern for the discovery of original documentation seems understandable, but it is also reasonable to call for a little academic tolerance here; historical knowledge and understanding can surely be
generated both by the discovery of new documents and by the imaginative reinterpretation of old ones. The discovery of the Dead Sea

Scrolls in 1947, for instance, imposed a new agenda of interpretation irrespective of contemporary political assumptions. At the same time, Charles Beard's reinterpretation of the American Constitution owed little to newly discovered documents, yet transformed our knowledge and generated massive debate that led to a real advance in historical understanding.[30] Historians are always led by their present-day concerns; the truth does not simply emerge from an unprejudiced or neutral reading of the sources, even if such a thing were possible; the Dead Sea Scrolls themselves have been the subject of huge controversy almost since their discovery. Not all sources are equally open to a variety of interpretations or uses, and some indeed can only reasonably be interpreted in a single way. Others, like philosophical texts, can be, and have been, subject to almost constant reinterpretation over the years. Some sources are used to get at a historical reality beyond themselves; others are studied for their own sake. Historians work in a variety of ways, and specialists in one field should not censure their colleagues in another for failing to conform to the pet methods they employ in their own.

III

THE traces left by the past, as Dominick LaCapra has observed, do not provide an even coverage of it. Archives are the product of the chance survival of some documents and the corresponding chance loss or deliberate destruction of others. They are also the products of the professional activities of archivists, which therefore shape the record of the past and with it the interpretations of historians. Archivists have often weeded out records they consider unimportant, while retaining those they consider of lasting value. This might mean, for example, destroying vast and therefore bulky personnel files on low-ranking state employees, such as ordinary soldiers and seamen, manual workers, and so on, while keeping room on the crowded shelves for personnel files on high state officials. Yet such a weeding policy reflected a view that many historians would now find outmoded, a view which considered "history" only as the history of the

elites. Documents which seem worthless to one age, and hence ripe
for the shredder, can seem extremely valuable to another.

Let me give an example from my personal experience. During
research in the Hamburg state archives in the 1980s, I became aware
that the police had been sending plainclothes agents into the city's
pubs and bars during the two decades or so before the First World
War to gather and later write down secret reports of what was being
said in them by socialist workers. The reports I saw were part of larger files on the various organizations to which these workers
belonged. Thinking it might be interesting to look at a wider sample, I went through a typewritten list of the police files with the
archivist, and among the headings we came across was one which
read: "worthless reports." After going down into the muniment
room, we found under the relevant call number a vast mass of over
twenty thousand reports which had been judged of insufficient
interest by the police authorities of the day to be taken up into the
thematic files where I had first encountered this material. It was only
by a lucky chance that they had not already been destroyed. They
turned out to contain graphic and illuminating accounts of what
rank-and-file socialist workers thought about almost every conceivable issue of the day, from the Dreyfus affair in France to the state of
the traffic on Hamburg's busy streets. Nobody had ever looked at
them before. Historians of the labor movement had been interested
only in organization and ideology. But by the time I came to inspect
them, interest had shifted to the history of everyday life, and workers' views on the family, crime and the law, food, drink, and leisure
pursuits had become significant objects of historical research. It
seemed worth transcribing and publishing a selection, therefore,
which I did after a couple of years' work on them.[31] The resulting
collection showed how rank-and-file Social Democrats and labor
activists often had views that cut right across the Marxist ideology in
which previous historians thought the party had indoctrinated them
because they had lacked the sources to go down beyond the level of
official pronouncements in the way the Hamburg police reports
made it possible to do. Thus from "worthless reports" there emerged
a useful corrective to earlier historical interpretations. This wonder-

ful material, which had survived by chance, had to wait for discovery and exploitation until the historiographical climate had changed so as to make someone think it was worth using.

The survival or otherwise of historical source material is undeniably a matter of history itself. The record left us by the past is fragmentary, and the process of selection has not always been arbitrary. But historians have always known this, and have always thought it important to situate the fragments that do remain in the broader context of other remaining fragments, thus gaining some idea of the whole even where significant parts are missing. Doing historical research is rather like doing a jigsaw puzzle where the pieces are not all present in one box but are scattered over the house in several boxes and where, once it is put together, a significant number of the pieces are still missing. The nature of the resulting picture will depend partly on how many boxes you find, and this of course depends partly on having some idea of where to look, but the picture's contours can also be filled in, even when not all the pieces have been located. Of course, we imagine the contours in this situation and have to speculate on a bit of the detail; at the same time, however, the discovery of the existing pieces does set quite severe limits on the operation of our imagination. If they only fit together to produce a picture of a steam engine, for instance, it is no good trying to put them together to make a suburban garden; it simply will not work. The fragmentary nature of the traces left to us by the past is thus no reason for supposing that historians' imagination is entirely unfettered when it comes to reconstructing it.

But this raises the further question of how we translate these traces into a language that we ourselves can understand. Often they are written not only in a different tongue (Latin, Greek, Anglo-Saxon, or whatever it might be) but also metaphorically, so that the same word used in the seventeenth century as in the twentieth or twenty-first may have a subtly different meaning. "Family" is a case in point; in the seventeenth century it was liable to include living-in servants, which is no longer true even in the rare households where they still exist. So serious is this problem of source interpretation that one group of German historians has produced a multivolume encyclopedia tracing the shifting meanings of such words and concepts (alas, only in German) through the centuries.[32] But of course, such readings are a matter of interpretation, too. If different historians translate historical sources from the historical language in which they are written in two different ways, how do we know which translation is "correct"? How can we convey to today's readers the meanings such words had for historical contemporaries? Are these meaningful questions anyway? Some have argued that they are not, that there is in effect no means of deciding between one translation and another, no means therefore of accurately reconstructing the past meanings of language and therefore the past to which it refers.[33] But of course, it *is* possible to reconstruct the meanings which past language had for those who used it because the individual words and concepts we come across in it were part of a system of meaning, so their meaning can be pinned down in terms of the other words and concepts used in the system. We do not read just a single document from, say, Tudor England, but hundreds, even thousands of documents in the course of a single research project, and by seeing the same words and concepts used in conjunction with many others, we can eventually isolate their meaning in terms of the overall linguistic and conceptual system being employed.

As a historian who works not only on a very different society from our own but also one which used an entirely different language—German—I have of course been faced by a double challenge in this respect. Yet I do not think it has been insurmountable, not least because many of the sources I have used—civil service minutes from the Justice Ministry in Berlin, for example, or surveillance reports from the police files in Hamburg—employ a stereotyped and repetitive language in which the same words and concepts appear all the time. In many ways indeed these sources are linguistically impoverished compared with the writings of the great poets and philosophers of the day. The kind of translation work the historian does is rather different from that carried out by someone who is translating Heinrich Heine or Immanuel Kant. What the historian is usually concerned with is language and thought at a fairly basic level, unless of course the subject is the history of poetry or philosophy.

Relatively few historical controversies turn on the meanings of specific words or concepts of even documents. Insofar as they involve disagreements about the interpretation of source material at all, they tend, rather, to center on disputes as to what sources are relevant rather than what the sources actually mean. Moreover, it is perfectly possible for one source to have only one permissible interpretation in itself if two historians are asking the same question of it and therefore to conclude that if the two historians disagree as to what that interpretation is, one historian's reading is true and the other's is false. The fact that this is not always the case does not mean that the possibilities of "translation" are necessarily and inevitably open or infinite. The fact that there are historical controversies, moreover, does not mean that there are no definitely ascertainable historical facts. There are, after all, thousands of historical facts which are undisputed and which are not the subject of historical controversy.[34]

These points cast a somewhat negative light on the argument, originally put forward by R. G. Collingwood and subsequently elaborated by E. H. Carr, that all history is the history of thought because ultimately, as Carr put it, "no document can tell us more than what the author of the document thought." When we read a source, he claimed, we reenact in our minds the thought of the person who wrote it.[35] But this is too limited. Historians are accustomed to elicit meaning from documents by comparing them with other documents, and in this way a document can indeed be made to reveal more than its author thought. The gaps in a document—what it does *not* mention—are often just as interesting as what it contains. A statistic in a document can look quite different from what its author thought when we put it together with other statistics of which the author was unaware. We bring our own thoughts to bear on documents, and these can have a material effect on how the document is read. Many sources are not written at all. Getting inside the head of someone who buried treasure in a grave in the fourth century, or made a newsreel in the twentieth, is far from easy. Collingwood's notion of historical explanation is far too closely tied to the explanation of political events. If we are looking at the causes of the price rise in sixteenth-century Spain, for instance, it does not make much

sense to say that we are reenacting the thoughts of the contemporaries who compiled the sources from which we derive the statistics.[36] Moreover, as two American historians have pointed out,

> Documents cannot be viewed as simple manifestations of a creator's
> intentions; the social institutions and material practices which were
> involved in their production played a significant part in shaping what
> was said and how it was said. The historian's meticulous reading of the
> evidence may therefore have little in common with what the author
> intended to say or what the contemporary reader understood to be
> said.[37]

Historians have to know about these institutions and practices, of
course, and must bear this context in mind even while they detach
the document from it. Otherwise they run the risk of violating the
boundaries of its possible meanings in the service of their own particular interpretation. Still, in the end, the conscious motive or
thought of the writer of a document might be quite irrelevant to the
purposes for which we wish to use the document, though of course,
we always have to take it into account.[38] What the historian writes,
and what the documents say, are two different things, or at least most
historians have hitherto supposed them to be. But this distinction,
too, as we shall now see, has come under fire from postmodernist
critics of historical method.

I V

HOW do we derive historical facts from historical sources? The great
Italian historian of the ancient world, Arnaldo Momigliano, once
described the foundations of modern historical scholarship in the
following terms: "The whole modern method of historical research
is founded on the distinction between original and derivative
authorities. By original authorities we mean statements by eye wit-
nesses, or documents and other material remains that are contemporary with the event they attest. By derivative authorities we mean
historians and chroniclers who relate and discuss events which they

have not witnessed, but which they have heard of or inferred directly or indirectly from original authorities."[39] This distinction, for
which the terms "primary" and "secondary" sources are more commonly used, was introduced above all by German scholars in the
nineteenth century. The contrast between their practice of always
going to the primary or original sources and that of, say, the
Enlightenment historians, who relied heavily, though not exclusively, on chronicles and other secondary or derivative sources, has led
many, if not most, historians to date the establishment of the subject
on a professional or scientific basis to the nineteenth century and not
before. It is this distinction which postmodernist critics of this historical tradition are now radically calling into question.

Perhaps the most far-reaching, comprehensive, and explicit challenge to history as a discipline in this sense has been mounted by the
French linguistic theorists Roland Barthes and Jacques Derrida. As
early as 1968 Barthes charged that historians' claim to reconstruct
past reality rested on a pretense. History as written by professionals
(or for that matter by anyone else) was, he said, "an inscription on the
past pretending to be a likeness of it, a parade of signifiers mas-
querading as a collection of facts." Objectivity was "the product of
what might be called the referential illusion." The illusion lay in the
fact that the past was only *imagined* to be out there, waiting to be discovered; in practice it was an empty space waiting to be filled by the
historian. Verbatim quotations, footnote references, and the like were
simply devices designed to produce what Barthes described as the
"reality effect," tricking the reader into believing that the historian's
unprovable representations of the past were no more than straight-
forward reporting. Historians' own understanding of what they did
remained, as Jacques Derrida noted, stubbornly "logocentric"—that
is, they imagined they were rational beings engaged in a process of
discovery. But this, too, was an illusion, like all forms of "logocen-
trism."

Such ideas derived—at some distance, to be sure—from theories
originally advanced by the Swiss linguist Ferdinand de Saussure, who
had noted early in the century that the relation of words to their
meanings was usually completely arbitrary. The word "dog," for

instance, no more suggested in itself a carnivorous, barking quadruped than *chien* did in French, or *Hund* in German. Saussure argued therefore that words, or what he called signifiers, were defined not by their relation to the things they denoted (the signified) but by their relation to each other (e.g., "dog" as opposed to "cat"). But while Saussure regarded language as a system of differentiation constructed from signs, in which the signifiers were consistently related to one another in a logical way, subsequent theorists such as Jacques Derrida went much further and argued that the relation changed each time the word was uttered. Language was thus an "infinite play of significations." There was no "transcendental signified" which determined meaning in itself. Everything was a mere arrangement of words; everything was "discourse" or "text." Nothing exists, in this view, outside language. Because we apprehend the world through language and nothing else, everything is a text.[40]

Advocates and critics alike are right in thinking that such views have radical implications for both literature and history. They imply that authors can no longer be regarded as having control over the meaning of what they write. In the infinite play of signification that constitutes language, the meaning of a text changes every time it is read. Meaning is put into it by the reader, and all meanings are in principle equally valid. In history, meaning cannot be found in the past; it is merely put there, each time differently, and with equal validity, by different historians. There is no necessary or consistent relation between the text of history and the texts of historians. The texts which survive from the past are as arbitrary in their signification as any other texts, and so, too, are the texts which use them. "If there is nothing outside the text," as Lawrence Stone has remarked, "then history as we have known it collapses altogether, and fact and fiction become indistinguishable from one another."[41] The medievalist Gabrielle Spiegel has noted that "if texts—documents, literary works, whatever—do not transparently reflect reality, but only other texts, then historical study can scarcely be distinguished from literary study, and the 'past' dissolves into literature."[42] This is not merely an alarmist diagnosis on the part of disciplinary conservatives. Postmodernists themselves have taken a similar view. Patrick Joyce, for example, has argued that because "the events, structures and processes of the past are indistinguishable from the forms of documentary representation, the conceptual and political appropriations, and the historical discourses that construct them," the idea of the social as something separate from discursivity disappears, and with it social history, too.[43] In practice his argument would seem to undermine the enterprise of history as commonly understood on a wider scale still.

For present reality can be felt and experienced by our senses, but the past no longer exists; it is not "real" in the same sense as the world around us in the present is real. It, too, has become a text. Documents are the texts through which we apprehend the past, and there is no reality beyond them except other texts. "Historians," complains the philosopher Hans Kellner, ". . . routinely behave as though their researches were into the past, as though their writings were 'about' it, and as though 'it' were as real as the text which is the object of their labours." This he declares to be "naive realism."[44] "The *reality* of the past," Alan Munslow, another postmodernist writer on the theory of history, proclaims, "is the written report, rather than the past *as it actually was*. . . . The past is not discovered or found. It is created and represented by the historian as a text."[45] Moreover, in principle historical documents are no different from the writings of historians themselves. The reader, the historian, invests documents and history books alike with meaning; there is no meaning there otherwise. So the distinction between primary and secondary sources is abolished, and with it the principle, enunciated by Momigliano, on which most modern historical scholarship effectively rests goes out of the window, too. The primary and secondary distinction, charges Keith Jenkins, "prioritises the original source, fetishises documents, and distorts the whole working process of making history."[46] It is therefore time to abandon it.

It follows from this, Jenkins argues, that "when we study history we are not studying the past but what historians have constructed about the past. In that sense," he continues, "whether or not people in the past had the same or different natures to us is not only undecidable but also not at issue. In that sense, the past doesn't enter into it. Our real need is to establish the presuppositions that historians take to the past." It is thus "more constructive," in his view, to "get into the minds of historians than the minds of the people who lived in the past and who only emerge, strictly speaking, through the minds of historians anyway."[47] This view echoes that of the Dutch philosopher Frank Ankersmit, who argues that the nature of differences of historical opinion cannot satisfactorily be defined in terms of research; it is rather a matter of style. Differences of opinion between historians are in his view primarily grounded in aesthetics. "Content," he says, "is a derivative of style." What the historian should do therefore is to stop investigating the past and start instead to think about ways in which it figures in the present. "History . . ." he says, should "no longer [be] the reconstruction of what has happened . . . but a continuous playing with the memory of this."[48] In a similar way, Jenkins says that it is wrong to insist that history students should properly look at history itself rather than what historians have written about it. "If history is interpretation, if history is historians' work(s), then historiography is what the 'proper' study of history is actually about," because history itself is simply a discourse, a "congealed interpretation."[49] History and historiography are the same thing. "History," as Munslow observes, "is the study not of change over time *per se*, but the study of the information produced by historians as they go about this task."[50] The point of history is to study historians, not to study the past.

Thus, as commentators have been quick to note, the historian's conventional concern with the past would be replaced in a postmodernist history with a focus on self-reflexivity and on problems of literary construction: How does the historian as author construct his or her text, how is the illusion of authenticity produced, what creates a sense of truthfulness to the facts and of closeness to past reality (or the "truth effect")? The implication is that the historian does not in fact capture the past in faithful fashion but rather, like the novelist, only gives the appearance of doing so. In literary theory we do not study the characters and actions Jane Austen wrote about in her novels as if they were something that existed outside her mind; why should we proceed differently with historians and the characters and actions they write about?

Such an approach follows a prominent vein in postmodernist

thinking, in which the secondary rather than the primary becomes paramount; rather than study Shakespeare, it is often argued, we should study what critics have written about him, because one reading of Shakespeare is as good as another, and the text itself has no particular priority above interpretations of it, since all are forms of discourse, and it is wrong to "privilege" one discourse over another. What all this might mean in practice is exemplified in a recent book by the feminist historian Diane Purkiss, *The Witch in History*. Purkiss explicitly rejects the idea of even attempting to answer "the empirical questions that preoccupy many of my contemporaries" because of "the impossibility of defining the witch." Her purpose rather is to "tell or retell the rich variety of stories told about witches." The sources are too fragmentary to say with any degree of certainty why people believed in witches. Her interest in the treatment of witches by academic historians who have studied the sources under the illusion that they can say something meaningful or certain about witches is therefore to delineate the role the witch plays in their "academic self-fashioning." She makes no attempt to assess the relative merits of these historians in relation to their empirical accounts and interpretations of the historical phenomenon of witchcraft.

Now of course, in practice, Purkiss actually has "assembled evidence," as she admits, about all these things and, in doing so, is not only carrying out the same procedures she so derides in others, but also carrying them out in the service of an "overall empirical purpose" she elsewhere deplores as a concept. Although she derides historical skepticism about empirical arguments as "masculine" and the very notion of "truth" in "empirical history" as "male," this does not stop her from criticizing the claims of some feminist historians about witchcraft as inherently "improbable," thus arrogating to herself a right of skepticism which she denies to men—a sexist double standard if ever there was one, and an impossible one, too, for if truth were really a masculine concept, then Purkiss could never even begin to claim that anything she said herself was true. Such contradictions aside, however, the important point about her account of witchcraft here is its refusal to make any distinction between historical, fictional, and poetical accounts of witchcraft and its concentration on the portrayal of witches in verse, drama, historical texts, and other forms of secondary literature, rather than on the witches themselves. In Purkiss's books, all these texts, from Shakespeare to Keith Thomas, are treated on an equal basis.[51]

So in this approach there is no real difference between history and fiction. For Hayden White, researching and writing a history book are much the same as researching and writing a novel. Both are made up of elements of real human experience. Both have to meet the demands of correspondence to that experience and coherence in the way they present it. Both use language as their means of representing reality. Just like novelists, historians, says White, prefigure their field of inquiry by applying to the selection and evaluation of the evidence the linguistic and imaginative tools that are also to be used in the construction of the resulting narrative.[52] There is something to be said for White's observation that the great nineteenth-century historians whose work he analyzed in his first major book, *Metahistory*—Michelet, Ranke, Tocqueville, Burckhardt—had a great deal in common with their contemporaries among the novelists, like Flaubert, though given the dominance of literary realism in the novels of the day, this was hardly surprising. But White goes on to argue that the literary and linguistic forms by which different historians and novelists construct their work are all equally valid ways of representing the past.

There is in consequence no single correct view of any event or process, but many correct views, "each requiring its own style of representation. . . ," he argues.

> When it is a matter of choosing among . . . alternative visions of history, the only grounds for preferring one over another are moral or aesthetic ones. . . . One must face the fact that, when it comes to the historical record, there are no grounds to be found in the record itself for preferring one way of construing its meaning rather than another. . . . We can tell equally plausible, alternative, and even contradictory stories . . . without violating rules of evidence or critical standards. . . . One can imagine not only one or two but any number of alternative stories of . . . any . . . culturally significant event, all equally plau-

sible and equally authoritative by virtue of their conformity to generally accepted rules of historical construction.

Thus White not only denies the possibility of objective knowledge
about the past but also claims that it is pointless to argue about it,
since each version forms a closed system of thought which is as valid
as any other as a form of historical representation (however it may be
judged on other grounds). Fictional narratives do not displace each
other if both are written about the same subject. We do not say that
one is true and the other false. White and those who follow him say
that the same holds good for historical narratives.[53] "No given set or
sequence of real events," White has declared, "is intrinsically tragic,
comic, farcical, and so on." Events can only "be constructed as such"
by the historian,[54] who is bound by the limited possibilities of literary representation to follow one or other of these models in constructing events and to draw on a strictly finite number of metaphors
and forms of "emplotment." Such literary models, in other words,
constructed the interpretation, rather than the interpretation emerging from the sources and finding a form of literary expression appropriate to the truthfulness of the argument and the material.

In all this theory, historical fact more or less disappears from view.
The distinction between primary and secondary source, on which
historical research rests, is abolished. Historians become authors like
any other, the object of literary criticism and analysis. The boundaries
between history and fiction dissolve.[55] The demarcation line between
history and historiography, between historical writing and historical
theory is erased. Whatever the opportunities this line of thinking
offers history as a discipline, there is no doubting the hostile intent
of many of those who have developed it. How far their ideas can
stand up to critical scrutiny themselves is the subject of the next
chapter.

CHAPTER FOUR

SOURCES AND DISCOURSES

I

BELIEF in the historian's almost unlimited power to shape interpretations of the past derives from the perception in postmodernist theory that a historical text, as the intellectual historian David Harlan has argued, can no longer be regarded as having wholly fixed and unalterable meaning given it by its author. But it is doubtful whether anyone in fact has ever believed that meaning can be fixed in this way. Anyone who has published a book and read the reviews of it will be well aware of the fact that many different interpretations of a text are possible, a number of them—whether motivated by malice, by carelessness, or by simple stupidity on the part of the reviewer— only remotely related to the interpretation intended by the author. An awareness of the multiple meanings of texts and their relative autonomy from the intentions of the author has long been part of the stock-in-trade of the historian. That most traditional branch of historical scholarship, diplomatic history, has been largely built on the analysis of the ambiguities of diplomatic documents—not all of them intentional—and has taken much of its analytical power from its knowledge of the possibility, even likelihood, that a treaty or a protocol can, and often will, be interpreted by different states in different ways. Political historians have always known that a speech by an individual statesman can often have the opposite effect from that intended, and they have always been aware that a politician may frequently fail to make his meaning clear to his audience and produce in consequence what Harlan describes as the poststructuralist paradigm of an "unruly text spewing out its manifold significations, connotations and implications."[1]

The language of historical documents is never transparent, and historians have always been aware that they cannot simply gaze through it to the historical reality behind. Historians know, historians have always known, that we can see the past only "through a glass, darkly." It did not take the advent of postmodernism to point this out. But what postmodernists have done is to push such familiar arguments about the transparency or opacity of historical texts and sources out to a set of binary opposites and polarized extremes. To an imagined historian believing that the language of texts is a transparent window onto the mind of its author, they oppose the equally unreal picture of a situation in which the author has no relevance to the content of a text at all. Sometimes this polarization of the debate is used as an explicit polemical technique, as in the writings of David Harlan.[2] At other times it has a more theoretical character, but is equally unconvincing for all that. The French theorist Paul Ricoeur argues, for example, that "the reader is absent from the act of writing; the writer is absent from the act of reading ... the text thus produces a double eclipse of reader and writer."[3] But this is not so. A text is always written for a readership and framed according to the writer's expectations of how the intended readers will take it. Similarly, the reader is always mindful of the purposes of the writer during the act of reading. All this remains true even if a document is read by people for whom it was not intended—people like historians, in fact.

When we read, for example, a diplomatic dispatch from, say, the U.S. secretary of state to the Spanish foreign minister in the 1880s, we bear both reader and writer in mind; it would be foolish to do otherwise. We remain aware of the fact that the Spanish foreign minister may have taken the dispatch to mean something slightly different from what the secretary of state intended, so to understand the text, we have to know not only other texts of both writer and reader but also the political and diplomatic contexts in which they operated, knowledge which requires the reading of yet further texts. Moreover, we know what happened to Spanish-American relations in the course of the 1890s (they deteriorated until the Spanish-American War of 1898). We cannot help reading the dispatch in the light of this knowledge, whereas it was written not only without the knowledge of these later developments, but also without much idea of what was going to happen in the weeks and months after it was written, although obviously the secretary of state had some idea of what he *hoped* would happen as a result of writing the dispatch. In this sense it would not make much difference if we could by some magic summon both gentlemen before us and grill them in person on what the dispatch actually meant; we would still have to read those other documents to make sense of it and to inform ourselves sufficiently to ask intelligent questions, and even if they were made aware of later developments, too, we still could not wholly rely on the answers they gave, for who can wholly rely on what diplomats and politicians say in any case?

As historians we clearly cannot recover a single, unalterably "true" meaning of the dispatch simply by reading it; on the other hand, we cannot impose any meaning we wish to on such a text either. We are limited by the words it contains, words which are not capable of an infinity of meanings as the postmodernists suggest. Moreover, the limits which the words of the text impose on the possibilities of interpretation are set to a large extent by the author who wrote them. The polarization of the debate by postmodernist theorists is simply unrealistic. The fact is, as Dominick LaCapra sensibly remarks, that historical research and writing are a dialogue between two kinds of significances—the historians' and the documents'. "The historian enters into a 'conversational' exchange with the past and with other inquirers seeking an understanding of it." Historians have to "listen attentively to possibly disconcerting 'voices' of the past and not simply project narcissistic or self-interested demands upon them." Thus in any history book there is in fact a multiplicity of voices, and the historian may also be using several.[4] Something like this can be seen in Roy Porter's description of Gibbon's *Decline and Fall of the Roman Empire:*

> Gibbon coped with bias by revealing it; by exposing the prejudices of his sources, and presenting, rather than suppressing, the personality of "the historian of the Roman Empire." Impartiality arose not out of a fetishism of facts but from the operations of the mind, from analysis, imagination, wit and a capacity to hold judgment in suspense. Gibbon's "great work" reads like a chorus of voices. The contemporaries speak; Gibbon's sources comment on them; Gibbon adds his glosses, often scolding away in the footnotes; and the reader is invited to listen and participate in the intellectual symposium.[5]

Reading any history book necessarily involves listening to this chorus of different voices sounding through the text.

Postmodernist critics have alleged by contrast that historians adopt an omniscient position, using the language of scholarship to suggest to readers that the knowledge they are conveying is neutral, objective, and derived from a transcendent source rather than linked to the historian's own purposes. Thus they claim to have succeeded in alerting "an unwary public, as well as their peers, to how the different perspectives of historians enter into their books."[6] But have the readers of history books, whether professional or otherwise, always been so "unwary"? It simply isn't the case that readers gullibly swallow everything the historian writes as if it were the absolute truth. Too many commentators, postmodernist and otherwise, seem to harbor an arrogant underestimation of the sophistication and critical discernment of those who read history books. As Roy Porter has remarked, "The reader seems to be a missing person in so much history-writing today, presumably because academic historians have largely lost all sense of writing for a public."[7] This goes *a fortiori* for writers on historiography, who seldom pause to think how their work, or, still more, that of the historians they are writing about, is actually read.

In practice, surely, no reader comes to a history book naively willing to believe everything it says. Postmodernists are right to say that readers bring to history their own presuppositions, their own beliefs and purposes. The point, however, is that these no more completely shape their reading of the book than do the intentions of the author. Reading is a matter of interaction between reader and writer, in which neither is necessarily or inevitably dominant. Moreover, historians on the whole do not write as if *everything* they say were *absolutely* true. On the contrary, the conventional language of historians has *always* made a specific point of detailing the varying levels of certainty or probability attaching to what they say. It is not just that the words "probably" and "perhaps" occur fairly frequently in historical work; the careful historian in fact deploys a large variety of stylistic devices to indicate the relative strength or weakness of the argument advanced and to indicate how tentative or otherwise are the conclusions reached. When, exceptionally, a historian like A. J. P. Taylor made what he liked to call "snap judgments" and issue statements of seemingly dogmatic finality about complex historical issues, it is clear that these were intended to provoke his readers into thinking about the subject rather than to convince them that he was telling the absolute truth about it.

By making their own preconceptions and purposes explicit, historians have customarily tried to provide readers with the knowledge to read their books against their own intentions if so desired. Moreover, in teaching undergraduates and graduate students alike, university historians' primary aim is to get them to adopt a critical and questioning attitude to the books and articles they read, including their own (otherwise what value would teaching be to a historian, and why do so many historians acknowledge in the prefaces to their own books the crucial contribution of their students in having forced them to rethink or reformulate many of their arguments?). One postmodernist writer, Beverley Southgate, has claimed that the "traditional" model of history as the pursuit of the truth about the past means "that students of history will be taught not so much to question as to conform to existing dogma." Nothing could be further from the reality of the situation; one wonders whether Southgate's colleagues in the History Department at the University of Hertfordshire, where he teaches, would recognize their own teaching techniques in this description; one hopes not.[8]

Historical writing as well as teaching makes a point of conveying the provisional and uncertain nature of interpretation and the need to test it constantly against the source materials used as evidence in its favor. This is why it is important not to confuse what happened with how we find out about it. Patrick Joyce may assert that "the events, structures and processes of the past are indistinguishable from the forms of documentary representation, the conceptual and political appropriations, and the historical discourses that construct them."[9] But this is self-evidently not the case. Discourse does not construct the past itself; the most that it is possible to argue is that it constructs our attempts to represent it. Joyce himself confounded his own theoretical claims in a book published at the same time as his polemic against Lawrence Stone in *Past and Present*. While arguing for a "semiology of the social order" in this work, Joyce also noted that "conceptions of the social order were related to attempts to bring order and decency to the experience of poverty, insecurity and labour."[10] However Joyce interprets the concept of "experience" here, the implication that poverty was materially real is clear enough. He insists indeed on underlining his belief, as expressed in his book, that discourses in the past structured perceptions "only because they articulated the needs and desires of their audiences."[11]

As Joyce's own historical work suggests, the historian's voice is important, but so, too, are the voices of the past which the historian is trying to transmit. It is perfectly true to say, as Keith Jenkins does, that most school and university students learn history almost exclusively through reading secondary work.[12] But this is not really relevant to arguments about the nature of historical knowledge, which relate in the first place to the extent to which it is possible to reconstruct the past from the remains it has left behind—or, in other words, to historical research based on primary sources. It is certainly true that to a large extent we use the same procedures in reading secondary sources as we do in reading primary: We ask who has written the document, and why, and to whom the document is addressed, and why; we check it out for internal consistency and for consistency with other documents relating to the same subject; and if it contains information derived from other sources, we ask where this information comes from and do our best to check it out, too. But this does not mean the objects of these identical procedures must be identical, any more than the fact that we may use a literary framework of interpretation in understanding the past necessarily means that what we are saying is untrue.[13]

To call the past a "text" is of course to use a metaphor, not to attempt a description.[14] As the French historian Roger Chartier has warned, " 'text' [is] a term too often inappropriately applied to practices (ordinary or ritualized) whose tactics and procedures bear no resemblance to discursive strategies."[15] The past is much more than a mere text, and to attempt to read it as a text is to capture only a small part of its reality. Social and political events are not the same as literary texts. Gabrielle Spiegel has claimed : "No historian, even of positivist stripe, would argue that history is present to us in any but textual form,"[16] and elsewhere she has referred to "the literary nature of all historical documents."[17] But a historical source is not the same as a literary text. It is not necessarily, indeed it is not usually a description of an event or a state of mind or a story. From Mommsen's use of Roman inscriptions through to the Rankeans' analysis of diplomatic documents, or the cliometricians' number crunching of parish records of births, marriages, and deaths to the medievalist's surveys of field systems, buildings, and archaeological remains, historians have long been skilled in dealing with documents that do not directly tell a story themselves or report events even in the most recent past. Moreover, radio and cinema, videotapes and camcorders, computer printouts and records, photocopying, microfilm, electronic databases, the Internet and the World Wide Web all are generating new forms of source material for future historians, even if a large proportion of it gets lost. It is foolish to suppose, as John Vincent does, that because the written word is declining as a form of communication, history is dying, too.[18]

The textual metaphor can easily be unhelpful to the discussion of history, by suggesting that history depends on the analysis and composition of literary texts just as much as literary criticism and scholarship do. Even where the historian's sources are written down, they very often bear little resemblance to any form of literature. They may be statistical series of corn prices or criminal offenses; they may be lengthy lists of individuals belonging to this or that organization; they may be brief inscriptions or graffiti carved into a Roman wall. The conventional tools of literary analysis are of little use in dealing with such materials. On the other hand, historians do not of course simply take such materials as direct reflections of past reality. Maps can deceive, as Mark Monmonier has pointed out in his entertaining manual *How to Lie with Maps.*[19] So can figures and graphs. Statistical series and lists, like visual materials, were all compiled by human beings with specific purposes in mind, and the methods used to gather serial data in the past were often somewhat haphazard and uncertain. But that is to say no more than that they have to be treated with the customary skepticism with which the historian treats more conventional written sources, and the same kind of source-criticism has to be applied to them as well.

II

SOME writers have claimed that it is impossible for historians to enable the past to "speak for itself" because if the past were to express itself, it would have to reenact itself.[20] This assertion would seem to depend on the belief that when you or I think we are expressing ourselves in speech or writing, we are not really doing so at all, but producing an arbitrary set of words that has no determinate relationship to ourselves at all. However, even if we develop, perhaps even "reinvent" our identity during our lifetime, and even if we have not one unitary self but an identity that is multifaceted, it is still usually possible to discern some consistency in our utterances over time, and indeed most people, unless they are politicians, go to some trouble to make sure that they do express themselves in a reasonably consistent and noncontradictory way. We do in fact invest our words with meanings which have a real relationship to our own life and our own existence; life would be very difficult for us indeed if we did not manage to do this.

Language and grammar are in fact not completely arbitrary signifiers, but have evolved through contact with the real world in an attempt to name real things. In a similar way, historical discourse or interpretation has also evolved through contact with the real historical world in an attempt to reconstruct it. The difference is that this contact is indirect, because the real historical world has disappeared irrecoverably into the past. It has to be established through a reading of the documentary and other fragments which the real world of the past has left behind. Yet these are not arbitrarily configured discourses either but were themselves created in a much more direct interaction with reality. Language is not in the end purely self-reflective. Experience tells us that it mediates between human consciousness and the world it occupies, as Hayden White himself noted in 1975.[21] If it did not describe and inform us about the past, then we would not be able to know that the past had any real existence at all. Hence admitting the existence of the past as extratextual reality implies recognizing that language can describe things external to itself. Content is not a derivative of style; it is possible to describe the same thing accurately in a number of different styles, just as it is possible to give a full and fair account of, say, Gibbon's argument about the causes of the rise of Christianity without making a misguided attempt to imitate the literary style in which he put it.[22]

Moreover, a postmodernist such as Jenkins or Ankersmit would also presumably wish to maintain that he is expressing his own beliefs in a consistent and rational way in what he writes, even if this is not always the case in reality. Now there is no real difference in principle between Jenkins writing something in 1995 in a book which I am reading in 1998 and, say, King Henry VIII of England writing something in a letter in 1532 which I am reading in 1998. Both have written these texts in the past, even if Henry VIII's past is more remote than that of Jenkins's. Both wished to express a meaning or meanings which had a bearing on their own lives in some way. When King Henry writes to Anne Boleyn of "the great affection I have for you,"[23] he does not have to reenact this affection in person in order to express himself, however much he might have wished to, any more than when Jenkins says his "new work is addressed primarily (though obviously not exclusively) to advanced and undergraduate students and their teachers," he has to gather a group of such people together and start haranguing them in order to give them access to the reality of what he is saying. In other words, if we take Jenkins's book *On "What Is History?"* as a historical text, it is simply not true to say, as he does, that we cannot have access to his meaning because the past, in its incarnation in the Jenkins of 1995, cannot express itself.

The postmodernists are caught in a paradox of their own making here. They want to argue that all texts are essentially the same, that there is no difference, for example, between a primary source and a secondary source, between Henry VIII's letter or Jenkins's book and what someone else has written about either of these documents later on (for example, J. J. Scarisbrick's standard biography of King Henry or my own account of Jenkins's book in the pages which you are now reading). Yet there is a very real difference between what somebody writes and the account someone else gives of it. I would like to think that I have quoted Jenkins fully and fairly in these pages and given an accurate representation of his views. But if any readers wish to check whether in fact this is the case, then surely they are going to go back to the book itself rather than to some third person's account of it. The principle at work here is no different from that operating in the case of Henry VIII's letter and the account of it given in a later biography.

The same kind of contradiction catches Jenkins's attempt to deal with Gabrielle Spiegel's argument that the "dissolution of the materiality of the verbal sign means the dissolution of history."[24] According to Jenkins, history as a discipline never did rest on a verbal sign whose materiality was not dissolved, since all verbal signs are immaterial anyway. But for Jenkins to attack Spiegel's position by calling it the product of "ideology and mystification" is disingenuous, because he himself is on record as saying that *everything* is ideology, which means that his own position must be ideological, too.[25] Why should we therefore accept his invitation to be "suspicious of the motives" of those with whom he disagrees and not be suspicious of his own motives as well? The point here is not merely the failure of postmodernist writers such as Jenkins to engage in the self-reflectivity they so passionately advocate for others; it is also the manner in which they take an unproven assumption from their own arsenal of beliefs (in this case, the immateriality of the sign) and berate their opponents for advancing arguments which are not based on an acceptance of it. If we believe that signs—words, language, concepts, arguments, books—do bear some relation to material reality, then Spiegel's fears begin to seem a lot more reasonable.

Because the past is constantly generating its own material remains, some have argued, "it can and does constrain those who seek to find out what once took place," even if those remains can never really speak for themselves. In their qualified defense of the historian's belief in past reality and the possibility of reconstructing it, Professors Appleby, Hunt, and Jacob reject the idea that the past can impose its reality on the historian through these remains, and prefer instead to argue that the constraints which they impose on the possible variety of interpretations depend on the existence of "a scholarly community whose principal task is to reconstruct, interpret, and preserve artifacts from the past" and which operates a "complex set of rules" in so doing. But surely the past does impose its reality through the sources in a basic way. At the most elementary level, one cannot simply read into documents words that are not there. Moreover, it is highly dangerous to make objectivity in this sense dependent on the existence of a scholarly community. There was, after all, a scholarly community in Germany in the 1920s which remained in existence, largely unaltered in personnel and ideology, under Hitler's Third Reich; scholars nowadays are generally in agreement that the set of rules it operated in approaching the German past was seriously flawed and delivered an interpretation of history that was highly distorted. If we accept that this was because these rules were themselves faulty, however, we also have to accept that good rules transcend scholarly communities and do not therefore depend on their acceptance by them.[26] Those rules might include very basic precepts, such as not altering documents or not leaving out or suppressing material damaging to one's argument or purpose. Historians are not producing mere fictions because, as the

French historian Roger Chartier has observed, they are dependent on the archives and other real, material traces of the past:

> The work of historians in analysing and unmasking forgeries . . . is a paradoxical and ironic way of reasserting the capacity of history to establish true knowledge. Thanks to its unique techniques, the discipline of history is skilled at recognizing fakes for what they are and, by that token, at denouncing forgers. It is by returning to its own deviations and perversions that history demonstrates that the discrete knowledge it produces is inscribed within the order of a confirmable, verifiable knowledge.[27]

In this sense, genuine historical documents do have an integrity of their own; they do indeed "speak for themselves." The constraints that past reality imposes through them on the historian are more than merely negative. That is why, as E. P. Thompson once said, "the historian has got to be listening all the time. . . . If he listens, then the material itself will begin to speak through him."[28]

I I I

THESE issues, and others besides, were made painfully concrete in the American historical profession in the 1980s by the so-called Abraham affair. When the young American historian David Abraham's book *The Collapse of the Weimar Republic* was published by Princeton University Press in 1981, many reviewers (including myself) hailed it for its originality, while at the same time finding its structural Marxism rather too schematic. Indeed I thought that its central arguments were at such a high level of abstraction that they could not really be empirically validated at all and that the book was best regarded as a work of political science rather than history, conforming therefore to a set of rules and conventions that were not strictly historical.[29] Other, more specialist reviewers were critical in a very different way. In particular, the conservative and avowedly anti-Marxist American historian Henry Ashby Turner, who had himself worked on the same source material, went on record accusing

Abraham of deliberately inventing and falsifying archival material in order to discredit German capitalism and blame it for the collapse of the Weimar Republic. Appalled at these allegations, Abraham went back to the archives to check his sources and replied to Turner, admitting some minor errors but rejecting the main charges leveled against him.[30]

At this point another American specialist in the history of big business in the Weimar Republic, Gerald Feldman, entered the fray with a further string of accusations. Feldman had originally recommended the book for publication by Princeton University Press, despite numerous errors which he had said should be corrected. But he then discovered that one of his former graduate students, Ulrich Nocken, was checking over every reference and every quotation in Abraham's book. Nocken reported that there were hundreds of egregious mistakes, including the printing of inaccurate paraphrases as if they were direct quotations from the documents, wrongly attributed letters and documents, mistranslations, misconstruals, inventions, and falsifications of the sources. This persuaded Feldman that he had been wrong to assume that because Abraham had been awarded a Ph.D., his scholarly integrity could be trusted. As if to atone for his earlier gullibility in passing the manuscript for publication, Feldman now unleashed a ferocious campaign of denunciation, in which a large number of specialists in modern German history, including myself, were sent circulars exposing the errors in Abraham's work and declaring him unfit to be a member of the scholarly community. Abraham replied with a vigorous self-defense, lobbying the German history community on both sides of the Atlantic in his turn. But in the face of Feldman's campaign, which included denunciatory letters and phone calls to universities considering Abraham for an assistant professorship, this was in the end to no avail. As a result of Feldman's untiring hostility, Abraham was hounded out of the profession and went to law school, where he graduated with distinction and duly reentered university employment, this time as a lawyer rather than as a historian and therefore in a subject which is perhaps more comfortable with the manipulation and tendentious interpretation of evidence than history is.[31]

The affair raised three crucial issues apart from the one of the professional ethics of the participants in the row. First, the relationship between Marxist and non-Marxist views of history. Was Hayden White right to argue that "the Marxist view of history is neither confirmable nor disconfirmable by appeal to 'historical evidence,' for what is at issue between a Marxist and a non-Marxist view of history is the question of precisely what counts as evidence, and what does not?"[32] Was this, as Abraham's defenders maintained, an attempt by anti-Marxists to discredit him for political reasons, by traducing his scholarship without justification? Was a Marxist construal of a document inevitably a misconstrual in the eyes of an anti-Marxist? There was no doubt about Turner's anti-Marxism, and it is relevant to note that he himself was about to publish a large book on *Big Business and the Rise of Hitler* which constituted a massive demolition of the Marxist view that capitalists brought Hitler to power. On the other hand, Turner was on record as respecting those Marxist historians, notably Tim Mason, whose scholarship he held to be sound. Mason himself went into print distancing himself from Abraham and endorsing the importance of historical accuracy in research.[33] Moreover, Feldman had been generous in his praise of "good Marxist and neo-Marxist history" and could in no sense be seen as anti-Marxist.[34] The controversy could not therefore be reduced to the status of a political disagreement. It was a disagreement over historical evidence and its uses.

The second issue that it raised was the relationship between fact and interpretation. Abraham's defenders claimed that his mistakes of detail made no difference to his overall interpretation. Indeed, when Abraham himself, having been back to the archives and checked over all his sources again, issued a "corrected" second edition of the book, it was only the quotations, attributions, footnotes, references, and other matters of detail that were corrected; he did not alter or amend one single aspect of his interpretation.[35] The critics of the second edition were able to point out that the citations and much of the evidence no longer supported the argument at a number of points. But in a sense they never had. Abraham's schema of rival agrarian and industrial power blocs in the Weimar Republic was taken straight from the Greco-French Marxist political theorist Nicos Poulantzas. Abraham, it seems, had merely scoured the archives for "evidence" that would back it up. When combined with Abraham's self-confessedly poor research skills and excessive haste in research, this had led to misreadings that, in more cases than not, supported his argument and in many instances actually went beyond it in the direction of the old agency theory (that capitalists were directly, instead of merely indirectly, supporters of Nazism), a theory which, ironically, he was claiming to transcend.

This leads on to the third point—namely, the importance or otherwise of evidence and the falsifiability of historical interpretations by means of an appeal to it. At one point in his book Abraham cited a major German industrialist as writing in a private letter in the early 1930s that it was desirable "to crystallize the bourgeois right and the Nazi Party into one," a declaration which admirably supported his overall interpretation. But the original document, cited accurately by Feldman, contained the crucial word "not," so that it actually said the reverse of what Abraham said it did and therefore went against his general argument.[36] On innumerable occasions Abraham, Feldman showed, invented evidence by supplying additions or glosses from his research notes as part of actual quotations. Abraham indeed admitted that while in the archives, he had failed to fence off quotes from original documents with quotation marks in his notes, so that he was often unable to distinguish them from his own (often, as it turned out, rather tendentious) summaries of other parts of the same documents. Thus he frequently quoted the latter as if they were the former. The book was so riddled with errors that some of them, as Abraham himself was quick to point out, actually went against the argument he was advancing.[37] But it is hard to quarrel with Feldman's conclusion that the general tendency of the mistakes was "to exaggerate the evil role played by industry, to overdramatize its power and self-assurance, and to make arguments far beyond what the evidence would allow."[38]

Abraham wrote in self-defense that as he carried out his research, there seemed to be "an exemplary fit" between his initial hypotheses and the evidence he found.[39] But every working historian knows how unlikely that is. The first prerequisite of the serious historical researcher must be the ability to jettison dearly held interpretations in the face of the recalcitrance of the evidence. If a letter from an industrialist says he does not want any crystallization of the bourgeois right and the Nazis, then no amount of theorizing will alter that fact, and there is no way around it. There is nothing mysterious about this; historians are perfectly used to trying out ideas on the evidence and throwing them away when they don't fit. Evidence running counter to the argument cannot be omitted or distorted, but must be explained, even at the cost of amending the argument or abandoning it altogether. Many historians and reviewers have commented on this point. Thus when the British Marxist historian Christopher Hill remarked in the preface to one of his books: "I was advancing a thesis. . . . I . . . picked out evidence which seemed to support my case," his critic J. H. Hexter rightly commented: "Far from just looking for evidence that may support his thesis, he [i.e., the historian] needs to look for vulnerabilities in that thesis and to contrive means of testing them. Then, depending on what he finds, he can support the thesis, strengthen its weak points, or modify it to eliminate its weaknesses."[40] It is clear that Abraham had failed to follow this basic procedure in researching and writing his book.

My own view is that while Abraham did not deliberately falsify evidence, he was extremely careless with it, far more so than is permissible in a work of serious historical scholarship, or indeed in any work of history, and that he *subconsciously* molded the evidence gathered in his research notes in order to fit the interpretation he had worked out beforehand. It was not a question of middle-aged "fact fetishists" against youthful champions of "historical imagination," as some of Abraham's partisans implied. Both in his book and in his replies to Feldman, Abraham proved distressingly unable to tell fact from fiction. This was not therefore, as Abraham himself and his supporters such as Peter Novick implied, a methodological dispute between theoretical and empirical historians in which the "objectivists" demonstrated their continuing and, by implication, malign and stultifying grip on the American historical profession.[41] Abraham implied, and his defenders maintained, that any history book would reveal as many errors as his if it were subjected to the same level of intense, detailed scrutiny. Lawrence Stone, for instance, said:

> When you work in the archives you're far from home, you're bored, you're in a hurry, you're scribbling like crazy. You're bound to make mistakes. I don't believe any scholar in the Western world has impeccable footnotes. Archival research is a special case of the general messiness of life."[42]

But this, too, was a debatable point.

Stone should know about "the general messiness of life" in the archives. He was far from being an unimpeachable witness on this issue. When he was Abraham's age, in 1951, his own work had been subjected to a series of devastating and merciless attacks by his Oxford colleagues Hugh Trevor-Roper and J. P. Cooper in the *Economic History Review*, which had shown a similar catalog of gross error to that discovered in Abraham's work. Stone had published an article arguing that English aristocratic landowners in the early seventeenth century were extravagant, financially inept, and declining in economic power. The conclusion was that this hastened the "rise of the gentry," which was regarded by left-wing historians like R. H. Tawney as one of the main causes of the English Civil War. Trevor-Roper, however, pointed out that Stone had confused different generations of aristocrats with the same title, got many, if not most, of his sums wrong, and altogether misunderstood the nature of landownership at the time. In arguing that aristocratic ownership of manors had declined, for instance, Stone took county samples without realizing that aristocrats owned land in many different counties, and would readily sell their holdings in one to build up their estates in another; moreover, manors differed substantially in size, a factor Stone ignored completely, so that his figures showing a decline in the number of manors held by aristocratic landowners in some cases concealed an actual growth in the acreage and quality of land they possessed overall.

Trevor-Roper's critique was described variously as "terrifying,"

"brutal," and "one of the most vitriolic attacks ever made by one historian on another." Stone himself was forced to admit that there were
"very serious mistakes" in his article and confessed to his "unscholar-
ly treatment" of much of the evidence.[43] When I was an undergraduate in Oxford, indeed, the dons, sniffy as ever about American universities, even Princeton, where Stone had gone to teach, were wont
to sneer that he had been forced to seek employment in the United
States because his position in Oxford had become untenable as a
result of the controversy. Although he in fact subsequently went on to
a highly successful career, publishing a series of major (though never
less than controversial) works in the process, his mauling at the hands
of Trevor-Roper clearly rankled even more than thirty years after-
ward, and his defense of Abraham, with whom he evidently had a certain fellow-feeling, has to be regarded with suspicion. More to the
point, however, was the fact that Stone had recovered from this early
débâcle and during his later career had exercised a major and undeniably significant influence on the study of early modern English history and, through his perceptive and readable review articles, the study
of history in general. To deny Abraham the same chance of making
amends, as Feldman ultimately did, was surely wrong.

I V

THE Abraham affair was taken up into the debate on postmodernism
not least because it touched on the issue which was proving the crucial test of the claim that history was incapable of establishing any
real facts about the past. Nazi Germany seemed to postmodernism's
critics to be the point at which an end to hyperrelativism was called
for. Postmodernists realized this. In replying to critics, Hayden White
pointed out (in a footnote to one of the essays in *The Content of the
Form*) that the Jewish historian Lucy Dawidowicz had attacked all
previous writers on Nazism for misrepresenting, neglecting, or trivializing the "Holocaust," thereby implying that they, too, were writing more in literary than in factual terms and that the Third Reich
was no different from any other historical subject in this respect. But

Dawidowicz's book *The Holocaust and the Historians* has rightly been generally viewed as distorted, exaggerated, overpolemical, and grossly inaccurate in its account of the subject. There is in fact a massive, carefully empirical literature on the Nazi extermination of the Jews. Clearly, to regard it as fictional, or unreal, or no nearer to historical reality than, say, the work of the "revisionists" who deny that Auschwitz ever happened at all is simply wrong. Here is an issue where evidence really counts, and can be used to establish the essential facts. Auschwitz was not a discourse. It trivializes mass murder to see it as a text. The gas chambers were not a piece of rhetoric. Auschwitz was indeed inherently a tragedy and cannot be seen as either a comedy or a farce. And if this is true of Auschwitz, then it must be true at least to some degree of other past happenings, events, institutions, people as well. What then are the implications of this for postmodernism?

In a conference devoted to this subject, published in *Probing the Limits of Representation*, edited by Saul Friedländer, a number of postmodernists and their critics sought to address this problem. Hayden White in particular retreated from his earlier position in order to defend himself against the accusation that his hyperrelativism gave countenance to the "revisionist" enterprise of "Holocaust denial." He conceded that the facts of the "Holocaust" closed off the possibility of using certain types of "emplotment" to describe it. But in making this concession, he implicitly acknowledged the primacy of past reality in shaping the way historians write about it, thus abandoning his central theoretical tenet. The past turned out not to be completely at the mercy of historical "narrativity" and "emplotment" after all.[44]

White himself summed up his change of position by saying that in his early writings he was more concerned to point out the ways in which historians used literary methods in their work and, in so doing, inevitably imported a "fictive" element into it, because their written style did not simply report what they had found but actually constructed the subject of their writing. In his later work he came to draw a sharper distinction between fiction, on the one hand, and history, on the other. Rather than imagine the object first, then write about it in a manner that was therefore mainly subjective, history

existed only in the action of writing, involving a kind of simultane-
ous production or identification of the author of the discourse and
the referent or thing about which he or she was writing. White made
this shift of position in response to the debate on postmodernism and
"Holocaust denial," and it seems to me to sum up more realistically
than his earlier arguments the way in which historians actually go
about their business. Historical imagination, he says, calls for the
imagining of "both the real world from which one has launched
one's inquiry into the past and the world that comprises one's object
of interest."[45] This is a view from which it is hard to dissent.

What does the whole debate add up to in practical terms, then?
According to Russell Jacoby, when postmodernists such as White and
LaCapra deign to descend from the lofty heights of abstraction to offer
concrete criticisms of actual works of history, "what begins as a call for
a radical departure in historical thought comes out sounding very
familiar: the importance, complexity, and ambiguities of the text are
continuously reiterated."[46] This is perhaps taking too negative a view.
Even Lawrence Stone admits that the "linguistic turn" has "taught us
to examine texts with far more care and caution than we did before,
using new tools to disclose covert beneath overt messages, to decipher
the meaning of subtle shifts of grammar and so on."[47] All this is to the
good. And if Hayden White has had few direct imitators, his influence
has been nonetheless real for being all the more diffuse. It can to some
extent be traced in the use by other historians of terms such as
"emplotment" and the like, terms originally used by White himself,
but more generally it can be seen in a growing awareness on the part
of historians of the literary and narrative elements in their own
work—research as well as writing—and that surely is no bad thing. Yet
most of White's earlier arguments do not stand up. The distinction
between primary and secondary sources on the whole has survived the
withering theoretical hail rained down upon it by the postmodernists.
The past does speak through the sources and is recoverable through
them. There is a qualitative difference between documents written in
the past, by living people, for their own purposes, and interpretations
advanced about the past by historians living at a later date.

Keith Jenkins has argued that historical method does not lead to historical truth. But in saying this, he confuses theory and method. Historical method is not what he says it is: feminist, neo–Marxist, structuralist, *Annaliste,* Weberian, or whatever.[48] These things are *theories.* Historical *method* is based on the rules of verification laid down by Ranke and elaborated in numerous ways since his time. It is common to all historians working in all these various theoretical modes, as a glance at their heavily footnoted works will easily show. Even major methodological differences, for example, between cliometricians churning quantitative data through their computers, intellectual historians engaged in a close reading of a small number of texts, or medieval historians deciphering archaeological finds still fade into the background in comparison with the shared duty of "getting it right": of copying out and punching in the figures accurately, of verifying the wording and authorship of the text, of reporting the correct location of each find in the dig. It is not true to say that historians are "not too concerned about discrete facts."[49] On the contrary, whatever the criteria for the facts' selection, the vast majority of the historian's efforts are devoted to ascertaining them and establishing them as firmly as possible in the light of the historical sources. Even Jenkins uses footnotes. Footnotes and bibliographical references really are designed to enable the reader to check the sources on which a historian's statement is made and to see whether or not they support it. They are not mere rhetorical devices designed to produce a spurious "reality effect." Postmodernists have claimed that

> Although historians often frame their criticisms of colleagues' work in terms of evidence—sources overlooked, misplaced emphasis, inappropriate categorization—such criticisms cannot demonstrate the superiority of one interpretation or story-type over another. These debates over evidence are largely diversionary; they are carried on as if the choice and use of evidence will determine a historian's perspective rather than that the historian's perspective counts as evidence.[50]

This claim is misconceived. As the Abraham controversy—and others, too, such as the famous "storm over the gentry" in the 1950s—

showed, interpretations really can be tested and confirmed or falsified by an appeal to the evidence, and some of the time at least, it
really is possible to prove that one side is right and the other is
wrong. What counts as evidence is not determined solely by one historian's perspective but is subject to a wide measure of agreement
which transcends not only individuals but also communities of
scholars. Still, it has undeniably been a frequent cause of dispute,
above all, perhaps, when historians have come to deal with the problem of causation, as we shall now see.

CHAPTER FIVE

CAUSATION IN HISTORY

I

IN his book *What Is History?* E. H. Carr famously declared that "the study of history is a study of causes."[1] Historians had to look for a variety of causes of any given event, work out their relationship to one another if there was one, and arrange them in some kind of hierarchy of importance. Causes had to be ordered as well as enumerated. Carr poured scorn on the views of Sir Isaiah Berlin and others who argued, in the style of Cold War attacks on Soviet historical "determinism," that history was governed by chance, accident, and indeterminacy and that individuals were autonomous and endowed with unfettered free will and were thus morally responsible for their own actions. These therefore could be explained only as the outcome of their will and not of some larger impersonal "cause." But in everyday life, Carr noted, not unfairly, people did not proceed on such extreme assumptions. To adduce causes was not to deny moral responsibility; nothing was less true than the dictum that "to understand everything is to excuse everything." Morality and causation were two distinct categories which should not be confused.

Admittedly, Carr conceded, accident and contingency in history were real enough. It would be futile, for example, to argue that Lenin's premature death at the age of fifty-four had had no effect on the subsequent course of Russian history. But, Carr insisted, broader trends were more important. Insofar as the essence of being a historian was to generalize, and accidents of this kind were not generalizable, then they were in practice of little interest; they belonged to the "facts" which it was the historian's duty to get right, not to the interpretations which it was the historian's real purpose to advance. It might be the case, for example, that Mark Antony would not have fought and lost the Battle of Actium if Cleopatra had had a big nose and so had failed to attract him (an example quoted by J. B. Bury from Pascal's *Pensées*). Thus, if Cleopatra had not been beautiful, Octavius would not have founded the Roman Empire. Carr said: "It is true that Cleopatra's nose had results. But it makes no sense as a general proposition to say that generals lose battles because they are infatuated with beautiful queens . . . . Accidental causes cannot be generalized . . . they teach no lessons and lead to no conclusions."[2]

Carr thought that historians operated a kind of commonsense approach to explanation which might not satisfy the philosopher but would operate perfectly well in everyday life. If Mr. Jones, driving a car with defective brakes, ran over Mr. Robinson on a blind corner, Carr said, we might explain the incident in terms of the corner, or the brakes, or by reference to Mr. Jones's excessive consumption of alcohol at the party from which he was returning; but we would not get much credence if we argued that the cause lay in the smoking habit which had led Mr. Robinson to cross the road to buy a packet of cigarettes at the corner shop. For Carr, this last-named cause lay in the realm of chance and contingency and therefore effectively had to be ruled out of court. You could say that blind corners, defective brakes, or drunk driving made road accidents more likely, but you could not say that cigarette smoking by pedestrians did.[3]

Carr's example of Mr. Jones and Mr. Robinson has been reexamined recently by Professors Appleby, Hunt, and Jacob. "Doesn't any analysis of this case," they ask, "depend on whether Mr. Robinson and Mr. Jones were white or black, homosexual or heterosexual (perhaps one of them was on his way to a gay bar and was preoccupied), or even accident-prone or rock-steady?"[4] Appleby, Hunt, and Jacob seem to be objecting to Carr's account because it is not a politically correct way of approaching history in the 1990s. But their argument is itself open to objections which point to the limitations of rewriting history from a particular political perspective. In the first place, while it might indeed have been important that one of the two men in question was thinking about the bar he was going to visit instead of the oncoming traffic, if indeed he was, and if indeed this could be proven, it is not immediately apparent why it should matter whether the bar in question was straight or gay. In any case, however, we know that Mr. Jones was on his way home and that Mr. Robinson had simply popped out to buy cigarettes, so Appleby, Hunt, and Jacob just haven't read the evidence correctly, and we can rule out their speculative point as factually wrong. As far as the ethnicity of the two gentlemen is concerned, this, too, is irrelevant to an explanation of the accident unless we can show that Mr. Jones was a racist and deliberately ran down Mr. Robinson because he belonged to a different ethnic group. But there is no evidence for this in Carr's account, since Mr. Jones clearly stepped on the brake pedal when he saw Mr. Robinson crossing the road (otherwise it would not have mattered that the car's brakes were defective, since he would not have tried to use them; indeed he would have stepped on the accelerator). So we can rule this out, too, as factually incorrect as well as irrelevant.

The British historian A. J. P. Taylor used to delight in provoking more sober historians by positing tiny causes for vast events. The First World War, for instance, in his view was caused by railway timetables because this locked the belligerent powers into a sequence of troop mobilizations and war declarations from which they could not escape.[5] Even in his autobiographical writings he liked to emphasize the element of chance in his life.[6] Doubtless he would have been sorely tempted by the idea that Mr. Robinson was killed because he smoked cigarettes. But it is less than certain that he intended to be taken entirely seriously in this kind of thing, and more likely that he intended it to irritate his more pedestrian colleagues, an activity at which he was generally very successful.

A more fruitful way of indicating the importance and limitations of chance (or contingency, as the more theoretically inclined like to call it) in history is to imagine what might have happened had things been slightly different. Suppose, for example, that U.S. President John F. Kennedy had not been assassinated but had instead gone on to a full two terms in the White House. Would things have turned out differently from the way they did? Certainly his presidency would have been more glamorous than that of Lyndon B. Johnson or Richard M. Nixon, and the chances are that the latter would not have come to power and thus the whole Watergate scandal would never have happened. But the big issues—civil rights, welfare, the Vietnam War—would not have been much affected. We would still most probably have had Medicare. The student and other radical disturbances of the late 1960s would not have been prevented by a Kennedy presidency. America would still have been involved in Vietnam and would still have been defeated. Nothing in Kennedy's record up to 1963 makes us think that he would have differed strongly from his successors on these issues. Of course we can never know for sure what would have happened. The relevant point here is that despite very significant differences, it is unlikely that the overall pattern of events would have diverged totally from what actually happened had Kennedy not been assassinated. Accident, chance, and contingency certainly have a real effect, but that effect is almost always rather limited in practice.

As far as this goes, therefore, Carr's argument, though put in a rather extreme way, certainly has a good deal to recommend it. But there are problems with it, too. To begin with, Carr went on to argue that causality is a matter of interpretation and therefore inevitably bound up with value judgment. History must serve the present, and so, too, must our view of the causes of historical events. In the case of Mr. Jones and Mr. Robinson, for example, we could cite the blind corner, the defective brakes, or the alcohol intake of the driver, because we could do something about these things—alter the corner, for instance, or introduce tougher laws about the standards of maintenance and repair of motor vehicles and the level of alcohol with which people are permitted to drive them. But although we could ban cigarette smoking, and thus prevent Mr. Robinson from killing himself in another way, this would have no effect at all on traffic accidents of the kind which took place when Mr. Jones ran him over. The enumeration of accidental causes, therefore, concluded Carr, is "from the point of view of the historian dead and barren," because it cannot contribute anything to our ability to shape the future.[7] Our search for the causes of Mr. Robinson's death is guided by our objective of reducing deaths on the road.[8]

But while the citation of accidental causes may be dead and barren from the point of view of the politician or the social reformer, it is difficult to see why it should be dead and barren from the point of view of the historian, whose primary purpose is to understand the past. If your main aim is to shape the future, then it is not a good idea to devote your life to studying history; it would be far better to avoid academic or intellectual life altogether and go into politics or business or the civil service or some other kind of practical career. If the sources suggest that an accidental cause was at work, it would not be right to rule it out just because it could not be made to serve our purposes in the present. Indeed an even greater danger lurks here. Suppose a cause, accidental or otherwise, suggesting itself powerfully from the documents, goes against our ideas about the present and the future? Was Carr really saying that we should suppress it in the interests of present-day ideology?

It is hard to escape the conclusion that Carr did not really think his argument through. Nor, in the end, was the example of Mr. Jones and Mr. Robinson particularly well chosen. For historical explanation is not just about finding causes for discrete events like car crashes or world wars. Historians are just as interested in what events or processes decide, what they mean, as in what causes them. Consequences are often more important than causes.[9] "Why" is far from being the only question historians ask. Categorizing past societies or political systems or structures of belief is no less legitimate than inquiring into the causes of past events. Historians can "explain" something by putting it into a context (i.e., arguing it was part of this movement rather than that, belonged to one period or trend rather than another, and so on). Nor is explanation itself all that history is about. Allan Megill's view is typical: "It is a rather widely held opinion among professional historians that the truly serious task of historiography, making it a contribution to knowledge and not a triviality, is the task of explanation."[10] But are description and the recovery of empirical fact really no more than trivialities? Few historians would wish to concede this point in practice, given the enormous amount of time they spend on these activities. Moreover, some historians at least have become somewhat dismissive of the search for causes in recent years. Geoffrey Barraclough, a specialist on medieval Germany whose experiences in the Second World War converted him to the idea that history had to be relevant and oriented toward the present, argued in 1967 that historians should stop teaching their pupils about causes, which could only be speculated upon and had no relevance to the present, and concentrate on results instead.[11] More recently John Vincent has declared that the search for causes is futile; it is better in his view to look for explanations, though he never makes the distinction between the two very clear. "Cause," he says, "is a constriction on historical thought; let it be unbound."[12] Writing in 1976, Theodore Zeldin rejected narrative history and the search for causes in favor of what he called a *pointilliste* method, which would compose a picture out of unconnected dots, from which the reader could make "what links he thinks fit for himself."[13] "Causation," he observed, "has been almost as merciless a tyrant to historians as chronology."[14] He, too, thought it was time for historians to escape its clutches.

In his own great work *A History of French Passions*—originally published as *France 1848–1945* in the *Oxford History of Modern Europe*—Zeldin looks at French society over the century in question under a variety of novel perspectives—ambition, love, politics, intellect, taste, anxiety—and includes surveys of almost every aspect of French life, illustrated with telling and often entertainingly told examples of individual Frenchmen and women whose lives seemed to come into the perspective in question. The book is indeed remarkable for its refusal to engage in large-scale theories or explanations and its rigorous avoidance of narrative and chronology. But at the same time all is not quite so innovative as it seems. Often, for example, the novel-sounding titles conceal quite old-fashioned subjects. "Ambition," for example, introduces the reader to a masterly synthesis of recent research on French social structure, with chapters on the peasantry, the bourgeoisie, and the working class. A chapter on "Hypocrisy" turns out to be mainly about the Communist party. And so on. The book's section on politics not only has a chronology concealed beneath the thematic approach, moving from Legitimism and Orleanism via Bonapartism to Republicanism and so on, but also in practice delivers numerous quite cogent and persuasive explanations of French political history, for example, of the reasons why the Third Republic managed to last so long. Since Zeldin's previous experience had been as a straight political historian specializing in the Second Empire, it is perhaps hardly surprising that the political coverage was the most coherent in the book. But the rest, too, consisted not only of attacks on historical orthodoxies but of numerous explanations of the subjects with which it dealt.[15] There is indeed a refusal to put forward any overarching thesis to bind the various parts of the book together. But perhaps this is inevitable in a survey of a century of modern French history that aimed to be totally comprehensive in its coverage.

At the opposite end of the spectrum, other historians have emphasized the importance of causation and the prominent role of accident and personality in history. Geoffrey Roberts, an expert on Soviet Russia, has argued for a

> human action approach to the study of history [which] emphasizes the freedom of individuals to act, the importance of reconstructing what happened from the actor's point of view, and the role of accident, miscalculation and unintended consequences in shaping historical outcomes. . . . The idea that people do things for a reason, that their individual and collective actions are the stuff of history and that it is possible to construct an evidence-based account of why past actors acted as they did is, for most of us, plain common sense.[16]

But this is not true at all. Historians by and large do not concentrate on the accidental, do not assume that individuals have unfettered freedom of choice, and do not confine themselves to reconstructing the past actor's point of view. To argue, as some philosophers of history have done, that historians are only interested in discovering what individual actors thought and intended in the past, and frame their causal explanations in terms of what they find out about these things,[17] is plainly wrong, as a glance at any one of a whole variety of major areas of historical scholarship, from economic history to the history of climate, will show. Long ago, Sir Herbert Butterfield pointed out in his little essay *The Whig Interpretation of History* that many of the greatest and most important developments in modern history were the unintended consequences of actions whose originators had had something entirely different in mind. The Protestant Reformation, for instance, and its Catholic counterpart in sixteenth- and seventeenth-century Europe had intended to make people more godly, but the religious upheaval and conflict which followed eventually produced such widespread disillusion that the secular rationalism of the eighteenth-century Enlightenment was the result.[18] Friedrich Engels expressed this view much earlier and far more succinctly when he famously spoke of historical change as resulting from the operation of a "parallelogram of forces"; one person moved one corner of the parallelogram, moving all its arms and thereby affecting things far away from the point of origination and far removed from the intentions of the actor.

Moreover, while "common sense" may not exactly be coterminous with "prejudice" and imbued with "a potential for repressive bigotry," as Christopher Lloyd has charged, it certainly varies widely from epoch to epoch and culture to culture.[19] "Common sense" in the medieval and early modern periods, for example, included the notion that human action was guided by divine (or diabolical) inspiration and that disease was frequently caused by black magic or witchcraft. The recounting of miracles was part of the "common sense" of medieval historiography. The giveaway here is of course Roberts's phrase "for most of us," a phrase which implicitly ejects from the community of historians those who do not write political or diplomatic history and are therefore not one of "us." This does not really do justice to the breadth and diversity of historical scholarship today. Nor does the view taken by Sir Geoffrey Elton, that because historians are concerned with particular events, they should only look for particular causes. Even the most empirical of political historians must make some attempt to look for broader explanatory factors, and in a wider sense all of us mobilize explanations that depend on broad assumptions about how human beings think, feel, and behave in a given culture and society.[20]

II

WHILE Roberts would have us concentrate on explaining historical events in terms of their relation to the aims and intentions of the people who took part in them, Carr's concept of causation has often been labeled "determinist"—that is, it rests on the assumption that events are generally caused by factors independent of the will of the people involved in them. In an early piece, written in 1966, for example, Hayden White declared that history's claim to discover true patterns in the past trapped human beings, as it were, in an inescapable net of causation and robbed them of freedom of action in the present; if this was abandoned, then people could use history to assert their control over the future, and this indeed should be history's primary purpose.[21] White's argument rested on the idea that it didn't matter whether the history we used to further our present concerns was true or not. Any history beyond the merely antiquarian was by definition a "metahistory" the truth or otherwise of which could never be determined since it was essentially the creation of the historian.[22] "Explanation" in history really consisted only of theories made up by historians without reference to the source material and imported into it from outside. It rested on a series of poetic insights into how things happened, formalized into a philosophy of history which was to be found, if only implicitly, in every historical work, in one variant or another.[23] This argument collapsed a number of distinct, though, to be sure, clearly related phenomena into one another, abolishing altogether the distinctions between them, and reducing them all in the end to the single phenomenon of the poetic insight.

Empirical research into the causes of specific events is arguably more than the expression of a philosophy of history, though admittedly the historian has to have some basic theory of how and why things happen, some fundamental idea of human motivation and behavior, to begin with. Moreover, White did not say why historians' explanations of the causes of things were "poetic" rather than rational. Given the dull and pedestrian manner in which many historians write, "poetic" seems something of a misnomer. His argument was also remarkable for its trivialization of questions of evidence and its elevation of interpretation to a position of almost exclusive preeminence in the nature of historical scholarship. Historians, according to White, are less concerned to establish *that* certain events occurred than to determine what certain events might *mean*. But establishing that events occurred is a central part of the historian's business and cannot be dismissed as a secondary problem or a side issue.

In the hands of some postmodernists, White's argument can be turned into a general criticism of the historian's enterprise as a whole. Thus Keith Jenkins, for example, declares roundly that "historians are not too concerned about discrete facts. . . . No," he says gleefully,

> historians have ambitions, wishing to discover not only what happened but how and why and what these things meant and mean. This is the task historians have set for themselves (I mean they did not have to raise the stakes so high). So it is never really a matter of the facts *per se* but the weight, position, combination and significance they carry *vis-à-vis* each other in the construction of explanations that is at issue. . . .

He proceeds to reprimand historians for this folly. "Working historians," he says, "clearly ought to recognise" that interpretations do not just arise from the facts, but are put there by historians themselves and will have only a limited temporal and local validity before they are superseded by other interpretations. The concept of historical causation is itself merely an element in the arbitrarily constructed discursive formation of professional historiography.[24]

Even more radical criticisms have been leveled at the concept of historical causation by some postmodernists. The idea of a cause depends rather obviously on the concept of sequential time. Something that causes something else generally comes before it in time, not after; thus the causes of the American Declaration of Independence of 1776 are to be sought in the years 1775 and before, not 1777 and after. If sequential time is recognized as no more than an intellectual construct, of course, then the consequences of this recognition for historical research are very serious, as a number of writers have recognized. Frank Ankersmit expresses a widespread view when he says, "Historical time is a recent and highly artificial invention of Western civilization." Writing historical narrative based "on the concept of time," he has declared, is "building on quick-sand."[25] Drawing on Einsteinian physics, many postmodernists are skeptical of the notion of time as even and regulated; in political terms, they see such a view of time as oppressive and controlling, legitimating hegemonic discourse and privileging Western ways of viewing the world over non-Western.[26] A democratic history written according to the precept of abandoning sequential time would be, as one postmodernist writer has argued approvingly, an "inter-minable pattern without meaning," rather like some forms of con-temporary music or some contemporary experimental novels. This would lead to a new form of history which would abandon "the time of clocks and capital" altogether.[27] Yet those who argue in this manner are caught in a paradox; indeed the very use of the concept of "*post*modern," which is inevitably tied to a particular time period of history, is contrary to the postmodern notion that there are no particular time periods of history. As a perceptive critic has remarked, when a postmodern writer puts forward the claim that "historical time is a thing of the past," she does not seem to see all the ironies present in the statement, for declaring something to be a thing of the past itself uses the historical concept of time which the statement is intended to dismiss.[28] Besides, a historical—that is, basically linear—concept of time continues to be used the world over by people both in the conduct of their everyday lives and in their preference for, say, novels which narrate a story over novels which do not, for John Grisham over Alain Robbe-Grillet, for example. Historical time is thus in no way merely adhered to as a concept by people who, as some argue, are "privileged by the prevailing hegemonic arrangements."[29] It is in essence far too powerful a principle to be dispensed with, even by those who reject it. Indeed any attempt to deny historical time necessarily presupposes the very thing it denies. *How* we count the years—whether we use the Western calendar, or the Jewish, or the Chinese, or whatever—is completely irrelevant to this point, and it is hard to escape the conclusion that postmodernists here are confusing the Western hegemony implicit in the worldwide use of the Christian calendar with the culturally neutral, universal sequence of time which calendars are designed to count.

III

TIME passes, therefore; yet no historian can hope to capture every passing moment. As I am writing this, I can hear the click of my fingers on the word processor, the faint whine of the computer in the background, the dull but constantly varying roar of the traffic in the main road behind the houses across the garden, the twittering of the birds outside, the light ticking of the clock on my desk, the soft padding of my cat as he comes up the stairs, the sound of my own breathing, and so on. All this in a handful of seconds, and already it is gone beyond any hope of complete or accurate reconstruction, least of all in the exact sequence in which these noises have come to my ears. So we all pull out from the seamless web of past events a tiny selection which we then present in our historical account. Nobody has ever disputed this. The dispute arises from those who believe that the selection is largely made by the narratives and structures which occur in the past itself and those who think it is largely made by the historian.

Is it the case, as Hayden White has maintained, that most professional historians believe that they are constructing their narratives as simulacra of the structures and processes of real events in the past, not as the product of their own aesthetic sensibilities and purposes?[30] It seems unlikely. Every historian is aware of the complexity of the facts, their irreducibility to a single narrative strand, and everyone writing a history book, or, come to that, a Ph.D. thesis, is confronted by the problem of how to separate out the still rather inchoate material collected—or to be collected—during research into a series of more or less coherent narrative and structural strands and then of how to weave these strands together into a more or less coherent whole. Often the decisions taken are a direct consequence of the interpretation advanced. What might appear to be a conventional historical narrative is often nothing of the kind, but the outcome of a series of aesthetic and interpretative choices by the historian. For example, LaCapra has described *The Defeat of the Spanish Armada* by Garrett Mattingly rather patronizingly as "a lovely old-style tale" and Le Roy Ladurie's *Montaillou* as a "highly conventional narrative" presenting a "traditional story."[31] But in both cases he misses the point. First, of course, a conventional narrative account of the Inquisition register on which Le Roy Ladurie based his book would use it to describe the inquisitorial process in Montaillou. The whole point about Le Roy Ladurie's book is that it reads it *against the grain*, for a structural analysis of everyday life and relationships in the village, in which a whole battery of modern anthropological theories is brought to bear on everyday life.[32] Similarly, Mattingly's book is a highly complex and sophisticated narrative, moving from one geographical center to the next (London, Madrid, Antwerp, and so on), in a rather cubist fashion, trying to give us a multiplicity of viewpoints and interweave a number of different narratives. It seems to me to be very much aware of modern novelistic techniques, despite LaCapra's dismissal of it for belonging to the "traditional narrative" genre unaffected by the modern novel. Mattingly cast his classic book in this multistrand narrative form because as an American he wanted to get away from the common habit of British historians of narrating the whole thing from the British point of view. Historical narrative, then, seldom simply consists of a single linear temporal strand.

Perhaps I may illustrate some of these problems of interweaving narrative and causal argument by referring to my own work. When I began researching the cholera epidemic of 1892 in Hamburg at the beginning of the 1980s, it was because I was attracted by the immense amount of source material this major disaster generated, revealing details of the structure and dynamics of everyday life, social inequality, politics and administration, mentalities and behavior in a major European city which remain largely concealed from the historian's view in more normal times. As I went through the material, it became clear that explaining why a major epidemic happened in Hamburg that year and nowhere else in Western Europe would be even more revealing of the social and political assumptions and practices of nineteenth-century liberalism than the epidemic itself. It became clear that a whole range of factors was involved, from the amateurism of the city administration through the overcrowding of the city slums to the peculiar theories of disease transmission held by the city's medical profession. The major cause seemed to be the failure to modernize Hamburg's water supply, and this, too, required lengthy explanation.

The question then arose of how to present all these causes over a period stretching from the 1830s to the eve of the epidemic in 1892. Eventually, after a good deal of experimentation and shifting great chunks of text around as I wrote, I came up with a mixture of narrative and analysis which I hoped would generate an increasing sense of suspense and excitement in the reader as we came closer and closer to the actual narrative of the epidemic itself in the second half of the book. So I divided the causes into twelve groups or sets, each of which, readers would be clear, was to play a major role in the epidemic itself; narrative tension was generated by withholding information about precisely what this role was to be until we arrived at the epidemic itself. The book narrated each causal group from around 1830 or so up to the spring or summer of 1892 (the epidemic began in August), so that in effect it presented twelve separate narratives, each piling another layer of causation upon the previous ones and modifying them in the process. Starting with the most general—the amateurish nature of the city administration—it moved through the analysis of political inequality, poverty, and the social tension which governed the expenditure priorities of the city administration to the growth of environmental pollution and lack of public hygiene, the failure to build a properly purified water supply, and the inadequacies of popular nutrition, all of which, it was implied without explicitly being so stated, would act as multiplier effects in one way or another in the spread of cholera in 1892 until more than ten thousand people died of the disease in the city within the space of six weeks or less. The next six narratives, each once more beginning early in the century and moving up to the eve of the epidemic, dealt with the unfavorable patterns of death and disease in the city even in normal times, the laissez-faire dogma which prevented the local doctors from intervening in epidemic situations, the inadequacies of their responses to earlier, lesser epidemics, and finally the arrival of cholera in Germany in 1830, its recurrence at intervals thereafter, the medical theories evolved to account for it, and its reemergence in the course of 1892, setting the scene for the narrative of the epidemic in Hamburg itself.

There was never any doubt in my mind from the very outset that what I was doing was constructing an ensemble of narratives that added up to a set of causal explanations of why the epidemic broke out in Hamburg and (as comparisons with other cities like Bremen showed) nowhere else in 1892. This set of causal explanations was then recapitulated and weighted at the end of the book in a much briefer, more schematic fashion, where I argued that the epidemic occurred because the causative agent, the cholera bacillus, brought in by Russian emigrants on their way to America, passed through a series of safety nets. All or some of these were present in other cities, none in Hamburg. Medical skepticism in Hamburg about the infectious nature of the disease prevented proper isolation of the emigrants and delayed the notification of the outbreak. The failure to filtrate the water supply sent the bacillus through every household tap. Overcrowding, poor sanitation, and unhygienic housing aided person-to-person transmission. Administrative inefficiency made it difficult to contain the epidemic once it had broken out. It would have been perfectly possible to have put this argument in a completely different way; the reasons for devising twelve parallel causal narratives were mainly aesthetic. It simply seemed the neatest, most economical, most exciting, and most interesting way of organizing and presenting the evidence. Above all, it seemed the best way of using the wonderfully rich source material generated by the epidemic to explore all these various aspects of daily life, social structure, and political action in a city where—and this was the book's overarching thesis—laissez-faire liberalism proved incapable of dealing with the problems generated by massive urban-industrial growth and was forced by the ensuing disaster to give way to "Prussian"-style state interventionism.[33] There could never be any question of presenting a "simple" chronological narrative in this case—not even of the epidemic itself—because there were simply too many strands of events going on at the same time. Arranging it all purely in terms of chronology would have delivered a chronicle with no explanatory power whatsoever. The book's structure was the result of a series of deliberate aesthetic and intellectual choices in which I sought the most effective way of putting across a mass of empirical material to support a series of causal arguments and hypotheses.

Most historical narratives consist of a mixture of revealed, reworked, constructed, and deconstructed narratives from the historical past and from the historian's own mind. We start with a rough-hewn block of stone and chisel away at it until we have a statue. The statue wasn't waiting there to be discovered, we have made it ourselves, and it would have been possible for us to have made a different statue from the one we finally created had we wanted to. On the other hand, we are constrained not only by the size and shape of the original stone, but also by its nature; an incompetent sculptor runs the risk not only of producing an unconvincing statue that doesn't much resemble anything, but also of hammering or chiseling too hard, or the wrong way, and shattering the stone altogether. We have to work within the limitations of the material, the way a wood carver has to work with the grain of the wood, not against it. These limitations are often strict and severe.

Nor is it true to say, as many postmodernists do, that narratives do not exist in the past itself but are all put there by the historian.[34] In some cases the narrative is there in the sources, lived and thought by the people we are writing about: German or Italian unification in the nineteenth century, for example, or the making of the United States in the eighteenth. In other cases it is not. Yet even where historians are aware of the fact that people in the past were consciously living a story they believed in and sought to shape, they can never rest content with simply reproducing it; it must be juxtaposed with others, hidden meanings must be discovered, flaws and contradictions in the story must be exposed. Historians not only deconstruct the narratives of other historians but deconstruct the narratives of the past as well.

Hayden White has suggested somewhat condescendingly that history has become "a refuge" for people who want "to find the simple in the complex and the familiar in the strange."[35] But if this ever applied to historians in the past, it certainly doesn't apply today. It may be part of the postmodern turn in historical studies that so much work is now being done on the irrational, the bizarre, and the exceptional in the past. But in truth, ever since the early nineteenth century, one of the main purposes of historians has been to find the strange in the familiar, to increase the distance between ourselves and the past. Empirical historians are constantly telling us that the past is far more complex than the great, suprahistorical metanarratives would seem to allow. Back in the 1950s the great liberal American historian Richard Hofstadter was even worried that historians' commitment to the "rediscovery of the complexity of social interests . . . may give us not only a keener sense of the structural complexity of our society in the past, but also a sense of the moral complexity of social action that will lead to political immobility."[36] It was precisely this kind of political consequence, of course, that conservatives like Sir Geoffrey Elton most welcomed. Professional historians have more often than not been hostile to "oversimplification" rather than indulging in it.

The postmodernist critic Sande Cohen has gone further than Hofstadter and argued that historical narrative in itself is inherently anti-intellectual. Historians, he says "use narration in order to deflect thinking," and he condemns their "outrageous recreation of tutelary narration" where "the reader is not even allowed to *think*." Thus history, he thinks, is part of "the discourse of bourgeois society." By focusing attention on the past, historians are engaging in "aggression against the present," which is part of "capitalism's promotion of thought forms that make the present as something that matters all but inaccessible." Cohen goes on to condemn the Marxist historian Edward Thompson's polemic against French structuralist Marxism, *The Poverty of Theory,* as "an aggressive rejection of the nonnarrated" demonstrating a "sad" conformity to "bourgeois historiography" and a most un-Marxist rejection of "critical thinking," while even Hayden White's analyses of historians' writings are dismissed as "defensive protections of the historical discipline," something which would surprise the many historians, such as Elton and Marwick, who have seen them in a rather different light.[37] But like many postmodernists, Cohen vastly underestimates the critical capacity of people who read history and hugely overestimates the historian's ability to discipline the reader's thought, even by the use of "tutelary narration." Other versions of postmodernist thought suggest, at the opposite extreme, that the reader's ability to impose meaning on narratives is virtually unlimited. Neither extreme, however, comes anywhere near the reality.

Many historical narratives have been devoted to providing historical justification or inspiration for political and social movements in the present. Reading or writing about the feminist struggle for equal rights and human dignity for women in the nineteenth century in no way closes off the possibility of contemplating women's situation in the present. Rather the contrary, in fact; that is why present-day feminists have devoted so much attention to it. It is quite wrong to see narratives as constricting and essentially reactionary myths that have little to do with historical truth or to argue, as some postmodernists do, that narrative is essentially conservative or even fascist.[38] The official historiography of Soviet Russia and the Eastern bloc was, in the view of the French originator of this particular critique, Jean-François Lyotard, a "master-narrative," imposed and sanctified by the state. What he termed local narratives were by contrast forms of resistance, individual stories told by prisoners, students, peasants, and deviants of various kinds, impossible to incorporate into the state's version of events and thus directly subversive of it. Unlike the master-narrative, local narratives did not claim omniscience or universal validity, and they were subjective rather than lay claim to objective historical truth.[39] Hence history in general consisted—and should consist—of a mass of local histories. "Postmodernism" indeed was defined by Lyotard simply as "incredulity toward master-narratives."[40] But of course it is not true to say, as Lyotard tended to, that master-narratives are the hegemonic stories told by those in power. The Marxist master-narrative itself, in many different variants, was developed over decades by an oppressed minority. The same may be said of the master-narratives of feminist history, or gay history, or black history. Even master-narratives do not have to be oppressive.

Historians in general have not only always been active in constructing local narratives or counter-narratives but also taken special pleasure in attacking master-narratives of every kind. Sir Geoffrey Elton was particularly insistent on the historian's duty in this respect. Many historians have seen their task not in creating narratives but in destroying them. "Ever since historical study became professional," Elton declared toward the end of his life, "—that is to say, systematic, thorough and grounded in the sources—it has time and again destroyed just those interpretations that served particular interests, more especially national self-esteem and self-confidence."[41] The continued prevalence of national historical myths in the Third World was for him a matter for regret. "The world is now in the hands of adolescents," he moaned.[42] "Historians," Theodore Zeldin has written, echoing Elton in his own, less apocalyptic manner, are "the counterpart of the social scientists; they say what cannot be done, rather than what should be done. Their function is less glamorous than that of the soothsayer. They are only court jesters."[43] It was a function of the court jester in medieval times, of course, not only to entertain and amuse, but also to tell his audience unpalatable truths. History has always been seen by historians as a destroyer of myths as much as a creator of them.

In destroying myths, historians have often sought to substitute for them narratives which are more closely grounded in the sources. But narrative of course is by no means the dominant mode of historical representation that postmodernists, fixated on the great narrative histories of the nineteenth century, like to claim it is among contemporary historians. Indeed the sequential presentation of historical material has often been entirely abandoned by modern historical scholarship, under the influence of the social sciences. Probably the majority of histories other than introductory textbooks have in the last three or four decades done their best to avoid having their structure shaped by the passage of time, and this is even more the case with articles and theses than it is with monographs. Moreover, some of the most famous history books of earlier periods have avoided narrative too: Namier's *Structure of Politics*, like Braudel's *Mediterranean*, sought to uncover the deep and largely unchanging structures which underlay the surface froth of events. Stephan Thernstrom's *The Other Bostonians*, Eugene Genovese's *Roll, Jordan, Roll*, even Wehler's *Kaiserreich* all were structural histories in which the passage of time was either frozen in the period studied, and change consigned to periods before and after, or abolished altogether in the continuities being posited. The first injunction history tutors in universities give to their students is "avoid narrative"; only thematic analysis gets the top grade, a judgment which also reflects wider attitudes in the twentieth-century historical profession to the presentation and communication of historical research and scholarship at every level.[44]

I V

HISTORICAL narratives do not necessarily have to be bound to a forward direction of time's arrow. Some of the most celebrated historical works of modern times move backward in time instead. For an English legal historian like F. W. Maitland, in his book *Domesday Book and Beyond*, it could mean peeling off the layers of time which had accumulated in the returns made about custom and law to William the Conqueror's massive landholding survey of 1086, Domesday Book, to reveal earlier and earlier patterns of tenure and settlement as he went back through the centuries; "beyond" in this sense meant moving toward more and more remote periods of the past, seen from the perspective of the late eleventh century. For the nationalist German historian Hellmut Diwald, writing a history of the Germans in reverse chronological order, starting with the present (in his case, the 1970s), meant moving backward from what he saw as his country's humiliation, division, and impotence in the third quarter of the twentieth century to a more and more glorious past—a past he clearly hoped the book would help his readers want to recover.[45] Whatever its purpose, writing history backward has long been part of the stock-in-trade of historians, one of a large variety of ways in which they have managed to smash what the French historian François Simiand called at the beginning of the twentieth century "the tyranny of chronology."[46]

Postmodernist critics of linear notions of time ignore the fact that historians have long been accustomed to employ a variety of concepts of temporality in their work; indeed one could say that it is precisely this that distinguishes them most clearly from chroniclers, whose notion of time is by definition confined to the tale of years.[47] Even in the most traditional kinds of political history, historians skate quickly over years or even decades when nothing much changed, to concentrate on periods, like the revolutionary years of 1789–94 in France, when as much of political importance happened in a month as happened in a year for most of the time under the *ancien régime*. There are periods when political history seems to speed up, as in America in the 1770s, others when it seems to move in slow motion, as in Spain in the postwar years of General Franco's dictatorship. Historians are also used to the idea that historical processes of a similar kind occur in different countries at different times. Industrialization, for example, got under way in Britain in the1780s, but not in Germany until the 1840s or Russia until the 1890s. The "demographic transition" from a society of high birth and death rates to one of low birth and death rates began in France in the eighteenth century but in Italy only a century or so later.

Historians have long been familiar with the notion that there are different kinds of periodization for different kinds of history. Most obviously, economic change moves at a different pace from political change. The history of changes in, say, military technology also has its own particular periodization, as does that of culture and the arts; recently it has been argued that women's history should also be periodized differently from men's. Change in any one of these areas obviously had an effect on the others, but to cram them all into conventional boxes of time framed by major political turning points, although it has been done often enough in textbook surveys of national histories, is artificial and unhelpful, and insofar as the postmodernist questioning of linear notions of time has contributed to a realization of this, it is to be welcomed.[48] But of course, conventional, politically defined periods have always provided their own testimony to the unevenness of historical time and its malleability in the hands of the historian. In modern European political history, for example, the nineteenth century is conventionally dated from 1815 to 1914, or in some versions from 1789 to 1914; the "short twentieth century," from 1914 to 1989. In American history the conventional time spans are framed by events such as the Declaration of Independence or the Civil War, not by abstract and evenly spaced dates like 1700, 1800, or 1900.

Some historians have also built the notion of different kinds of historical time into their own work, most famously Fernand Braudel, who said that his major problem in writing his great book *The Mediterranean and the Mediterranean World in the Age of Philip II* "was to show that time moves at different speeds."[49] At the top level were political events, which Braudel recounted in the third part of his book. Here things happened quickly, if unevenly. Battles, treaties, court intrigues, and political rivalries were "surface disturbances, crests of foam that the tides of history carry on their strong backs."[50] These tides of history were covered in the second part of Braudel's massive work: slow-moving social and economic trends, often imperceptible to contemporaries, changing military technologies, social structures, and state systems. Finally, at the very bottom of the ocean of time were the still, deep waters "in which all change is slow, a history of constant repetition, ever-recurring cycles." Treated at length in the opening section of *The Mediterranean*, this was the level of "immobile history," the "*longue durée*," in which preindustrial society's possibilities of change were confined by the unchanging powers of the natural environment.[51]

In turn this generated persistent systems of belief or "mentalities" which other historians, such as Jean Delumeau in his history of fear in the West, charted over a period of several hundred years in which they seemingly underwent little change or no change at all.[52] In retrospect, the French historians often seem to have exaggerated the extent to which these things did not change: Braudel was heavily criticized for taking the natural environment of the Mediterranean littoral as a given, instead of investigating the ways in which it was transformed by human activity, for instance, in the massive deforestation carried out to supply wood for shipbuilding, construction, and fuel. Nor did he always show very clearly how his three different levels of time related to one another. The *Annales* model was never very good at accounting for historical change at any level; its interest in causation was often rather limited. Nevertheless, for all these undoubted problems, the point here is that it made explicit in a way that had seldom been done before the manner in which historical time is not the same as linear time. It is in many ways the opposite: not a given, unchangeable series of dates, but a construct which the historian has to argue rather than take for granted.

Postmodernism's new view of time can be seen in a more concrete sense in architecture. Postmodern buildings jumble together the architectural styles of several centuries to achieve a new synthesis; postmodern novels mix up genres popular at different periods or even interweave action scenes set in different eras.[53] But this is not really rejecting historical concepts of time; it is simply using them in a new way, rather like the way the authentic performance movement in music now prefers to perform eighteenth-century music on eighteenth-century instruments instead of modern ones, or at least on replicas of them (something which of course itself raises key questions of authenticity in a more subtle form). This aspect of postmodernism can perhaps be seen as extending an invitation to historians. Why should not we, too, raid the many and various genres of historical writing which have been developed over the past couple of centuries, to enrich our own historical practice today? Why do we have to stick rigidly, for example, to one particular model; why can't we take what we want from Macaulay, Braudel, structural history, and the history of events, diplomatic and economic history, cultural and social history, and so on, and weave them into a new synthesis?

Periodization is in large measure a function of teaching syllabuses in universities, with their division into neat chronological sections, each of which is then served by a textbook from a multivolume series, further solidifying the boundaries, and if postmodernism helps us escape from the straitjacket which this imposes on our segmentation of past time, that can only be to the good.[54] More generally, if postmodernism makes us more aware of the possible models available to us within the history of historical writing and research, this can only be a source of enrichment for our own practice as historians in the present.[55]

V

IN the end, therefore, time does pass, a fact we experience only too obviously in the process of human aging to which we are all subject ourselves, and we cannot abolish it by simply declaring, as Ankersmit does, that there is no difference between the fourteenth century and the twentieth, or that time is merely a collection of unrelated presents, or that the textuality of the world abolishes the principle of cause and effect. To argue that we can only know causes from their effects and that therefore the effect is the origin of the cause, as some postmodernists do, is to mistake the process of inquiry for its object. History rests on the belief that the present differs from the past and derives from it; it also points to the future, which will be different again. In the end everybody knows that the present is affected by the past, that what happens today can affect or cause what happens tomorrow or the day after, and that the texts and other material objects we produce today provide the basis on which the future can attempt to know us. "It is an illusion," therefore, as Perez Zagorin has concluded, ". . . to assume that historiography can dispense with the concept of causality."[56]

If time is inescapable in its inexorable sequentiality, that still does not solve the fundamental problem of historical causation; it only makes it possible to contemplate it. It is obvious enough what a cause is; we can have *necessary* causes (if A had not happened, then B could not have happened) and *sufficient* causes (A's happening was enough to make B happen). Within the first category at least, we can have a *hierarchy* of causes, *absolute* causes (if A had not happened, then B *definitely* could not have happened) and *relative* causes (if A had not happened, then B *probably* could not have happened). Accustomed as they are to stating their arguments in a careful gradation of assessment of probability and plausibility, historians do not in practice approach the discussion of causation in concrete historical instances in such a schematic way. They prefer to talk of the disposition of things to bring about certain outcomes in certain circumstances, and many argue counterfactually that if a cause had not happened, then the probability of the effect's having happened would have been lessened to a determinable degree.[57] Most historians will go to some lengths to avoid a "monocausal explanation." They often approach the question of causes by turning it around and thinking of whatever has to be explained as the consequence of something else. This is what Sir Geoffrey Elton meant when he observed, reasonably enough, that historians explained events by "deducing consequences from disparate facts."[58] Almost all historians are used to the idea that historical events are frequently *overdetermined*—that is, they may have several sufficient as well as necessary causes, any one of which might have been enough to trigger the event on its own. Generally, however, they see it as their duty to establish a *hierarchy* of causes and to explain, if relevant, the relationship of one cause to another. "Opposition to a strict hierarchy of causation," one defender of this procedure has argued, "*can* lead to a refusal to admit any sense of causative priority, to a mere description of 'free-floating,' relatively valid and equally significant forces."[59] This is something most historians usually try to avoid.

Historical explanation commonly proceeds by relating an event or a process or a structure to a broader historical context, for example, locating a text in the society in which it was produced, relating the behavior of a political party to the social identities of the people who belonged to it, or linking rising death rates to an increase in poverty, malnutrition, environmental deterioration, and disease. Some postmodernist theory denies any possibility of separating text from context and so involves a rejection of this procedure. However, if, as we have seen earlier in this book, it is in fact possible to distinguish a historical source from the past reality to which it (in part) refers, and if it is meaningful to set this source and this reality against other sources and other realities, then the procedure remains defensible. It is true that contexts themselves are in a sense infinite. For reasons of time and effort historians cut out a small segment or segments from this infinity, and this is where their own preconceptions and intentions come in. Relating a source to its context depends above all on what questions one is asking of it; once the decision has been made to ask one set of questions rather than another, then it follows that one particular set of contexts has to be examined rather than another, and in this sense, once more, there are certain inescapable routes the historian has to follow. Historians do therefore, in a sense, reconstitute the historical contexts in which they read sources, but once again, the possibilities of reconstitution are far from infinite once the initial direction of research has been decided; moreover, research itself usually throws up new contexts of which the historian was originally unaware, but which are of obvious relevance to the project nonetheless, while undermining or drastically altering the originally conceived shape of others.

The contexts which historians choose to bring into play are far from arbitrary, however roughly the seamless web of history is torn asunder. Historians usually stop looking for explanatory contexts once they reach areas that are so remote from what they are trying to explain that the connection becomes minimal. Nevertheless, different historians will discover different contexts. Some have drawn far-reaching conclusions from this obvious fact. David Harlan, for instance, writes:

> The overwhelming abundance of possible contexts and perspectives, the ease with which we can skip from one to another, and the lack of any overarching meta-perspective from which to evaluate the entire coagulated but wildly proliferating population of perspectives—all this means that the historical fact, once the historian's basic atomic unit, has jumped its orbit and can now be interpreted in any number of contexts, from a virtually unlimited range of perspectives. And if

the historical fact no longer comes embedded in the natural order of things—if it is no longer bred in the bone, so to speak—then what happens to the historian's hope of acquiring stable, reliable, objective interpretations of the past?[60]

The answer is: not much. Because Harlan here is confusing two issues. On the one hand, he is right to say that individual facts may be interpreted in a variety of different contexts, according to what question the historian is asking. On the other hand, this is quite a different matter from saying that none of these interpretations can be reliable or objective in themselves.

Much more serious for the nature of historical explanation is the question of exactly what kind of context we are looking for. The recent turn to cultural history and *mentalités* has seriously undermined the notion of historical causation as understood by someone like Carr. The new focus on culture and language undermines the common prioritization of causes common to Marxism, the *Annales* school, and neo-Weberian social history, in which economic causes work through social and on up to politics and culture. The new cultural history has removed the idea of socioeconomic determination while replacing it with cultural determination in which culture is itself of course relative and so lacks any universal explanatory power. Just as Foucault and Derrida have rejected the search for origins and causes as futile, so postmodern theories of interpretation in general challenge any attempt to interpret cultural artifacts in terms of anything besides themselves, as we have seen, because there is in this view nothing outside the text anyway.[61] While cultural history, intellectual history, and even the history of high politics have received something of a fillip from the new theories and approaches of the late 1980s and 1990s, the principal victim, as we shall now see, has thus been social and economic history, precisely the areas which experienced the greatest growth and expansion in the 1960s and 1970s.

CHAPTER SIX

SOCIETY AND THE INDIVIDUAL

I

FOR a long time political history dominated the historical profession. "History is past politics," as Sir John Seeley, Regius Professor of History at Cambridge in the late nineteenth century, put it, "and politics is present history."[1] For political historians, indeed, "history" is still coterminous with political history. Thus, when the conservative American historian Gertrude Himmelfarb argues that "more history has to be put into social history," she means of course "more politics."[2] History as it emerged during the professionalization process of the nineteenth century was emphatically the political history of the nation-state and its relations with other nation-states. The history of high politics and international diplomacy was king. History in this view was made by great men, who were taken to be morally and politically autonomous individuals whose decisions reflected in the first place the peculiarities of their own personality rather than wider forces of any kind. So dominant was this approach within the profession that social and economic historians actually had to set up their own separate university departments to get a foothold in the world of academia and to claim that their own specialism constituted a separate discipline entirely distinct from history proper. Two world wars reinforced rather than undermined the hegemony of the "kings and battles" approach. Even in the 1990s the view that history is essentially political history remains widespread within the profession, and the associated belief that it is made by morally autonomous individuals, as we have already seen, is far from dead.

Declarations by eminent historians dismissing the history of the great majority of human beings in the past as trivial, meaningless, or impossible to study are legion. The great Sir Lewis Namier, for instance, examining a Ph.D. thesis in London on a popular movement in the French Revolution of 1789–94, asked the candidate pointedly: "Why do you bother with these *bandits*?"[3] The history of every age, he thought, was shaped by a handful of men who possessed the necessary freedom of will and action for this task, and history was therefore no more than the business of finding out what made them tick. "Whatever theories of 'free will' theologians and philosophers may develop with regard to the individual," he wrote, "there is no free will in the thinking and actions of the masses, any more than in the revolutions of planets, in the migrations of birds, and in the plunging of hordes of lemmings into the sea." The point of history was to study "people who *mattered*," in the words of Namier's assistant and disciple John Brooke, and "the workers, the peasants, collectively, had hardly ever mattered," so "a historian rarely had to take notice of them."[4] In this rather snobbish and elitist attitude, Namier was curiously not so very far away from the views of G. M. Trevelyan, a historian who in many ways represented the opposite pole in historical thinking from his own. Trevelyan was a patrician who looked back nostalgically to the ordered world of the eighteenth century, in which his own class, the landed gentry, had held sway, and he loathed the Industrial Revolution and the age of the masses. His paternalistic and condescending stance toward the lower orders in history is the main reason why he is no longer read today and why he will continue to be neglected, despite the advocacy of supporters such as his biographer David Cannadine.[5]

Historians like Sir Geoffrey Elton and Gertrude Himmelfarb have advocated a return to traditional political history based on the study of the nation-state.[6] But this is whistling in the wind. Even in the 1960s, when Elton made his plea for politics, administration, and the state to be at the center of the historian's concerns, and relegated such matters as the history of ideas to the status of optional extras, he already knew that it was unlikely to be listened to. This approach was all very well when university history degrees were a means of training the political and administrative elite of the next generation, but by the 1960s they were fulfilling functions far wider and more diverse than that.[7] Himmelfarb may earn the plaudits of right-wing journalists in the intellectual magazines, but among professional historians her views cut little ice. History has become too diverse for such arguments to stand any chance of damming the new currents in history that have flowed so strongly in the decades since Carr and Elton wrote their books: social history, quantitative history, microhistory, cultural history, women's history, gay history, black history, psychohistory, and others. Political history is now written only by a minority. In Britain, indeed, ignoring or belittling these trends now seems so eccentric an enterprise that when Professor John Vincent, one of the few historians who still do this, submitted the manuscript of his *Very Brief Introduction to History* to Oxford University Press, which had commissioned it, the publishers lost no time in rejecting it for this very reason.[8]

Yet Himmelfarb, Vincent, and the other defenders of the elite view of political history have had some surprising allies in their battle to confine history to the study of the elite and dismiss the thoughts and deeds of the vast majority of people in the past as irrelevant and unimportant. E. H. Carr, for example, thought that it was only over the last two centuries or so that "the mass of people . . . enter fully into history," because it was only in this period that "social, political and historical consciousness has begun to spread to anything like a majority of the population."[9] By "history" in this context, of course, Carr meant what he called "the expansion of reason" and the march of progress. Thus he clearly thought the history of ordinary people was not worth studying until they became organized in political movements and so contributed to the making of the modern world. More recently John Vincent has claimed that because history depends on written sources, and most people in the past could neither read nor write, "history can only speak directly of minorities."

The history of preliterate or illiterate societies, he has declared, is "unsound."[10] These arguments have generally failed to convince the historical profession at large. Historians have displayed great ingenuity in exploiting unwritten sources to construct the history of preliterate social groups, assisted by many kinds of written records compiled about these groups by the state and by their social superiors. There are many reasons why the history of the powerless masses before the modern era is worth studying and the popularity of books about them, such as Le Roy Ladurie's *Montaillou,* has shown that there is a large readership interested in the past for its own sake and for what it tells us about the human condition in a wider sense. Historians have stubbornly ignored the advice of Namier and Carr and spent increasing amounts of time and energy over the past few decades on taking notice of the majority of people in history whom these sages dismissed as unworthy of their notice.

Historians have broadened their perspectives in a methodological sense, too. At the end of the twentieth century historians are writing about almost every conceivable kind of human activity in the past, as well as about animals, plants, the natural environment, and the constructed world of machines and human habitations. Under the influence of the *Annales* school in France, there have been studies of the history of fear, of smell, of madness, of childhood; under the impact of radical neo-Marxists in Britain, "history from below" has tried to adopt the perspective of ordinary men and women in the past, to write about their experiences and to look on the state, politics, and society as they might have done; under the influence of neighboring or indeed not-so-neighboring disciplines, there have been studies of the body, of medicine and science, of health and disease, of popular culture, of seemingly irrational and inexplicable folk beliefs in the past; under the tutelage of the social sciences in Germany and America, there have been quantitative structural studies of urban and rural communities in the past, of religious practice, of crime and criminality. Virtually everything of meaning or importance to humanity in the present day now has a history, and that means everything of importance to all kinds of people, not just to a small elite of the educated and the powerful. However humble or powerless, however illiterate or uneducated, almost every group of people in the past has now been rescued from what E. P. Thompson called, in a phrase which struck a resounding blow against the arrogance of the political historians, "the enormous condescension of posterity."[11]

II

THE major influence in this broadening out of the historian's perspective on the past in the last few decades has been the rise of social history. This has taken place in every country. To begin with, it originated in Britain in the nineteenth century under the influence of the celebrated third chapter of Macaulay's *History of England*, which was devoted to a survey of the state of English society in the later part of the seventeenth century. This spawned many imitations, above all in the work of Macaulay's disciples, right down to the similar surveys devoted to the social history of early-eighteenth-century England in the first two volumes of Sir John Plumb's unfinished biography of Sir Robert Walpole. It achieved its apotheosis in the enormously popular *English Social History* of Macaulay's greatnephew G. M. Trevelyan, the best-selling English history book of its time. Trevelyan unashamedly took his cue from the history of English literature, with which he assumed all his readers would be familiar, and entitled his various chapters "Chaucer's England," "Shakespeare's England," "Defoe's England," "Dr. Johnson's England," and so on.[12] The problems of this kind of work were manifold. It relied too heavily on imaginative literature for source material, and so was often led astray. Its basis in literary sources meant that it concentrated too much on the history of literate minorities. It was entirely innocent of social theory or indeed explanation.

Above all, however, it defined itself negatively, as "history with the politics left out," in G. M. Trevelyan's notorious phrase. The history of this approach ultimately went back again to Macaulay, whose third chapter was deliberately written as a contrast with or background to the political history which dominated the rest of the narrative. It received its first book-length incarnation in J. R. Green's *Short*

History of the English People, published in 1874, in which the author announced that he had "preferred to pass lightly and briefly over the details" of political history and to dwell instead "at length on the incidents of that constitutional, intellectual and social advance in which we read the history of the nation itself."[13] Yet this approach was soon superseded. Social history in the universities emerged as an adjunct of economic history, and as departments of the latter were set up in the first decades of the twentieth century, they usually included a small minority of historians whose field was the history of living standards, trade unions, and the "labor" side of industry in the nineteenth and twentieth centuries, linked to the history of industrialization (where Macaulay, Trevelyan, and their followers, such as Sir John Plumb, had preferred to concentrate their gaze somewhat nostalgically on the rural world).

This pointed to a second root of social history, more common on the European continent, where the term "social question," coined in the mid-nineteenth century to refer to the emergence of a class of impoverished industrial workers, led naturally on to the concept of the "social movement," which these workers formed to liberate themselves, the "social revolution," by which they would supposedly achieve this, and thus the "social history," which described these conditions and these aspirations. "Social history" thus meant in effect for many years the organizational and ideological history of the labor movement, and especially the Marxist labor movement, a version of the term still incorporated for example in the French periodical *Le Mouvement social*, the German *Archiv für Sozialgeschichte* and above all the Dutch-based *International Review of Social History*, produced by the International Institute for Social History in Amsterdam, which houses the papers of Marx, Engels, and many of the leading German Social Democrats of the late nineteenth and early twentieth centuries. The identification of social history with nineteenth-century labor history is evident even in a more recent periodical, such as the British journal *Social History*, which concentrates heavily on this particular area of investigation and gives prominence to debates and controversies between labor historians working largely within the overall framework of a Marxist, neo-Marxist, or post-Marxist approach to the past.

But this concept of social history has long since been outflanked by a far broader approach developed in France and subsequently in Germany and the United States. The 1970s and 1980s saw a massive shift from social history in this old sense, to the history of society, in Eric Hobsbawm's phrase.[14] In America the catalyst for this was the publication and reception of British historian Edward Thompson's *The Making of the English Working Class*, published in 1963, a book which profoundly influenced young, radical American historians inspired by the informally organized politics of the student and civil rights movements of the time. Social history broke out of its ideological and institutional straitjacket. History "from the bottom up" became the key practice of left-wing historians, as they turned to rediscover examples of radical protest and rebellion in American history that had been forgotten because they had had no formal organizations or written programs. Marxism was an influence on many of these historians, including Herbert Gutman, Natalie Zemon Davis, and David Montgomery, but it was a Marxism shorn of dogma and cut loose from its former moorings in the Communist tradition.

As time went on, not just the proletariat but other social classes, from the landowning aristocracy and the propertied and professional bourgeoisie to the mass of the peasantry and the criminal underclass, came into the purview of the new social history. Social institutions such as the family, clubs and societies, leisure organizations, and the like entered the picture. There were studies of social structure in individual towns and villages, of demography and population movements, of generations of men and women, of childhood and old age, of social rituals, mores, and beliefs. Old-fashioned labor historians who believed in the centrality of class and labor movement politics to social history protested that the politics were being taken out of history again.[15] But the fact was that the very concept and nature of politics were changing around them. The personal had become the political. It was no longer adequate to confine it to matters of formal organization and formal ideology. The Marxist tradition of social history was merging with other, broader traditions, and before long, social historians were staking a claim to have created a major new discipline, separate from "traditional" history altogether. A mark of its success was provided by the fact that between 1958 and 1978, the proportion of history doctorates in the United States devoted to social history quadrupled and overtook political history.[16] Peter Stearns's tenth-anniversary editorial in the *Journal of Social History* in 1976 was a typical example of the aggrandizing political style of social history at this time. Kitted out with sub-headings such as "Us and Them" and assessments of how many social historians had managed to get appointed in university history departments in Britain and the United States, the article laid out ambitious claims for the dominance of social history ("social history *is* history") over the rest of historical scholarship.[17] This view was widely shared. "Social history," the British historian John Breuilly remarked in the mid-1980s, "is not a particular kind of history; it is a dimension which should be present in every kind of history." This, he said, was because every kind of action and institution had a social dimension.[18] "Social history," as his colleague Geoff Eley observed, was not just another branch or subspecialism, it had a "totalizing" commitment "to understand *all* facets of human existence in terms of their social determination."[19]

This kind of claim has provoked the more aggressive postmodernists into lambasting what one of them has recently called "the ludicrous nature of the pretentions of the social historians."[20] Indeed there have been indications for some time that the social history boom has passed its peak. As early as 1976, ironically enough in a companion piece to Stearns's editorial in the *Journal of Social History*, Theodore Zeldin was already proclaiming that social history had failed in its ambition to become the "central pivot of research" into the past. It had "lost its direction amid the variety of its achievements."[21] This was not least because of its growing fragmentation, which reflected the disintegration of history as a whole. Some two decades later two British labor historians, Jon Lawrence and Miles Taylor, noted similarly that the "totalizing ambition" of social history had collapsed during the 1980s into a mass of largely unconnected subdisciplines, such as demography, urban history, and so on.[22] "What is History?" E. H. Carr asked in 1961, and he went on to give an answer that was both clear and coherent and applied to all kinds of history everywhere, no matter what the subject covered or who the historian was covering it. A quarter of a century later, when the editor of the magazine *History Today* came to ask the same question of a number of its contributors, all of them professional historians and many of them distinguished practitioners of the discipline in their own right, she found it impossible to elicit a single answer and instead split the question up into a series of no fewer than twelve subquestions, covering issues such as "What is social history?" "What is women's history?" "What is intellectual history?" and so on. Introducing the collected answers, she voiced the fear that the sub-division of the discipline in this way "fragments and atomises the past so that we are left with nothing but the loose change of history . . . the chances of a coherent narrative history, the possibility of putting the story of the past back together again, are lost forever."

But this, she went on, was no cause for despair. Rather it was time to celebrate "a new pluralism," which had been animated by "the retreat from faith in impartial 'truth,' the loss of the belief in the past as a jigsaw which will one day be complete."[23] Other commentators on this phenomenon have not been so sanguine. Even in 1961 E. H. Carr deplored the fragmentation of knowledge and ascribed the "vast and growing mass of dry-as-dust factual histories, of minutely specialized monographs of would-be historians knowing more and more about less and less, sunk without trace in an ocean of facts" to the continuing influence of the nineteenth-century idea "that history consists of the compilation of a maximum number of irrefutable and objective facts."[24] But in practice even the most dauntingly specialized of monographs usually has an argument of some kind or other. Doctoral dissertations succeed not just by virtue of delivering new research on a detailed topic but also by using that research to revise existing interpretations in a wider field. Carr ascribed the growth of specialization to a failure to distinguish between what was important and what was not in the past, yet his own ideas of what was important were in fact quite narrow, as we have seen, and excluded the history of the vast majority of the human race through-out recorded time. It may not have been surprising therefore that he dismissed as unimportant the new wave of social historical studies which was just making its presence felt as he was writing at the beginning of the 1960s.

The historical profession, and with it the generation and further specialization of historical knowledge, have undergone a vast expansion since the early 1960s, when Carr was writing. Membership of the American Historical Association, the national organization of professional university and college historians in the United States, which numbered a few hundred in the 1950s, had climbed into the thousands by the 1980s. It has been calculated that there were more historians alive already in 1960 than in all previous ages of history put together, and the expansion of the profession has continued at an even faster pace since then. In Britain the new universities founded in the 1960s almost all established history departments, some of which—as at York, for example, or Warwick—quickly won reputations for important and innovative research. Similar developments took place in West Germany and France. It was never so easy to get a job as a paid, professional historian as it was in the second half of the 1960s. This meant, however, that historical knowledge was increasing so fast that it became more and more difficult to hold it together in a single discipline. New, increasingly specialized journals were founded, from the *Journal of Transport History* to the *Journal of Holocaust Studies*, and new specialized groupings of historians were established, such as the German History Society or the Society for the Social History of Medicine, in which the majority of historians spent their entire professional careers.

In 1979 an American commentator lamented what he called the "truly awesome" degree of subdivision within the historical profession:

> Historians are subdivided quadruply, by nation or region of the globe, by time period, by thematic category . . . and by cognitive predilection. . . . All that unites historians is a concern for the evolution over time of whatever it is they study. . . . This is something, . . . to be sure. . . . But it is far less compelling as an attribute in most contexts than the diversity of outlooks and interests that splinter historians into minute subgroups, each with its own hierarchy of respected authorities.

What this meant was that historians were finding it increasingly difficult to agree about what was important about the past. Take E. H. Carr's claim, for instance, that while millions of people have crossed the river Rubicon, the historian is interested only in Caesar's crossing of the river because it affected the course of history. By the 1980s Carr's statement was manifestly untrue: Social historians would have been interested precisely in those millions of ordinary people and the patterns of communication their crossings and recrossings of the river Rubicon revealed; economic historians would have been interested in the trade patterns and cycles of these millions of crossings; medical historians would have been interested in the ways in which the masses' crossings of the river communicated disease; and so on. The confidence of the Rankeans and their successors that the political history of the nation-state was the central object of study had gone.[25]

So, too, has the assumption of E. H. Carr that what was significant in history was defined by its contribution to social progress. Each subspecialism of the discipline nowadays has its own definition of what is important, and several historians may study the same object, or the same documents, with completely different questions in mind, and without having the least interest in the questions that other kinds of historians have asked. History, many now believe, is no longer an integrated body of knowledge; it has fragmented almost beyond recall. Historical scholarship has become vastly more diverse, and the sheer volume of historical knowledge generated by the thousands of historians at work in the last thirty years makes it impossible for any one person even to master the literature in such a relatively specialized field as, say, nineteenth-century American history or even the history of the French or Russian Revolution. In view of this proliferation of historical knowledge, it is scarcely surprising that there seems to be a greater demand for historical syntheses than ever before. Moreover, the needs of history teaching at every level create an unstoppable demand for syntheses. A glance at the catalogs of any academic publisher will reveal a plethora of multivolume general textbook series, from the *Oxford History of Modern Europe* and its companions, the *Oxford History of Early Modern Europe* and the *Shorter Oxford History of the Modern World,* to the *Cambridge Medieval History* and its companions, such as the *Cambridge History of India,* from the new *Penguin History of Britain* to the *Longmans History of Italy,* the *Fischer Europäischie Geschichte,* and many, many more. In Germany, the appetite for multivolume histories seems undiminished, and the ghost of Ranke stalks the corridors of academe, driving senior historians to attempt to emulate his immortality by putting similarly serried lines of books on the library shelves alongside his. To the late Thomas Nipperdey's three huge volumes on Germany from 1800 to 1918 one can now add Hans-Ulrich Wehler's three even larger tomes. Both authors attempt to cover social and cultural history as well as political and economic.[26] In France, the preference seems to be for multivolume surveys dealing with large subjects over extremely long time spans and coauthored by teams of historians rather than by individuals. Here, too, the aim is to be comprehensive.[27]

Yet these syntheses are all to a greater or lesser extent self-consciously selective in the treatment they accord to their subjects. The contrast, for example, between the *Cambridge Modern History,* published at the beginning of the twentieth century, and its successor, the *New Cambridge Modern History,* which appeared fifty or more years later, is instructive. In 1900 the authors commissioned by the series editor, Lord Acton, still shared the basic post-Rankean assumptions about the subject matter of history, and delivered detailed empirical narratives of the political history of European nation-states and the relations between them that made a coherent and satisfying whole. If you want to find out which party was in government in Denmark in 1895, or what were the diplomatic objectives of the Austrians in the Seven Years' War, you can safely turn to the relevant volume and find what you want there. By the time the *New Cambridge Modern History* came to be written, however, all consensus on the subject matter of such a history had disappeared, and what resulted was a disparate collection of essays covering a rather haphazard variety of subjects, so that you can never be quite sure what you will find there. The fact that it gives far more room to interpretation than its predecessor also ensures that it has dated far more quickly. If I want to get basic information about modern European political history, it is to the old Cambridge volumes that I turn, not the new ones. The whole idea of a multivolume and "authoritative" synoptic history is out-of-date, and it is not surprising that the latest series of this kind, the sixty-volume *Fischer Europäische Geschichte*, makes no pretense at being comprehensive, but instead aims to provide a series of comparative studies covering broad aspects of European history, in which authors are given their head and allowed to express their individuality; indeed this is reflected in the very title, which claims to be not a "history of Europe" but simply "European history." In other series currently in production, the coverage varies widely according to the predelictions of the author of each individual volume. In the new *Penguin History of Britain*, for instance, the volume on the seventeenth century, by the American historian Mark Kishlansky, sticks largely to an old-fashioned narrative of high politics, while the coverage of the twentieth century, by the English historian Peter Clarke, is much broader (though still giving the "view from Westminster" and neglecting the crucial determining factor of Britain's imperial crisis and decline). What is safe to say is that the publisher's claim that "these volumes will furnish the definitive history of Britain for our day and generation" will not be fulfilled. There can be no definitive history anymore. Sensible readers and teachers will select the best volume on any given period from the range of multivolume series available, and their judgment as to which is the best will vary, of course, according to how they think history should be studied and taught.[28]

The notion of a complete synthesis of historical knowledge in a particular field has all but disappeared. Those written in the present day, like Norman Davies's panoramic *Europe: A History*, tend to present an avowedly personal view of the field and to provoke as much as to inform.[29] We take from them what we want—in Davies's case, the argument that Europe should be seen as a whole, stretching across as far as the Urals, and not just identified with "the West" or the current membership of the European Union—and their idiosyncrasies encourage us even more than before to read with a critical and skeptical eye. The virtual disappearance of the idea of a com-

plete and comprehensive synthesis is one reason why Peter Novick
concluded in 1988 that "as a broad community of discourse, as a
community of scholars united by common aims, common standards
and common purposes, the discipline of history had ceased to
exist."[30]

III

DESPITE the increasing specialization and fragmentation which
many have observed in the historical profession in recent decades,
there is still in some respects reason to doubt Novick's pessimistic
view of its future as a community of scholars united in a single discipline. With the globalization of communication, more historians in
more countries are saying more to audiences in other countries than
ever before. Certainly, for instance, the translation of books by French
and German historians into English has been undertaken on a far
greater scale in the last two or three decades than previously, while
English and American historians now find a much wider readership
in other languages than they did even a generation ago.

Historians in every country have been steadily more influenced by
their colleagues elsewhere. Nothing could be further from the truth
than John Vincent's assertion that historical writing "remains conspicuously national in character. French, Germans, Americans,
English, go their separate ways."[31] In fact, the *Annales* school has had
an enormous influence on scholarship in England and America,
while the work of the British Marxist historians has had a similar
international impact, despite Vincent's curious belief that E. P.
Thompson has had no influence on other historians or in any way
"affected historical practice."[32] Postmodernist theories have been
imported into the United States from France and spread back from
there to the historical profession in Europe. Translations of history
books from one language into another are now more frequent than
ever before; cheap international travel and instantaneous transconti-
nental communication through E-mail and the Internet have effectively abolished the boundaries between scholars of different nations;

conferences and seminars on an international basis are held almost daily; international scholarly centers have sprung up everywhere, from the Institute of Advanced Study at Princeton to the Wissenschaftskolleg in Berlin, the Maison des Sciences de l'homme in Paris to the Humanities Research Centre in Canberra, and no historian's curriculum vitae can be held to be complete without the now virtually obligatory listing of lectures and seminars given in London, New York, Jerusalem, or San Francisco. In the international marketplace of ideas, no one can afford the luxury of intellectual autarky any longer.

The fact that Novick's own excellent book on the "objectivity question" in the American historical profession has been so widely debated in so many different branches of the profession in the United States is itself a persuasive falsification of his views. Just because we all have a different idea of what history is, or should be about, does not mean that we no longer read one another's works. But there is no denying that this has become more difficult, for over the last thirty years in history there has been an almost exponential increase in the total volume of historical knowledge, occasioned not least by the unprecedented growth in the number of historians that has taken place over this period. Not only has there been an expansion of history's subject matter, but there has also, just as important, been a widening of the historian's geographical horizons from the days when the profession in the West continued to write mainly on the political history of the European and North American nation-state. Recognition of this fact has still not dawned on a number of stubbornly parochial specialists in European history, above all perhaps in Britain. Hugh Trevor-Roper, too, writing as Regius Professor of Modern History in the University of Oxford in 1965, declared that Africa had no history, merely "the unrewarding gyrations of barbarous tribes in picturesque but irrelevant corners of the globe."[33] As late as the 1990s John Vincent was still writing off Asian history as an impossibility ("we do not understand Asia and will not need to"),[34] surely a rather unwise statement in an age when the global influence of the new Asian economies was already exerting a major impact on the advanced industrial economies of the West. All this underlined the commitment of the grandees of the historical profession in Great Britain to the view that history was properly the study of literate minorities in the West, preferably minorities with political power.

Nearly thirty years after Trevor-Roper, another British historian, the seventeenth-century specialist John Kenyon, observed with satisfaction that in "history departments, hastily cobbled-up courses on Indochina or West Africa faded away as soon as these areas ceased to be of immediate current concern; students also found," he added, "that such arcane courses, for which external examiners at degree level could rarely be provided, left them at the mercy of their tutor's whims and prejudices." But this observation, reflecting a now-fashionable tendency among British conservatives to deride the 1960s, and delivered from the safe distance of a "Distinguished Chair" at the University of Kansas, merely reflected the mental insularity and prejudice of its author, even more so than did his equally misguided claim that the contribution of British historians to European history did not "constitute an important or influential corpus of work."[35] Far from European and overseas history's being on the decline in Britain, it has grown and flourished in the 1990s as never before, and the number of distinguished publications, pathbreaking theses, learned journals, university courses, and even competent external examiners is greater than ever. Even in 1961 E. H. Carr had poured withering scorn on "the parochialism of English history, which already weighs like a dead hand on our curriculum" and argued for an expansion of continental European and indeed non-European history on a considerable scale.[36] Thirty years on, there was a good deal of evidence that his plea had been heard.

Here, too, Carr ran into criticism from Sir Geoffrey Elton, who devoted his inaugural lecture as Regius Professor of Modern History in the University of Cambridge to the demand that English history be placed at the center of the university curriculum.[37] Others have echoed this view, particularly during the debate on the contents of the national history curriculum introduced by Britain's Conservative government into the schools.[38] There has been a parallel debate in the United States, too, though it has scarcely found any echoes on the European continent, where history has on the whole remained obstinately insular. To demand that more time be spent on French history in France or German history in Germany, for instance, would be entirely superfluous. In France the assumption of cultural superiority has guaranteed that the vast majority of historians do not really consider the history of other countries worth studying, although there is a partial exception in the case of Britain, where the contribution of French historians, such as Halévy and Bédarida, has been notable.[39] Multivolume French surveys of aspects of the history of "the West" have in practice been devoted to the history of those particular topics in France, which has been taken axiomatically—and of course quite wrongly—as typical of the history of Western humanity as a whole, and treatment of other countries has been somewhat cursory. Books by French historians claiming to deal with general trends in the history of "the West" have in practice been based almost entirely on French evidence and have completely ignored the experience of any country east of the Rhine.[40] In Germany the understandable obsession with national self-examination after the genocidal debacle of Hitler's Third Reich has ensured that virtually no one can make a successful career in the historical profession by studying the history of another country, and despite the opening up of German historical institutes in London, Paris, Washington, and Rome, to assist German scholars studying the history of these other countries, the fact remains that the contribution of German historians to the history of countries other than Germany in recent decades has been negligible. By contrast, no German historian can afford to ignore the vast corpus of first-rate work produced on modern German history by historians in Britain and America. The cosmopolitanism of the historical profession in Britain and America contrasts starkly with the insularity of the profession on the European continent in this respect.

In the twentieth century, European history has always been strong in Britain and America, driven on by the involvement of these two countries in two world wars fought to a large extent on European soil and centering in considerable measure on European Great Power rivalries, but in Britain decolonization has led to a shift of perspective from imperial history—also a long-established tradition—to the history of Africa and Asia from an African or Asian rather than a European perspective, while in the United States and Australasia, the attention of historians has been shifting for some time away from Europe and toward the Pacific Rim. Even in Germany there are at last signs that as the obsession with explaining the causes and consequences of the Third Reich becomes a little less central, historians are beginning to make a reputation for themselves with serious research on other European countries. Interest in the history of extra-European civilizations is growing, and books like those of the Anglo-American historian Jonathan D. Spence on the history of modern China are reaching a wide audience.[41] Historical scholarship is thus not only more eclectic than ever before, but also becoming gradually less Eurocentric and more cosmopolitan in its coverage and approach. While this has meant a greater fragmentation of history as a field of knowledge, this has also been balanced out by the greater opportunities which modern communications and the modern organization of historical scholarship have provided for specialists in different fields to talk to one another and exchange ideas with their colleagues in other fields and in other countries.

IV

TO some extent, the battles that have raged over the nature of history have been fought between different kinds of historian: economic, political, intellectual, and social. In practice each of these branches of historical inquiry has a somewhat different methodology, and the assumptions which these generate have been translated upward into different attitudes to theory and epistemology on a broader scale. Political historians, like Elton and Himmelfarb, have advocated a return to traditional political history based on the study of the nation-state and denigrated other approaches as trivial, irrelevant, or misguided.[42] Economic historians, like Robert Fogel, Morgan Kousser, and Christopher Lloyd, have argued for a reorientation of history onto a structural or quantitative basis and regard their own discipline of economic history as the only truly scientific, and hence reliable, way of studying the past. Social historians, like Peter Stearns, condemn the dullness of traditional political history, excoriate the impudence and ignorance of the postmodernists, and claim that social history is the only approach that combines intellectual excitement with scholarly solidity. Intellectual historians, like Hayden White and Frank Ankersmit, assert that all the world's a text and want to make us all into intellectual historians since the text is all that can meaningfully be studied. In this sense, history has become a multicultural domain, where different groupings struggle for intellectual supremacy in the marketplace of ideas, courses, and university history syllabuses. It is surely not out of place in this situation to plead for a little intellectual tolerance and to warn any one particular orientation against the arrogant assumption that its own methods and procedures are necessarily better than those of its rivals.

Such a warning is particularly apposite at the moment in the case of intellectual and cultural history. Here, as the American labor historians David Mayfield and Susan Thorne have pointed out, the "linguistic turn" has sought in effect to dethrone society and the economy as the moving forces in history and to reinstate politics and the state. Ideas and institutions become central instead of social and economic structures and processes. Society-centered explanations are sweepingly dismissed as "reductionist" because they allegedly either ignore politics altogether or reduce it to a direct and unmediated product of the social. The result is a "paradigmatic shift" which is bringing about "nothing less than the dissolution of the dominant modes of interpretation, both liberal and Marxist, which have informed social analysis for most of this century and much of the last." Mayfield and Thorne suggest that this may simply herald a "full circle" return to old-fashioned political history, in which political historians no longer think they have to pay any attention to the "social factors" which some of them at least have been forced to take account of in recent decades. It might therefore be a step backward instead of a step forward; alternatively, the focus on the social which has been so influential in history over the years might be seen as a pointless detour rather than a significant advance in understanding.[43] Yet, as Mayfield and Thorne remark, it is "quite wrong to suggest, as is commonly done in revisionist polemics, that the old social history simply neglected the constitutive effects of politics, language and culture."[44] This is true even though much of the debate has taken place within the tradition of Marxist-oriented labor and social history. Marx and Engels themselves were very conscious that the behavior of many political groups could not be reduced to a one-way product of the economic or social, as even a cursory glance at their classic studies such as *The Condition of the Working Class in England*, *The Eighteenth Brumaire*, and the *Class Struggles in France* will confirm.

Despite all the various pronouncements of its demise by postmodernists, social history is not dead. What has happened, undeniably, is that it has lost, or is in the course of abandoning, its universalizing claim to be the key to the whole of historical understanding. To this extent, the postmodernist critique has been not only successful but also liberating. By directing historians' attention to language, culture, and ideas, it has helped free them to develop more complex models of causation and to take seriously subjects they may have unduly neglected before. There is much to be said for paying closer attention than ever to the surface patterns and meanings of language. At its best, the work that is now appearing under the influence of postmodernist theory provides a new dimension of understanding that moves well beyond the limitations of social history. Studies of popular mentalities, of memory, commemoration, and celebration, of the cultural dimensions of power and authority, of gender and the micropolitics of everyday life, and of many other subjects have added significantly to historical knowledge. The achievement of cultural history in the postmodern mode is not merely additive; it has also helped reorient our understanding of many areas of political and social history, from the French Revolution to the First World War and beyond.

But this does not mean that we should abandon social history altogether. There is no reason, for example, why historians should not continue to use concepts like class as a means of understanding the behavior of human groups in the recent past.[45] Or why they should not carry on believing that the experience of poverty, misery, and oppression under which it is reasonable to suppose that some groups in the past had to suffer had some relevance to their culture and beliefs and to their political allegiance as well. We should not forget the fact that the poor in the past paid for their poverty in the real, physical coinage of disease, suffering, and death. There is a real danger that the "linguistic turn" in history may make us forget this fact. One postmodernist author, Elizabeth Deeds Ermarth, for example, has realized that by reducing everything to text and discourse, she has eliminated the notion of society as something real and with it "what used to be called social justice." The term "social," she says, was coined in the nineteenth century and is one of many classical notions which postmodernism has rendered obsolete. Aware of the embarrassing political implications of this, she claims that "other gains" have been achieved to make good the "loss of the terms 'reality,' 'truth,' and 'man.' " As one of her critics acidly marks, however, quoting from the relevant passages of her work,

> it is very unclear what those gains are. Perhaps the following: "to restore health to psychic and social life and to heal the damage done by long-term and ever-increasing discursive emphasis on the symbolic, syntactical, thetic disposition of language at the expense of the semiotic, paratactic, rhythmic disposition" (147). Since Ermarth is one of those who believe that "everything is writing" (177), perhaps this is how we are now supposed to refer to "what used to be called" poverty, hunger, torture, oppression.[46]

Thus the postmodernist concentration on words diverts attention away from real suffering and oppression and toward the kinds of secondary intellectual issues that matter in the physically comfortable world of academia. It has become commonplace to argue, for example, that words do matter just as much as deeds, that reading about an execution is the same as attending one or even carrying it out, or that pornography is indistinguishable from rape.[47] But while the pornography of sex and violence should not be trivialized or treated lightly, to equate it with real physical assault, bodily violation, and death is to restrict one's vision to the imaginative world of reader and writer, to give this a grossly inflated significance in the wider lives of the majority of people who for most of the time are neither of these things, and to avoid tackling the real world of people in history and society.

That is not to say that "mere words" have no effect, just that they should not be enthroned as the supreme beings of modern life and experience. In practice, most people recognize that there is some connection, on the one hand, between people's standard of living, occupation, gender, sexual orientation, ethnicity, and social status— all of which have real physical referents of one kind or another—and their social, moral, and political attitudes and general view on life and the language in which they express these things, on the other. What postmodernism has helped us to do is to underline the fact that this connection is not one-way. All these lessons can be useful when applied to the past. But their usefulness diminishes when the ideas in which they originate are pushed too far, so that we get an intellectual reductionism instead of a socioeconomic one, or abandon anything other than politics and ideas as irrelevant to an understanding of human motivation and action in history.[48]

V

IN one respect at least, the clash between social history and postmodernism is by no means so stark as some of the combatants would have us believe. In particular, both, in contrast with traditional political and diplomatic history, have a marked tendency to downplay the importance of the individual. As a champion of a particular social interpretation of history, E. H. Carr, for example thought that the cult of the individual was a pervasive Western myth which it was time to debunk. Mass democracy had brought it to an end.[49] Neither historians nor the people about whom they wrote were isolated individuals; they were all social beings. Carr argued that to distinguish between individuals and impersonal historical forces was false, for the former were the product and indeed embodiment of the latter. He exemplified this principle well in his own *History of Soviet Russia*, following Trotsky in depicting Stalin as the product of the new Soviet bureaucracy of the 1920s rather than as an individual with any marked personality traits of his own. But had he lived to carry his *History* on into the mid-1930s, he would have been confronted with the phenomenon of Stalin as the ruthless, paranoid dictator of the great purges and the reign of terror which killed untold millions of Soviet citizens for the most trivial of reasons or for no reason at all. Perhaps he would have subscribed to the view, advocated by some American historians in the 1980s, that these events were the products of the structure of Soviet rule, driven on "from below," rather than the consequence of Stalin's own individual pathology.[50]

Carr himself actually included a chapter on "Personalities" in the fifth volume of his *History of Soviet Russia,* where he dealt with the major players in the intraparty power struggles of the 1920s: Trotsky, Zinoviev, Kamenev, Bukharin, and Stalin. The chapter opens with a general statement about the role of the individual in history:

> The events of history are set in motion by the wills of individuals. But what individuals will is governed in part by the historical conditions in which they find themselves; and these conditions impose still narrower limits on what they can effectively will. Hence the explanations of events given by the historian cannot be confined to simple statements of the will of the individuals concerned, and tend for this reason to create the illusion of "impersonal" forces at work in history, though the historian is well aware that the acts through which these forces find expression are the acts of individuals and are set in motion by the individual will.

In a similar way, Carr thought that a "great man" was great because he embodied on a larger than normal scale the wills and aspirations of his contemporaries or anticipated those of their successors. Thus Trotsky represented Westernizing tendencies among the Bolsheviks, Stalin anti-Western. Carr believed that the key to the ambiguities of Stalin's character—"an emancipator and a tyrant, a man devoted to a cause yet a personal dictator"—could not be found in the man himself. They had to be found in his environment. "Few great men have been so conspicuously as Stalin the product of the time and place in which they lived."[51]

Carr thought that "great men" gave expression to their times and were always representative of wider historical forces. Hitler, for example, would have remained a disregarded figure on the lunatic fringe of German politics but for the depression of 1929–33 and the attendant crisis of the Weimar Republic. However, once such an individual attains a significant degree of power, then personality traits which may have little or nothing to do with "vast impersonal forces" come into play, and Carr was perhaps a little too quick to dismiss them. In the years after he wrote *What Is History?* Carr came, in fact, to concede a somewhat greater role to the individual in history than he had previously done. He thought, for example, that Lenin, had he remained in power, would have managed the industrialization of Russia more humanely than Stalin did.[52] Nevertheless, the social historical approach which he championed undeniably left relatively little room for the individual actor in history.

On the face of it, postmodernism, with its dethroning of the author and its elevation of impersonal discourses to the center of historical analysis, echoes this view. Yet ironically, perhaps, in view of its suspicion of the notion of individuality, postmodernism has also done a great deal to reestablish the place of the individual in history, though this has been in a very different mode from the political historians' traditional cult of "great men." Postmodernism's suspicion of the mainstream, its privileging of the marginal, the bizarre, and the obscure, has produced a good deal of historical work re-creating the world of little-known individuals such as Mennochio, the Italian miller, in Carlo Ginzburg's *The Cheese and the Worms*.[53] One of the very great drawbacks of generalizing social science history, with its reliance on averages and statistics, is its virtual elimination of the individual human being in favor of anonymous groups and trends. To reduce every human being to a statistic, a social type, or the mouthpiece of a collective discourse is to do violence to the complexity of human nature, social circumstance, and cultural life. On the other hand, to claim that an individual such as Stalin was simply a monster and a freak does little to help us understand why he behaved the way he did and hugely overestimates the freedom of maneuver people, even when they are dictators, have to impose their individual will on others.[54] In the end no one has managed to better Marx's dictum that people make their own history, but they do not do it under circumstances of their own choosing. It is precisely the interaction between the individual and the circumstances that makes the study of people in the past so fascinating. Postmodernist history's return to the individual, to the human element in history at every level redresses the balance and is an unqualified gain in this respect.

CHAPTER SEVEN

KNOWLEDGE AND POWER

I

IT is time, one postmodernist writer has recently declared, to abandon the kind of history that

> lets us think we know the past. History in the post-modern moment
> ... asks: Whose history gets told? In whose name? For what purpose?
> Postmodernism is about histories not told, retold, untold.... Histories
> forgotten, hidden, invisible, considered unimportant, changed, eradicated. It's about the refusal to see history as linear, as leading straight
> up to today in some recognisable pattern—all set for us to make sense
> of. It's about chance. It's about power.[1]

Some of these were sentiments with which E. H. Carr might have felt a certain sympathy. He thought that "the function of the historian is neither to love the past nor to emancipate himself from the past, but to master and understand it as the key to the understanding of the present."[2] Needless to say, such arguments did not cut much ice with Sir Geoffrey Elton. He admitted that one could learn at least a few lessons from the past, about the possibilities open to human thought and action, and the "magnificent unpredictability of what human beings may think and do."[3] But essentially, however difficult it may be, historians had to make the effort to understand in a cognitive sense the actions, ideas, and motivations of people in the past without direct reference to their own beliefs in the present.[4]

Yet even for Elton, in practice this could never be enough in itself. Consciously or unconsciously we also want to use our knowledge of the past for our own purposes in our own time. Marxist historians, for example, have always given present politics primacy in their approach to history. Nor should it be thought that such arguments apply only to Marxism. The historians of the *Annales* school in France insisted on scientific rigor in their research and were busily engaged on trying to construct an alternative set of ideas to Marxist historicism. None of this was politically neutral. Fernand Braudel wrote his magnum opus, *The Mediterranean and the Mediterranean World in the Age of Philip II*, in a German prisoner of war camp, according to his own confession, in order to recapture some of the deep structures of history and identity which he hoped and believed had survived the defeat of France by the Germans in 1940. Toward the end of his life, he returned to this ambition in his study of *The Identity of France*, in some ways a profoundly conservative, nationalist text. It argued that France and its borders had not changed in essence since the thirteenth century and declared that French blood had not been diluted since prehistory. This claim went together with Braudel's racist belief that between the French and other nations, including by implication all kinds of immigrants, "there may be some intermingling but there is no fusion."[5] Pierre Chaunu, another *Annales* historian, is similarly located on the right. Chaunu has described legalized abortion as "absolute murder" which will have "disastrous demographic consequences" for France.[6] The links between the pioneering role of French demographic history and the conservative-nationalist obsession with the traditionally low birthrate in France becomes explicit in Chaunu's work. Thus behind the seemingly scientific neutrality of these historians there lurks a welter of political purposes.

Even Elton had a political agenda and political preconceptions which he brought to his historical work. He thought, for example, that what mattered in historical training was to learn the methods of historical research; the historical subject to which they were applied was of secondary interest since no historical subject of any kind could in his view have anything of interest or importance to teach the present. "Elton's fundamental reason for wishing to emphasise technique over content," one of his sharpest critics has remarked, "appears to have been a deeply ironic one: a fear that historical study might have the power to transform us, to help us think more effectively about our society and its possible need for reform and reformation."[7] But whatever he might have said in theory, Elton did believe in practice that history had lessons to teach. In the preface to his first book, *The Tudor Revolution in Government*, he argued that "government must be strong to be worth having," and he devoted much of his subsequent career to building up a positive assessment of the "strong rule preventing anarchy and preserving order" which he saw as having been created under King Henry VIII of England and his minister Thomas Cromwell. He attacked the fact that "our history is still much written by whigs, the champions of political freedom," and declared his intention of stressing instead "the need for controlling that freedom."[8] His was far from being a history which sprang naked from the sources; on the contrary, it was clothed from the outset in strongly held conservative political beliefs. Elton's arguments about the historian approaching the documents free from all present-day preconceptions were refuted by his own explicit recognition of the role such preconceptions played in his own work.

In his book *Policy and Police*, Elton tried to exonerate his hero, Thomas Cromwell, from the charge that he practiced a "reign of terror" in his implementation of Henry VIII's Reformation decrees: the dissolution of the monasteries, the seizure of church land, and so on. The book relied mainly on denunciations of Catholics and opponents of these policies sent in by ordinary citizens ("without such activities," he commented, "society collapses"). In a devastating critique Lawrence Stone observed:

Dr Elton seems to be totally unaware of the damage done to the fabric of a society when governments positively encourage denunciations of neighbours by neighbours, thus opening up a Pandora's box of local malice and slander. No one who has read a little about life in occupied Europe under the Nazis, or has seen the movie *Le Chagrin et La Pitié* could share the satisfaction of Dr Elton as he triumphantly concludes that his hero encouraged private delation rather than relying on a system of paid informers. (Incidentally, it is on this issue that a serious case of *suppressio veri* occurs. In his discussion of whether or not Cromwell was planning or operating a police state, Dr Elton omits altogether to mention that sinister little sentence in one of his memoranda to himself in 1534: "to have substantial persons in every good town to discover who speaks or preaches thus" [i.e. "in favour of the Pope's authority"]).

Elton, charges Stone, considers that if a law was passed, the actions it sanctioned were therefore justified and cannot have amounted to terror or tyranny. This included a statute of 1536 which allowed persons spreading rumors contrary to the royal policy to be executed by torture on the denunciation of a single witness. Elton's preconceived partiality for strong government led him to engage in a distorted reading of the documents.[9] What is noticeable about this dispute of course is the way in which not only Elton's views but also Stone's derive from political positions occupied in the present. Yet this does not of itself invalidate Stone's critique or reduce the clash of views between the two historians to a mere difference of opinion about politics which cannot be resolved by recourse to the original historical documents. Ultimately Elton had to answer Stone's charge of *suppressio veri* by reference to Cromwell's memo of 1534, not by talking about the practice of delation in Nazi Germany.

I I

ALL history thus has a present-day purpose and inspiration, which may be moral or political or ideological. The question is, To what extent is this purpose paramount? Is it what history is really about in the end? It is one thing to admit that historians are swayed by their moral or political views in the present or to accept that theories derived from neighboring disciplines like sociology, anthropology, economics, or linguistics can be useful or even crucial in the study of the past. But it is going a major step farther to argue that whatever historians might say or believe, the main purpose of all historical writing and research is to gain power for historians or for those they represent in the present. The widely held postmodernist argument that it is derives, directly or indirectly, principally from the writings of the French philosopher-historian Michel Foucault, who saw truth and knowledge as the products not of cognition but of power. In every age, he argued, there was a dominant "discourse" among the sciences which—in the language and terminology it employed—framed and restricted the possibilities of thought and its expression in such a way as virtually to exclude the possibility of disagreement. Texts—novels, histories, and so on—were not, in Foucault's view, the outcomes of individual thought, but "ideological products" of the dominant discourse. History was a fiction of narrative order imposed on the irreducible chaos of events in the interests of the exercise of power. And if one version of the past was more widely accepted than others, this was not because it was nearer the truth, or conformed more closely to "the evidence," but because its exponents had more power within the historical profession, or within society in general, than its critics.

The Foucauldian linkage of power and knowledge went together in the 1970s and above all the 1980s with the rise of explicitly politically committed forms of historical writing and research. The model for these was labor history, which had developed out of the socialist movement in the nineteenth century and was written explicitly from the point of view of the industrial working class. Labor historians sought to recover the history of workers and their organizations as a means of strengthening their class consciousness and political commitment in the present and their hope of eventual triumph in the future. They told a story of resistance to oppression and of the forward march of the organized working class toward the twin goals of political power and personal emancipation, to be gained by the eventual transformation of capitalist society and the state. Labor history was thus a matter of recovering precursors of present-day socialists and labor organizations and charting the rise of the movement up to the present, from which its further rise was implicitly extrapolated into a distant, imagined, triumphal future.

The model of labor history was taken up by other interest groups from the late 1970s, but it was increasingly stripped of any overarching theory of historical progress or indeed to any claim to historical objectivity at all. Black history, women's history and feminist history, gay and lesbian history, all of which became increasingly assertive in the United States in the 1980s, began with an initial recovery of "lost" or even deliberately suppressed historical facts about one's own particular group which had been "hidden from history" and were now "becoming visible."[10] But by the late 1980s the interest groups had broken free from this largely empirical model and were expending much of their energies in offering a self-consciously partisan reinterpretation of wider and more familiar historical territory from the point of view of their particular group interest. At the same time, they condemned all previously existing historical writing as partisan, representing a white, male, heterosexual, Eurocentric point of view, purveying the discourse of the culturally dominant. The point of historical discourse, they argued, was to empower people—specifically, to empower the particular group or groups of people they represented. What made the difference between different ways of viewing the past was the framework of politics and morality, not the historical accuracy of the historical vision itself, which was in the end impossible to determine.

This development reflected in part the decline of the old working class in advanced industrial and postindustrial societies. The ebbing tide of Marxism and revolution in the West left labor history increasingly stranded as the 1980s progressed. Other sources of inequality in society—gender, ethnicity, sexual orientation—grew in relative importance, rendering social cleavages more complex. The changing nature of historical scholarship on the left began to reflect these wider changes in society at large. Moreover, the situation of the university academics who wrote history was changing, too. E. H. Carr's confident belief in historical objectivity as an accurate judgment of the direction in which history was moving had arguably become popular among historians in the 1960s and 1970s not least because this had been a time of vast and rapid expansion in the university systems of all the major Western nations and thus in the historical profession as well. Much of the excitement, optimism, and intellectual confidence of the generation of historians—above all, social historians—who entered the profession at that time stemmed from this fact. More confidence came from a belief in the possibilities of radical political reform created by the Democratic presidencies of Kennedy and Johnson in the United States, the Labour governments of Harold Wilson in the U.K., the Social Democratic coalition led by Willy Brandt in West Germany, and the events leading to the fall of General de Gaulle in France. History seemed to deliver the key to the future, the universities seemed to be the powerhouses of political and social change, and the recovery of whole forgotten areas of human struggle and human existence in previous ages through the huge expansion of social history in these years gave liberal and left-wing historians the feeling that they were engaged in a crusade to restore human dignity to the neglected masses of the past, as a means of making society more democratic in the present and the future.

At the end of the twentieth century, however, it no longer seems possible to most radicals to hold up the vision of a total transformation of society; instead all that is attainable is the assertion and recognition of particular interests. The dominance of assertive right-wing governments in the Reagan-Bush-Thatcher years gave the academic left in America and Britain a feeling of impotence which was underlined by the crisis of academia which began in the 1970s and reached its height in the 1980s. The conservative governments of the 1980s held the universities in scant respect and preferred to look to privately run "think tanks" for advice, often rejecting a good deal of received academic wisdom in the process. The expansion of the academic profession came to an end. The wave of new university foundations was over. Competition for academic jobs, so easy in the 1960s, was now extremely severe, as all the new institutions began to produce Ph.D.'s who in the new situation were unable to find jobs. The numbers of Ph.D.'s in all Western countries fell sharply by the middle of the 1980s as a result. History was particularly badly hit. It declined as a university and college subject while students began to look for subjects they considered more relevant to the present and turned to applied areas of study that would lead to direct qualifications for jobs at a time of growing unemployment. The number of first degrees awarded in history at American universities fell from forty-four thousand in 1970-71 to sixteen thousand in 1985-86.[11] But the malaise was more general. The relative economic position of academics declined, as their salaries now fell behind those of other groups, such as lawyers or civil servants, with whom they had traditionally been compared. Increasingly the autonomy of the academic profession was eroded by the growing power of professional university administrators; the declining influence of democratic institutions, such as university senates; the replacement of a collegial by a managerial ethos within universities; and the ending of a professional hierarchy based on a professorial power, status, and prestige to which all, in theory at least, could aspire. Government checks and controls on universities, especially in the U.K., added further to the declining autonomy of the academic profession.[12] History is no longer seen as having any overall direction or making any larger sense. The working class, with which so many historians on the left identified, has turned out to be a broken reed, both declining in numbers with the coming of postindustrial society and transferring its allegiance at least temporarily in part to ideologues of the right, such as Mr. Reagan and Mrs. Thatcher.[13]

Many aspects of postmodernism can be understood, sociologically, as a way of compensating for this loss of power within the world at large and within the university as an institution. For it places enormous, indeed total intellectual power in the hands of the academic interpreter, the critic, and the historian.[14] If the intentions of the author of a text are irrelevant to the text's meaning—if meaning is placed in the text by the reader, the interpreter—and if the past is a text like any other, then the historian is effectively reinventing the past every time he or she reads or writes about it. The past no longer has the power to confine the researcher within the bounds of facts. Historians and critics are now omnipotent. To underline this, the postmodernists have developed a new level of specialized language and jargon, borrowed largely from literary theory, which has rendered their work opaque to anyone except other postmodernists. The enterprise thus seems not only self-regarding but, ironically in view of its criticism of hierarchy and prioritization, elitist as well. Its narcissism and elitism both can be seen as compensatory mechanisms for the loss of real power, income, and status suffered by its academic practitioners over the past ten to fifteen years. It all reminds one of Oscar Wilde's saying that any fool can make history; it takes a genius to write it.

The narcissism of much postmodernist writing can be even more directly personal than this. Postmodernism's legitimation of subjectivity in the historian's work encourages historians to intrude their own presence into the text to such a degree that in some cases it all but obliterates the historical subject. The word "I," "me," or "my" appears no fewer than eighty-eight times in the first four pages of the postmodernist historian Diane Purkiss's book *The Witch in History*, for instance. Where is the witch herself in all this? Purkiss attacks male academic historians of witchcraft for instrumentalizing the witch in pursuit of their own academic careers, but does not pause to think how she is doing precisely the same thing herself.[15] Another recent article by an avowedly postmodernist historian, Rudy Koshar, is only a little less excessive in including thirty-two references to himself in the first five pages.[16] The prioritizing of historical debate and prescriptive writings about the study of history over the study of the past itself also encourages a self-regarding obsession with where the historian stands on these issues, at the expense of the issues themselves. If historians begin to regard themselves as more important than the people they are writing about, it they start to refer to one another—and to themselves—more than they refer to the past, as theorists like Ankersmit and Jenkins would like them to, then inflated self-importance, solipsism, and pretentiousness can be the only results. A return to scholarly humility is surely called for here. It was after all Sir Isaac Newton who reminded his fellow scientists that if he could see farther, it was because he was standing on the shoulders of giants; what he was doing was possible only because of the work carried out by his predecessors.[17]

A modicum of humility would be in order not least because it is not just the postmodernists, but also in their time the quantifiers, the psychohistorians, the Marxists, feminists, and many others, who have arrived on the intellectual scene arrogantly proclaiming all previous ways of doing history to be redundant, biased, useless, or false because they had unsophisticated theories or methods, because they neglected central organizing concepts, or because they were simply unscientific. The originators of this rhetoric in modern times were of course the Rankeans of the nineteenth century. Seen in terms of the sociology of professionalization, such claims might be regarded as a way of legitimating the professionalism of those who advance them and of convincing the rest of the scholarly world that they are important. Ironically, they are part of the culture of modernism, in which to gain a hearing, intellectuals have to claim that they are saying something radically new.[18]

But the pattern of such interventions in the past has been that after an initial period of controversy, in which its universalizing pretensions are disputed, the new approach settles down to become yet another subspecialism. When cliometrics appeared on the scene, for example, its adherents claimed that it rendered all previous approaches obsolete and that *all* historians would in future have to be trained in its methods. Twenty years or so later, in the 1990s, the debate has calmed down, the claims of the cliometricians to solve fundamental historical problems by the application of statistics have largely been discarded, and quantitative history has become a subspecialism with its own societies, its own journals, and its own specialized language, coexisting reasonably happily with all the other subspecialisms. The same has happened at various times with other new waves of historical theory and practice.

As a classic example of this process, one can take the case of social history, which as we saw made extensive claims to permeate the whole of historical study when it first arrived on the academic scene in a major way in the 1960s. The opening article in the *Journal of Social History* by its editor Peter N. Stearns, written in 1967, used the language of the pioneer ("few significant topics have been explored in any depth"), talked of the subject's "advancement," and proclaimed its ability to "recast . . . traditional questions of historiography."[19] In 1976, however, Stearns was already complaining after a decade of the journal's existence that "social historians are viewed with misgiving or are simply mislabeled, so that a history department can merrily do what it has traditionally done while adding the word 'social' to a few course descriptions and research projects." "The rigidity of traditional historians" was of course to blame in his view for this sorry state of affairs, alongside "conventional historical thinking" which perpetuated "the common assumption that social history is another topic rather than a total approach." Thus "the resolute desire of traditional historians to put social history into another neat cubby hole" was being effectively realized. In something of a despairing mood, Stearns called for the foundation of separate social history departments to escape the "boring" nature of "conventional history" and achieve proper equality as a "recognized discipline."[20] Fortunately, perhaps, no one heeded his call.

Here, therefore, was a crucial retreat back from social history's hegemonic claims to dominate the whole of historical study toward the more modest demand for its recognition as a legitimate subspecialism. This process, replicated with many other subspecialisms in history, is very similar to the phenomenon the jazz singer George Melly encountered in his study of popular music in the 1950s and 1960s: Groups like the Rolling Stones or the Beatles began with a revolt which within a short space of time was reduced to a style.[21] The same process is currently happening with postmodernist history. In the guise of a specific kind of cultural and intellectual history, it is already equipped with its own apparatus of specialized journals and associations, conferences and seminar meetings, book series and so on. Rather as history departments especially in the United States thought it necessary to hire one or two quantitative historians in the 1970s and one or two women's historians in the 1980s, so they now think it necessary to hire one or two postmodernist cultural or intellectual historians in the 1990s. These are likely to add in the long run to the already bewildering postmodern diversity and fragmentation of the historical profession, rather than revolutionize its theory and practice as a whole. In due course, no doubt, a new challenge to existing methodological and theoretical orthodoxies will emerge; in due course it too will be absorbed into the overall structure of the historical profession as one of its many, and continually proliferating, subdisciplines.

III

ARE professional historians engaged just in producing justifications for things as they are, including the maintenance of their own privileged position as middle-class academics? Many postmodernists argue that this is so, for "in the end," as Keith Jenkins says, "history is theory and theory is ideological and ideology just is material interests."[22] A postmodernist perspective sees "professional historians . . . as being not so much outside the ideological fray but as occupying very dominant positions within it . . . professional histories as expressions of how dominant ideologies currently articulate history. It seems rather obvious," Jenkins continues,

> that, seen in a wider cultural and "historical" perspective, multi-million pound institutional investments such as our national universities are integral to the reproduction of the on-going social formation and are thus at the forefront of cultural guardianship (academic standards) and ideological control; it would be somewhat careless if they were not.[23]

Many postmodernists rail against the imagined intolerance of the historical profession, in which, according to one of them, "non-conformists, doubters and non-believers have been treated as heretics fit only for the stake."[24] They seek therefore to destroy the notion that "the profession can duly be applauded as having some importance" which rests on its claim to be engaged in uncovering an "objective" historical truth, for the professionals' truth is no more true than that of any other group in society. Postmodernist history would dispense with professional university historians altogether in this vision and encourage instead the "empowerment" of oppressed social groups by showing how "our own history" can "serve as a validating foundation" for political programs in the present and the future.[25] The rules of historical research and the belief in the attainability of historical truth would be jettisoned because the "distinction between propaganda and good history serves mainly to delegitimize histories which challenge dominant ideology." Historical writing and teaching would thus be based on the belief "that history is propaganda, that it is about the present."[26]

Yet this is the voice not of postmodernism per se, of which, as we have already seen, there are many varieties, but of vulgar postmodernism, transforming into the jargon of the 1990s the crude reductionist Marxism of the Stalinist era. That Keith Jenkins sees university historians in this jaundiced way may, if one wishes for a moment to borrow his own mode of argument, have something to do with the fact that he is only a lecturer in an Institute of Higher Education and so feels excluded from the multimillion-pound university institutions he is criticizing so aggressively. Doubtless this would be an unfair charge, but no more unfair than the charges he is leveling at the university historical profession as a whole. It is in any case simply naive to see cultural institutions such as universities functioning as mere transmitters of dominant values; they are rather one of many sites of contradiction within society, bases for the launching and debating of new and often disturbing, subversive knowledge and ideas. The very notion of a dominant discourse or ideology—liberalism, in Jenkins's formulation—is itself a sweeping oversimplification in our multifaceted and fragmented postmodern society. Many of the advocates of postmodernism itself after all are located at major teaching and research institutions like Cambridge and Manchester, Princeton and Cornell, Berkeley and Yale, the Collège de France and the Sorbonne. There are numerous examples of historians and philosophers, not to mention politicians, who have enunciated and stuck to principles that run counter to their material interests. One could do worse than start with the middle-class intellectual Karl Marx and the factory owner Friedrich Engels. A primary thrust of postmodernism is to stress the independent force of ideas and to uncouple them from material factors altogether, and it is difficult to avoid the conclusion that Jenkins and those popularizers who think like him do not really understand what postmodernism is about if they regard ideology as just a way of expressing material interests. In any case, there are and always have been many reasons why historians choose one theory, method, or interpretation rather than another; often the impulses driving them are hidden deep inside the subconscious mind and cannot be explained in terms of any kind of rationality, let alone economic.

If history is a "bourgeois" ideology, then how does it function as such, and what is its importance in society? According to another postmodernist writer, history is a "disciplined means for the production of a 'historical past' which exercises a regulatory function in relation to the 'public past.' Its role in this regard is enormously important," he goes on, because the historical debates conducted by professional historians "decisively influence the public face of the past over the long term."[27] Another postmodernist has even gone so far as to declare: "Written history . . . is the primary vehicle for the distribution and use of power."[28] On the other hand, Wulf Kansteiner, a German observer of the postmodern cultural scene, has identified "the growing insignificance of traditional historiography" in public discourse as a major source of history's current malaise.[29] In fact, both these positions arguably miss the major point, which is that public knowledge of the past—public memory, in other words—has always been structured by influences other than professional historians, from folk song, myth, and tradition to pulp fiction, broadsheets, and the popular press. The thrust of professional history has more often been toward puncturing the clichés of popular historical myth than toward sustaining them. Moreover, from the outset professional historians have usually addressed themselves only to an educated minority. To regard university-trained professional historians as simple one-way producers of historical knowledge which structures public perceptions of the past is to overestimate their public influence several times over.

Nevertheless, this is what a number of postmodernist writers persist in doing. Jenkins argues that "the bourgeoisie" believes history to be neutral, an academic discipline above and beyond politics, because it does not need a historical trajectory (such as progress) which has not arrived at its ultimate future destination since it has long since arrived at its own—namely, the dominance of society and the exploitation of everyone else in it. History serves the interests of the bourgeoisie. The notion that history serves the interests of the past cannot be true because "the past does not have a self."[30] Like many postmodernist critics of history, Jenkins lumps all historians together into a single category ("bourgeois liberals") and refuses to recognize the enormous variety of political and methodological positions that characterize the profession as it is today. Moreover, the "bourgeoisie" does not have "a self" either, any more than does the "proletariat" or, come to that, "women" or "gays" or "African-Americans"; in all these cases the "self" is just as much constructed ideologically as the past is, and just as hotly contested by varieties of liberalism and conservatism, rival doctrinal interpretations of socialism, mutually hostile concepts of feminism, and so on.

It is quite wrong to suppose that professional historians all agree on certain aspects of history because these conform to a "dominant ideology" which helps them keep their posts and their salaries. Those who claim that the historical profession is "disciplined by power relations to say and do certain things"[31] are wide of the mark. Visions or versions of history are not simply accepted because their authors have power within the historical profession or the universities. Consider, for example, E. P. Thompson's book *The Making of the English Working Class*, published in 1963. Its author could scarcely be called an adherent of liberalism or an academic careerist. At the time of writing the book, he was not a university historian at all, but taught mainly in extra-mural studies and the Workers' Educational Association, and the only spell he ever spent as a fully paid-up academic historian, at Warwick University, ended in chaos when he led a group of radical students in an occupation of the university's administration and published an excoriating attack on the academic world's subservience to capitalism in his book *Warwick University Limited*.[32] Yet in terms of its method and approach, *The Making of the English Working Class* has surely been one of the most influential works of English history published in the last forty years.

Consider, in contrast, the thesis of Sir Geoffrey Elton that Thomas Cromwell inaugurated a "Tudor Revolution in Government." For all the cogency and learning and persistence with which this thesis was advanced by its author, it was never generally accepted by scholars in the field and indeed was sharply attacked not long after its enunciation, in a major debate in *Past and Present*.[33] Writing in 1980, Lawrence Stone noted that Elton had "failed to persuade more than a minority of his colleagues in the profession that the changes that took place at that time can reasonably be described as a 'revolution in government,' " and although Stone added that "every serious student of the period" had to "grapple" with Elton's argument, the fact is that this does not add up to Elton's thesis having become an accepted part of historical orthodoxy.[34] Yet its author was for decades a pillar of the academic establishment; he was president of the Royal Historical Society and Regius Professor of Modern History at Cambridge and was indeed given a knighthood on the recommendation of Mrs. Thatcher's government. Power and knowledge seem only indirectly related in both these cases.

It is perfectly possible to take a rather different view of the relationship from historians and power from that advocated by many postmodernists. As John Vincent has remarked, historians nowadays are mostly state employees in universities, who have experienced a perceptible decline in income and status over the last few decades of the twentieth century:

> Historians today are not holders of power—power over men, over money, over opinion. They live among the foothills of society, where they engage anxiously in downward social mobility. They see very little of power in their own lives; they do not catch its reflections in the lives of others. From the life of action in its modern form—business—they are quite especially remote. Their disconnection from things, their want of rootedness, their poverty of commitment, are those of the minor official class the world over.[35]

To regard them, in other words, as some kind of hegemonic elite is sadly misplaced.

This may be true, but what of the conclusion Vincent draws from all this? He argues that because they depend on the state for their employment and pension, historians today are congenitally biased in favor of the big state, of social reform, and (of course) of pensions, and deride "market forces" in history, for "left to the market, there would be few historians and little history." Thus it is extremely difficult for the historian to regain the intellectual position of a "freebooter or lone adventurer."[36] It may be of course that Vincent's own experience of earning big money as a columnist for the *Sun* newspaper encouraged him in his favorable view of freebooting tendencies. But anyone who knows the work he wrote before this, when he depended mainly on his salary, knows that it was as unconventional in its approach.[37] If we really believed his somewhat reductionist view, we would expect only robust right-wing opinions from historians who lived off private incomes, and while it is true that there are some individuals, such as Andrew Roberts, author of the neo-Thatcherite text *Eminent Churchillians*, who fit into this pattern, there are many more who do not. And there is a market for history and historians in the universities where students have not deserted their subjects quite as much as they have some others, such as physics. Within the universities there is as wide a variety of political views among historians as there is among other sectors of the population, not least because the universities which employ them have been deliberately created by society as intellectual spaces where a wide variety of thoughts can flourish. Such a role is not merely cherished by radicals. In Britain, when the Conservatives' educational reform bill of 1989 proposed to abolish tenure for university faculty, it was a Conservative revolt in the House of Lords which succeeded in writing in a clause stating that academics were not to be dismissed because of their beliefs.

IV

THE argument that each group in society creates its own history as a means of building its own identity has worrying implications. As the American historian Laura Lee Downs has noted,

> The politics of identity, feminist and otherwise, rests on a disturbing epistemological ground, in which the group's fragile unity, rooted in an emergent sense of identity as an oppressed other, is shielded from white male colonization by asserting the inaccessibility of one's experience. Only those who share the group identity and have lived its experience, whether seen as biologically given or socially constructed, can know what it means to be black, a woman, blue-collar, or ethnic, in an America constructed as white, Anglo-Saxon, and Protestant."[38]

One might of course argue that it follows that none of these oppressed groups can possibly write the history of white Anglo-Saxon Protestant males since they in turn have not shared the experience which makes the writing of such a history possible. The ultimate implication indeed is that no one can know anything beyond his or her own bodily identity. Experience is the sole arbiter of truth. There is no universal truth; there are only truths particular to specific groups of people.

Thus white male historians can write only about dead white males, and that, in the opinion of many postmodernists, is why the dominant perspective on the past purveyed by the historical profession has written so many other groups out of the story. Indeed some professional historians have explicitly defended this practice and argued that history is, and always should be, basically about the dominant (and in Western society, therefore, white, male) group or groups in society, because their "truth" is historically more important than that of subordinate groups. E. H. Carr was absolutely clear that those who had (in his view) contributed little or nothing to the creation of historical change as he saw it, such as women or the preliterate and politically unorganized masses, were not really deserving of the historian's attention. John Vincent agrees with Carr on this point: "History is about winners, not losers. . . . History is deeply male. . . . History is about the rich and famous, not the poor."[39] But this is merely a confession of the writer's deep ignorance of other kinds of history than the history of British high politics in the nineteenth century which he himself writes. In the broader world of historical scholarship in Western Europe and the United States over the past three decades and more, this kind of history has been increasingly in the minority, and it has been precisely the poor and the unknown, the losers, and indeed the female who have attracted the largest number of historians and been the subject of the greatest number of books.[40] This is only partly connected with the rise of "identity politics." The historians who have written about vagrants have almost certainly not been vagrants themselves, and the same (one hopes) goes, *mutatis mutandis*, for the history of crime. The recovery of the history of oppressed groups has had far more to do with the desire to expose fundamental structures of inequality in society than with any attempt to bolster political, social, ethnic, or gender identities in the present. When a postmodernist historian argues in the mid-1990s for a "rediscovery of history's losers," one wonders what planet he has been living on for the last thirty years.[41]

The idea that each group in society writes its own history breaks down in practice because by and large it is *not* the case that professional historians, who are still overwhelmingly white, male, and middle class, are still primarily engaged in writing the history of middle-class white males, even if some of them, like John Vincent, argue that they should be. Moreover, the argument that white middle-class men who wrote women's history or black history, heterosexuals who wrote gay history, and so on were "appropriating" the history of other groups in an illegitimate manner, because they lacked the experience necessary to do so, is itself unsustainable on a number of grounds. For the ultimate implication of such a view would be that the history of religion would have to be left to clergymen, of war to the generals, of fascism to fascists. In the end no history would be possible, only autobiography. That such a view can have right-wing implications was illustrated by Carl Bridenbaugh's presidential address to the American Historical Association in 1962, for instance, in which he charged that "many of the younger practitioners of our craft, and those who are still apprentices, are products of . . . foreign origins. . . . They find themselves in a very real sense outsiders on our past. . . . They have no experience to assist them."[42] Nationalist historians have frequently argued in this manner that they own the past of their own country and that foreigners have no business trying to appropriate it. Even Fernand Braudel, much of whose work had been devoted to the history of Spain, Italy, and other parts of the Mediterranean, argued paradoxically in his last work, *The Identity of France*, that "The historian can really be on an equal footing only with the history of his own country; he understands almost instinctively its twists and turns, its complexities, its originalities and its weaknesses."[43]

But French history is too important a matter to be left to the French, German history has affected other histories too greatly for it to be left to the Germans. Nor should anybody suppose that insisting on the principle that only Bosnians were capable of writing Bosnian history, or Serbs the history of Serbia, would be a way of guaranteeing the production of good, accurate, and untendentious historical research. History is as much about the obviously other as it is about the seemingly familiar. It is about bridging a series of gaps, in time, culture, and experience, through the use of a disciplined historical imagination. Certainly, the historian can gain by bringing personal experience to bear on the study of the past. Edward Gibbon, for example, was wont to remark that the time he had spent serving in the local militia had not been wasted when it came to writing the military history of the decline and fall of the Roman Empire. Similarly, David Knowles's experience as a monk was clearly helpful to him in writing the history of the religious orders in England, though it skewed his interpretation in a particular way, as we have seen. But there can be losses, too, from a narrowing of perspective or a facile sense of identification which obscures some of the crucial differences between past and present. Much, if not most, military history written by generals, for example, is hopelessly narrow and ignorant of the wider social, political, and diplomatic aspects of the subject; the many books by one of the most reputable writers in this genre, Major General J. F. C. Fuller, are a case in point.[44] The cultural gap which separates women in the 1990s from women in the 1790s or 1590s or 1390s is very much greater in some respects than the cultural gap which separates men and women in the present.

Moreover, no one would surely claim that women were not entitled to write the history of men or masculinity, or gays the history of heterosexuality, simply because they lacked the personal experience of being male or heterosexual which made this possible. Why should the oppressed not write the history of their oppressors? Yet this is the implication of such arguments. "If the powerful can't criticise the oppressed," the philosopher Paul Boghossian has observed, "because the central epistemological categories are inexorably tied to particular perspectives, it also follows that the oppressed can't criticise the powerful."[45] In practice, of course, this has not happened. There has been a great deal of important work on masculinity written by female historians in recent years.[46] Imagination makes good the experience which is lacking. Indeed distance may even lend a useful degree of detachment. The historian's identification with the object of study is by no means unproblematical; it caused widespread unease in Germany, for instance, when one senior historian and Second World War veteran remarked that he empathized with the soldiers of Hitler's army on the eastern front during the Second World War in 1944–45. His sense of identification led him to equate their sufferings with those of the Jews, and the mass expulsion of millions of Germans from Eastern Europe after the war with the mass murder of the Jews by the Nazis, in a way that most people found both distasteful and unacceptable.[47]

A growing awareness of the problems caused by the claim that experience and identification are necessary for the writing of history has led some historians at least to shift their attention from the empathetic reconstruction of the history of the oppressed groups they identify with to the linguistic analysis of the concepts which they perceive as having structured that oppression: from women, for instance, to gender. But this, too, can have its pitfalls. In championing the postmodernist use of gender as a concept, the American historian Joan Scott, in the view of one critic, has begun to pursue a project in which gender identity is not grounded in the experience of oppression but is acquired "solely through a process of differentiation analogous to that which Saussure identified as the structural ground of linguistic systems of meaning." In this process the powerful— white middle-class males—created their own identity by setting themselves off against negatively defined others, such as women, nonwhites, and the poor. Thus women's gender identity was created by men, not by their own experience, which was merely forced on them by white middle-class males. Paradoxically, therefore, the implication of Scott's championing of gender as a useful concept for historians was that feminists should stop pursuing the illusion of a history of women's experience and devote themselves instead to examining the history and operation of "the inner workings of the ideological system which placed one in the unhappy position of the 'other' to begin with'": gender as a system of differentiation, rather than women as a group; racism as an ideology, rather than nonwhites as a category; and so on.[48]

Since Scott sees language as constituting social being and providing the only source of agency in history, she is unable to explain historical change at all, since there is nothing in her system of analysis which tells us how language may change itself, or why. Thus she offers no hope that the structures of inequality inherent in concepts of gender can be broken down. What we need, Downs argues, is to take account of the social and, one may add, political and economic context, in analyzing language in history, so that we can begin to explain why things changed in terms of the mutual influences of language and its context in the real world.[49] Scott's reply to these charges was vehement but unconvincing and failed to address any of the central points at issue.[50] Downs's plea for the restoration of a real historical context to language and thought was a powerful one.

History written by men about women is no more necessarily written from a male or masculine point of view than history written by women about men is female or feminine in perspective. One can point to many women historians who have written major works on political or diplomatic history in which there is nothing at all that might betray the fact that they are female except the name on the cover: Ragnhild Hatton's biography of King George I of Hanover and England comes to mind, for instance, or Olive Anderson's study of suicide in the Victorian era, or Annie Kriegel's book on French Communism, or indeed the writings of Gertrude Himmelfarb discussed at various points in the present book.[51] Postmodernists may argue that every historical work inevitably embodies both an interpretation and a philosophy of history and that this makes them essentially incommensurable and therefore incapable of generating any kind of controversy that can be meaningfully resolved. However, this does not commit them to tolerating any perspective apart from their own. When the feminist historian Diane Purkiss attacks the account of seventeenth-century witchcraft given in the standard work by Keith Thomas, she argues not that it is empirically flawed, but that

Thomas's portrayal of witches as powerless old beggar women is designed principally to purvey an "enabling myth" in which men's "historical identity is grounded in the powerlessness and speechlessness of women." At the same time, Purkiss castigates what she sees as Thomas's studious avoidance of the question of why so many witches were women as an example of male arrogance and indifference toward women's history.[52] Thus Thomas's work is delegitimized on political grounds; the question of whether witches really were mostly beggar women is regarded by Purkiss as irrelevant because as history, it can never be finally determined.

In practice, Purkiss's arguments are both contradictory and empirically flawed. Thomas's argument, backed by a mass of telling contemporary evidence, was that poor, single old women were often accused of witchcraft because far from being speechless, they cursed those who refused them alms. Guilt then drove the latter to link any subsequent accident or misfortune with the curse and to bring an accusation of witchcraft against the woman in question. This was an attempt to explain why so many witches were women, not an attempt to avoid the question. Of course, to say that such women were powerless in the face of witchcraft accusations, or that they had little status or influence in the local community, is to make an empirical observation of a strictly limited historical scope. There is no evidence at all to warrant Purkiss's charge that what Thomas is really doing is using these arguments to "ground" male identity in the present; there is only the sexist assumption that he must be doing so because he is a man. Other postmodernists are wont to claim that postmodernism has replaced the historian's supposed certainties of objective knowledge with "tentative" and "circumspect" hypotheses which are "subject to continual revision,"[53] but histories such as that of Purkiss, written with the explicit purpose of political empowerment in the present, are anything but tentative and circumspect, least of all in the handling of the empirical evidence on which they base their claims. Feminist history, like any other kind of history, has to be based on the facts if it is to carry conviction.

Postmodernists may claim that "there is no real object 'history,' only a philosophy of history; the historian's work reduces to its ideological positions,"[54] but neither of these statements is true. Ultimately, if political or moral aims become paramount in the writing of history, then scholarship suffers. Facts are mined to prove a case; evidence is twisted to suit a political purpose; inconvenient documents are ignored; sources deliberately misconstrued or misinterpreted. If historians are not engaged in the pursuit of truth, if the idea of objectivity is merely a concept designed to repress alternative points of view, then scholarly criteria become irrelevant in assessing the merits of a particular historical argument. This indeed is the ultimate goal of some postmodernists. David Harlan, for instance, describing objectivity in history as an "exhausted dogma," pleads for the reinstatement of a "pre-scientific" concept of history as a form of moral education. The study of American history has been degraded, he says, by "pragmatic, methodologically obsessed professionalism," and he calls for historians to address the "spiritual hunger" of Americans for moral guidance from the experience of the nation. Yet his argument is riddled with contradictions. On the one hand, he claims that "we do not have, and probably never will have, a widely agreed on and generally reliable set of objective criteria for evaluating historical accounts"; on the other hand, he goes on to say, "To claim that we cannot have objective knowledge about the past is not, as it turns out, to claim that the past has nothing to teach us." Yet how can we learn from the past if we cannot gain reliable knowledge of it? In practice Harlan ends up necessarily conceding that we can. "Certain texts," he admits, "resist certain readings." Historical research is a dialogue between historians and their sources, for historians cannot read into them anything they wish. So taken is Harlan with this point, indeed, that he even repeats the Eltonian injunction that the historian must approach the sources "with an open mind." Given this level of self-contradiction, together with his complete failure to define any of the terms he uses, from objectivity and relativism onward, it is difficult to take Harlan's argument entirely seriously.[55]

In similar vein to David Harlan, Ellen Somekawa and Elizabeth Smith argue that because "within whatever rules historians can articulate, all interpretations are equally valid," it is necessary for historians to "shift the grounds for the assessment of integrity from the absolute or objective truth to the moral or political. That is," they continue, "rather than believe in the absolute truth of what we are writing, we must believe in the moral or political position we are taking with it." They add that they "reject the assumption that if we abandon our claim to objective truth we must be writing in bad faith (writing propaganda in the most pejorative sense of the word),"[56] but they offer no reason to suppose why this should not be the case. In fact, of course, in classic postmodernist fashion they are caricaturing the position they are attacking by pushing it out to an extreme. No historians really believe in the *absolute* truth of what they are writing, simply in its *probable* truth, which they have done their utmost to establish by following the usual rules of evidence. In the end it simply isn't true that two historical arguments which contradict each other are equally valid, that there is no means of deciding between them as history because they are necessarily based on different political and historical philosophies. It is one thing to say that different historians use the same sources to ask different questions,[57] quite another to say that they use them for the same question and come up with diametrically opposed answers. If one historian argues that big business put the Nazis into power in Germany in 1933 and another argues that it did not, both these arguments cannot be correct. Claiming that each is true according to the perspective (in this case, Marxist or non-Marxist) from which it is written is a meaningless statement.

As Paul Boghossian has observed, "to say some claim is true according to some perspective sounds simply like a fancy way of saying that someone, or some group, believes it." Suppose, he goes on, we apply this view to itself:

> If a claim and its opposite can be equally true provided that there is some perspective relative to which each is true, then, since there is a perspective—realism—relative to which it's true that a claim and its opposite cannot both be true, postmodernism would have to admit that it itself is just as true as its opposite, realism. But postmodernism cannot afford to admit that; presumably, its whole point is that real-

ism is false. Thus, we see that the very statement of postmodernism, construed as a view about truth, undermines itself; facts about truth independent of particular perspectives are presupposed by the view itself.

Similarly, if it is argued that these claims are using different and essentially incommensurable rules of evidence from one another, so that there is no agreement about what might constitute the kind of evidence that would prove or disprove one or the other, then any claim could be justified simply by making up rules of evidence designed to provide such a justification. It would follow from this, as Boghossian observes,

> that we could justify the claim that not every rule of evidence is as good as any other, thereby forcing the postmodernist to concede that his views about truth and justification are just as justified as his opponent's. Presumably, however, the postmodernist needs to hold that his views are better than his opponent's; otherwise what's to recommend them? On the other hand, if some rules of evidence can be said to be better than others, then there must be perspective-independent facts about what makes them better and a thoroughgoing relativism about justification is false.[58]

Once postmodernist hyperrelativism's principles are applied to itself, many of its arguments begin to collapse under the weight of their own contradictions.

In a number of cases, political commitment, freed by postmodernist relativism from the shackles that normally bind historians to the facts, has produced deeply flawed work which clearly distorts or misinterprets the source material in the service of present-day ideology. One example is *Black Athena,* ironically written by a radical white male European scholar, Martin Bernal, whose argument is that white male European scholars had suppressed the uncomfortable truth that ancient Greek civilization was derived from Egypt. In place of what he regarded as the old Eurocentric view, Bernal offered an Afrocentric version according to which ancient Egypt was a black African culture. Since European and American civilization is generally portrayed in the "Western Civilization" course books used in universities throughout the United States as having derived from the ancient Greeks, this meant that it was ultimately black in origin. But this view was quickly revealed as incompatible with the evidence. The ancient Egyptians and Carthaginians were much as the modern Egyptians are in appearance—that is, most definitely not Negroid or Afro-Caribbean. The linguistic and archaeological evidence adduced by Bernal for Egyptian influence on Greece does not sustain the view that Egyptian culture was carried across the eastern Mediterranean by a series of invasions. Moreover, the argument that white thought was black in origin does not sit easily with the parallel contention that white thought is the source of the African-Americans' oppression. In all this, the point is not that political motivation in historical writing is wrong in itself. Rather, the point is that black history deserves to be treated with scholarly rigor and care as much as white history does, and that this was conspicuously lacking in Bernal's account.[59] Similar things may be said of the gay historian John Boswell's misguided attempt to prove that people explicitly identified themselves as homosexual throughout European history and that this was generally accepted in the Christian society of medieval Europe, in the face of a far more convincing historical literature which has located the emergence of homosexual identities at the end of the nineteenth century.[60]

Political commitment has been the source of a lot of good history and will continue to be a powerful influence on historians in the future. But history can provide convincing support for social and political empowerment in the present only if it can convincingly claim to be true, and this in turn demands a rigorous and self-critical approach to the evidence on the part of the historian, who must be willing to jettison political ideas if they prove unworkable without distorting or manipulating the reality of the past. History, as Roger Chartier has warned, "must resist the mythical constructions of the past governed by the needs of communities, imagined or real, national or not, that create or accept historical narratives to suit their desires and expectations." While historians are certainly swayed, consciously or unconsciously, by present moral or political purposes in carrying out their work, it is not the validity or desirability of these, but the extent to which their historical arguments conform to the rules of evidence and the facts on which they rest, by which they must stand or fall in the end. "If we give up striving for truth," Chartier has concluded, "an ambition that may be out of all measure but is surely fundamental, we leave the field open to all manner of falsification and to all the forgers who betray knowledge and therefore hurt memory."[61]

CHAPTER EIGHT

OBJECTIVITY AND ITS LIMITS

I

DESPITE his penchant for relativism, E. H. Carr did not think that all views of the past were equally valid. "It does not follow," he said, "that because a mountain appears to take on a different shape from different angles of vision, it has objectively either no shape at all or an infinity of shapes." Carr was close enough to the British empirical tradition to protest against the view that "the facts of history are nothing, interpretation is everything," and he saw real dangers in "extravagant interpretations"—such as those produced by extreme Soviet and anti-Soviet accounts of the Bolshevik Revolution—that "ran roughshod over the facts." Carr's account of the process of historical research and interpretation gave equal weight to both:

> The historian starts with a provisional selection of facts, and a provisional interpretation in the light of which that selection has been made—by others as well as by himself. As he works, both the interpretation and the selection and ordering of facts undergo subtle and perhaps partly unconscious changes through the reciprocal action of one on the other.

"History," he concluded, was thus "an unending dialogue between the present and the past."[1]

This brought Carr to another crucial point. An objective histori-an was thus not one who simply got the facts right. That was mere antiquarianism. A chronicler could do that. To be an objective histo-rian, you had to take a larger view:

> When we call a historian objective, we mean two things. First of all, we mean that he has a capacity to rise above the limited vision of his own situation in society and in history. . . . Secondly, we mean that he has the capacity to project his vision into the future in such a way as to give him a more profound and more lasting insight into the past than can be attained by those historians whose outlook is entirely bounded by their own immediate situation.

Like Ranke, Carr believed that history differed from chronicle because it tried to grasp how discrete historical facts were intercon-nected. Unlike Ranke, however, he thought that all history was therefore teleological, or in other words, to put it in more contem-porary terms, history was only history if tied to a metanarrative. The historian had to find objectivity not by virtue of some moral or reli-gious criterion outside history, or by eschewing any wider general-izations and sticking to a mere recital of the facts, but by looking for a larger meaning within history itself, an ongoing history moving from past through present to future.[2]

In his book Carr enjoined his readers to "study the historian before you study the facts." Let us follow this advice and study the man himself before we go on to a critique of his views on history. Edward Hallett Carr was born in 1892. Shortly before his death, some ninety years later, he wrote: "I must be one of the very few intellectuals still writing who grew up, not in the high noon, but in the afterglow of the great Victorian age of faith and optimism, and it is difficult for me even today to think in terms of a world in perma-nent and irretrievable decline."[3] This was an understatement of a very considerable order. Carr believed in progress with a capital *P*, and after a career spent partly in the Foreign Office, where he was a sup-porter of appeasement in the 1930s, and partly in academia, where he taught international relations at Aberystwyth, he moved to London and became an editorial-writer for the *Times* during the Second

World War. Here his enthusiasm for Britain's ally Stalinist Russia and his conversion to the belief that the planned economy was the way to the future caused him to be known as "the Red Professor of Printing House Square." After the war ended, he moved to Cambridge and immediately began work on a *History of Soviet Russia,* which was published over the following decades in no fewer than fourteen stout volumes, taking the story from 1917 up to its culmination in the *Foundations of the Planned Economy* in the early 1930s. As he indicated in an interview given to the *New Left Review* toward the end of his life, Carr never lost his faith in the Soviet Union as the embodiment of human progress. His multivolume history reflected this belief. As Carr said, his intention was "to write the history not of the events of the revolution ... but of the political, social and economic order which emerged from it." The book offered, he wrote, "not an exhaustive record of the events of the period to which it relates, but an analysis of those events which moulded the main lines of development." Thus, for example, he provided extensive coverage of "events and controversies before 1917 which, even if their immediate consequences appear small, played a vital part in the later history of the revolution."[4] By contrast, his three volumes on *The Bolshevik Revolution* ignored the drama of the Revolution itself, the defeat of the opposition to Lenin and the Bolsheviks, the military conflict of the civil war, the brutal suppression, murder, torture, and imprisonment in the "gulag archipelago" of opposition by the Cheka, Lenin's secret police, and all the other aspects of the subject which involved what one might call defeated alternatives to the Bolshevik vision of the future. Carr's purpose was simply to write about the origins and development of the institutions and policies, principally economic and social, which the Bolsheviks put into effect after they came to power and which he believed held the keys to humanity's future, and so he deliberately ignored everything else.

History was identified in this view with progress, and what was not progressive in Carr's view was largely edited out. "If Mr Carr's remaining volumes equal this impressive opening," wrote Sir Isaiah Berlin in a review of *The Bolshevik Revolution*, "they will constitute the most monumental challenge of our time to that idea of impartiality and objective truth and even-handed justice in the writing of history which is most deeply embedded in the European liberal tradition."[5] Sir Isaiah saw Carr's volumes as an attempt to rewrite the past in a manner that recalled George Orwell's *1984*. He was echoed in this view by Hugh Trevor-Roper, who thundered:

> What is the most obvious characteristic of *A History of Soviet Russia*? It is the author's unhesitating identification of history with the victorious cause, his ruthless dismissal of its opponents, of its victims, and of all who did not stay on, or steer, the bandwagon. The "might-have-beens," the deviationists, the rivals, the critics of Lenin are reduced to insignificance, denied justice, or hearing, or space, because they backed the wrong horse. History proved them wrong, and the historian's essential task is to take the side of History. . . . No historian since the crudest ages of clerical bigotry has treated evidence with such dogmatic ruthlessness as this.[6]

Extreme though this invective was, there is some truth in the view that Edward Hallett Carr was essentially a Stalinist, though his insistence on giving coverage to Trotsky as one of the architects of the Soviet system, his criticisms of Stalin as an individual, and other aspects of his *History* caused him to be anathematized by official Soviet historiography as long as he lived. For Carr, history was not about the past in itself or even about how the past came to be the present, but about how it contributed to the future the historian desired. The propositions advanced in *What Is History?* reflected this view of history as progress, as seen from the point of view of the future of the human race in a Soviet-style planned economy, an example, one might say, of the dictum that historians "remember the future and imagine the past," though perhaps not quite in the way that the originator of this uncharacteristic witticism, Sir Lewis Namier, intended. In taking this point of view, moreover, Carr was preaching with all the zeal of the convert, for he had spent the earlier part of his academic career writing about those very losers whom he later instructed historians to consign to what Trotsky called the dustheap of history, men such as the nineteenth-century anarchist Bakunin, who had failed in almost every political enterprise in which they had engaged.[7]

It is easy to see now the flaws in Carr's definition of objectivity in history. The sweep of history toward a Soviet-style planned economy in the light of which he required historians to judge the past if they were to be deemed objective came to an abrupt end in 1990. Moreover, those who thought, like the American political writer Francis Fukuyama, that history was now over because liberal democratic, free market capitalism had triumphed all along the line—another teleology, with the opposite signs to those of the kind of Marxism Carr espoused—were confounded, as religious fundamentalism spread in modernizing states like Iran or prosperous areas such as Israel or the American South.[8] Whatever else it is, historical objectivity is not conformity to an imagined future, not least because, as we saw earlier in this book, historians are no more capable of imagining or predicting the future accurately than anyone else is. Carr himself was a classic example of such failure.[9]

Well before Carr's vision of objectivity had been falsified by events, it had run into serious criticism not only from philosophers like Berlin but also from historians such as, most obviously, Sir Geoffrey Elton, whose political conservatism was strongly opposed to the notion of progress that underlay E. H. Carr's approach to historical objectivity. "One man's better," he remarked tartly, "is usually another man's worse." "The purpose of history," Elton declared, "is to understand the past, and if the past is to be understood it must be given full respect in its own right." The events of the past occurred, people lived and died, whether or not historians were interested in writing about them. They had an independent reality. The historian's job was to discover and analyze them through the study of the evidential traces they left behind. Establishing what happened, and when, and how, was a major part of historical research, he argued, and differences among historians over these matters often reflected the depth of the historian's knowledge of the sources rather than a contemporary standpoint or opinion. Good historians did not preselect the evidence according to their point of view. Bias and personal character came into historians' writing simply through impelling them to study one particular subject rather than another. Once they had selected their general topic or area of research, they became the servants of the sources, listening to them, and trawling as widely and as deeply as possible without asking any questions except those posed by the documents themselves.[10] Objectivity was simply a matter of reading the documents without prejudice and using them to reconstruct the past in its own terms.

Elton was surely right to demand openness to the sources, to deal fully and fairly with history's losers as well as history's winners, and to avoid the kind of distortion and suppression of evidence which would result if we all followed the prescription for objectivity laid down by Carr. But Elton's definition of historical objectivity has its problems, too. As we have seen, his own arguments were influenced at least in part by his strongly held political beliefs and his attraction for the order and strong government that had been so fatally lacking in the Central Europe of his childhood. He was deceiving himself when he supposed that good historians rejected theory and suppressed their present-day concerns when they researched the past. Historians, including Elton himself in his day, do not just listen to the evidence; they engage in a dialogue with it, actively interrogating it and bringing to bear on it theories and ideas formulated in the present. In this process of dialogue we must be conscious of the nature of our hypotheses; otherwise, if we abandon our self-consciousness and fail to develop the art of self-criticism to the extent that we imagine we are bringing none, then our prejudices and preconceptions will slip in unnoticed and skew our reading of the evidence in the way they did with Elton's reading of Thomas Cromwell's rule in early Tudor England.

If we engage in these conversations with the voices of the past speaking through the documents, will some kind of objective knowledge about the past emerge? Both Carr's and Elton's definitions of objectivity are clearly unsatisfactory as they stand. But does this mean we have to surrender to the hyperrelativism of the postmodernists and admit that in the end no kind of objective knowledge about the past, in the sense of the patterns of interconnectedness that make it history rather than chronicle, can ever be possible? The fundamental problem with this kind of extreme relativism is, as we have already seen, that it inevitably falls foul of its own principles when they are applied to itself. As Robert F. Berkhofer has remarked, "the theory and politics of poststructuralism and postmodernism demand the application of those theories and politics to themselves" and when this happens, they inevitably "undermine the grounds of poststructuralist and postmodernist theories as much as they do late modernist and structuralist ones, because they contradict themselves in application."[11] Why, after all, if all theories are equally valid, should we believe postmodernist theories of history rather than other theories? If all knowledge is relative, if it is impossible to give an accurate summary of a discourse without at the same time projecting one's own reading onto it, then why should we not give to the work of Barthes, or Derrida, or Jenkins, or Ankersmit, or White any significance that we wish to give it? At the most extreme fringes of postmodernism, indeed, an awareness of this problem leads to a self-conscious playfulness and arbitrariness of language, full of puns and metaphors, ambiguities, and different concepts linked by the postmodernist oblique stroke, so that the infinite play of significations begins within the text itself. But in practice, even the most extreme deconstructionists do not really accept that their own theories can be applied to their own work. They wish, on the contrary, to retain their own identities as authors and their own control over the interpretations to which their own texts are subject. Indeed, in their use of technical jargon, as we have seen, they lay implicit claim to the development of a scientific method of analyzing texts which they clearly believe has greater validity than other methods. None of this in practice, however, prevents anybody from applying to postmodernist writers the same concepts and methods as they apply to others. Once the intellectual gateway to total relativism has been opened, it cannot be closed again in the interests of one privileged theory or another.

Postmodernists mostly see themselves as situated on the political left. They argue that freeing history from the constricting shackles of objective fact will enable it to become more democratic, more skeptical, and more tolerant.[12] "Deconstructionist history," one postmodernist writer has observed, "openly accepts a dissenting role for the historian as someone who must challenge the established notions of authority within contemporary society by refusing to 'tidy up' the past by ascribing origins and causes with the claim to evidentially certified truth."[13] In the United States postmodernist relativism has gone together with multiculturalism, the idea that different, disadvantaged cultural groups in society have equally valid perspectives on historical truth and that these must be asserted in order to empower these groups in the face of the dominant concepts of historical truth held by the ruling white male elite. But if the only grounds we have for preferring one vision or interpretation of the past over another are aesthetic or moral or political, if the persuasiveness of a historical interpretation is simply a matter of the power of its advocates within society and within the historical profession, then it does not follow at all that history should necessarily be a democratic, a tolerant, or a skeptical enterprise or that it should in any way favor the politically or culturally disadvantaged. Some postmodernists in fact are deeply conservative in their politics and in their approach to the past. In arguing for the restoration of history as a form of moral education, for example, David Harlan attacks what he sees as the "overproduction" of studies on women's history, and regrets the negative and critical attitudes which he thinks the social scientific and radical influences of the 1960s encouraged historians to take to the American past. He devotes a whole chapter of his book to attacking historians of American Puritanism for their lack of a "sense of gratitude" to it. He laments the decline of "Western Civilization" courses and departures from the accepted "canon" of great literary and philosophical works and deplores the fact that today's historians no longer "write from within the main currents of American thought." Harlan calls for historians to concentrate once more on "what is good in American history, what they identify with completely, what is worth insisting on and saving." Postmodernist skepticism about the possibility of attaining truth in history goes together here with a deeply conservative hostility to minority points of view and an alarming desire to make history the unthinking servant of patriotism instead of encouraging critical thought about American institutions and the ways in which they might be improved.[14]

Social and political conservatism are also inherent in the postmodernist attack on "grand narratives." For the inventor of this term, Jean-François Lyotard, the fact that the historian's narrative inevitably in some sense reshaped and reworked the experience of oppression in the past made it immoral because it opened up the possibility of trivializing it. "The task of historical writing," he argued, "is not to give voice to the silence of the oppressed, which would only be to betray that silence."[15] But if the historian doesn't give voice to the silence of the dead oppressed, who will? Simply because some historians have trivialized or belittled suffering in the past does not mean that the whole enterprise of history will always and inevitably do so. Similarly, just because some of the very largest interpretative schema, such as Marxism, have been proved false, does not mean that all interpretation in history at every level is necessarily false. Not to try, for example, to analyze and explain the ideas and circumstances which caused innocent people to be prosecuted and jailed and their careers and livelihoods destroyed during the McCarthy era in postwar America would mean abdicating our responsibility to ensure that similar things did not happen again.[16] Frank Ankersmit has turned Lyotard's argument into a positive injunction. In his view, historical interpretation is impossible, and historians should therefore confine themselves to the minute study of tiny "historical scraps." If cutting historical research loose from any kind of context, abandoning the attempt to relate empirical studies to broader grand narratives, is what postmodernist theory is leading to, then we will soon have a new antiquarianism that few would be interested in pursuing and fewer still in reading.[17] Moreover, it would inevitably be politically conservative because there will be no way of learning from it. As C. Behan McCullagh has observed,

> The grand theories which Lyotard denounced might be false, but there are many generalizations about human social behaviour and about our institutions which are vital for our well-being in historically derived communities. . . . Those who would confine history to the particular would deprive us of the knowledge we need to protect and improve our communities."[18]

Acquiring this knowledge is not the only purpose of history, but it is undoubtedly one of the most vital.

Indeed, given the premises of extreme postmodernist relativism, history can with equal validity as history be not only a radical or a conservative undertaking, but a fascist or a Stalinist enterprise as well. Thus it can portray the past in terms of the struggle of different races for the survival of the fittest, or the inevitable progress toward the Stalinist utopia, as it did respectively in Germany and Russia in the 1930s, without fear of contradiction except on moral or aesthetic or political grounds. Historical controversy is here effectively reduced to moral or political debate. Does postmodernism therefore give a license to anyone who wants to suppress, distort, or cover up the past? Where do you draw the line between all this and legitimate reinterpretation?

II

THESE issues, and some even more serious, were raised in 1987, when a young Belgian scholar discovered that one of the leading post-modernists, Paul de Man, a professor at Yale University who had been born and grew up in Belgium, emigrated to the United States after the war, and died in 1983, had written some 180 articles for a Nazi-controlled newspaper in Brussels during the German occupation from 1940 to 1942. Their focus was cultural, but they included encomiums of collaborationist writers in France and—most contro-versially of all—attacks on the Jewish contribution to European cul-ture in the twentieth century, which de Man decried as mediocre and without great value. At a time when Jews were being rounded up in Belgium and deported to Auschwitz, de Man wrote an article arguing that if the Jews were deported to a Jewish colony outside Europe, European culture would suffer no great loss. After his emi-gration to the United States, de Man never mentioned this to any of his colleagues or pupils and indeed always denied any kind of col-laborationist involvement in Belgium during the war. Like the Austrian president Kurt Waldheim, he had rewritten his own past without reference to the evidence. On this basis he built a successful career in American academia and became an extremely influential literary theorist, leading the "Yale school" of literary "deconstruc-tionists" who argued for the irrelevance of authorial intentions and the multiple, indeed virtually infinite possibilities of textual interpre-tation.[19] The point of these revelations about his wartime writings was quickly grasped by deconstruction's critics. Literary criticism, for de Man, seemed to be a way of denying his own past. In his earlier, structuralist phase, he had argued that texts, as it were, wrote them-selves, thus implicitly denying authorial responsibility for them. Deconstructionism could be taken to have similar exculpatory impli-cations. As de Man wrote in his most influential work, *Allegories of Reading,*

> It is always possible to face up to any experience (to excuse any guilt) because the experience always exists simultaneously as fictional dis-course and as empirical event, and it is never possible to decide which of the two possibilities is the right one. The indecision makes it pos-sible to excuse the bleakest of crimes because, as a fiction, it escapes from the constraints of guilt and innocence.[20]

It was difficult in the light of the revelations of 1987 to see this as anything but a denial of the "empirical events" of the author's own wartime past. Still, to leap from this to a blanket condemnation of his entire output of literary theory as no more than a vehicle of person-al exculpation was going a long way. In the end the literary theories developed by de Man had to be confronted on their own terms.

Yet what was striking in the subsequent debate was the use of deconstruction by de Man's defenders to argue away not just the connection between his collaborationism and his literary theories but also the very fact of the collaboration itself. This involved the inevitable stress on the multiple possibilities of interpreting what de Man had written. De Man should not, his friends wrote, be con-demned on the basis of a single article; many other European intel-lectuals had done similar things, and de Man was being attacked only because he was a deconstructionist; and the early essays, in any case, had nothing to do with deconstructionism at all. The philosopher Richard Rorty defended de Man by arguing that his journalism was unconnected with his literary theory, just as the philosopher Heidegger's phenomenology was unrelated to his Nazi political speeches and his consistent refusal to condemn Hitler after the war. The death of the author and the independent life of each of his texts were used here to counter what Rorty called the condemnation of deconstruction "on the basis of the young Paul de Man's opportunistic antisemitism."[21] Moreover, other defenders of de Man argued that the attacks on him were no more than "a reaction to the genuine threat posed by de Man's work and by that of the so-called deconstructionists generally to a powerful tradition of ideological assumptions about literature, about history, and about the relation of literature to human life."[22] At the same time, de Man's defenders did not hesitate to make liberal use of the rhetoric of factual objectivity, and more than one of them made the explicit claim to "set the record straight" about the literary theorist's wartime past, condemning in the process the "misreadings, distortions, and selective slanting of quotations" which they believed had been employed by many of de Man's critics.[23]

For his part, Jacques Derrida argued that de Man's critique of "vulgar antisemitism" in his early articles, his insistence that the Jews were mediocrities rather than dangerous and potent racial pollutants, was tantamount to a condemnation of antisemitism itself, because antisemitism was "always and essentially vulgar." Thus, as others of his defenders among the deconstructionists argued, de Man was basically engaging in an act of resistance to Nazism when he wrote the article in question. Derrida accused de Man's critics of being Nazis themselves: "To judge, to condemn the work or the man on the basis of what was a brief episode, to call for closing, that is to say, at least figuratively, for censoring or burning his books, is to reproduce the exterminating gesture which de Man is accused of not having armed himself against sooner with the necessary vigilance." He accused de Man's academic critics of "collaborating" with the mass media in an outburst of journalistic hysteria and vulgarity. Derrida suggested that only deconstructionists were properly equipped to understand de Man's writings, and called his critics "confused, hurried, and rancorous professor-journalists," whose work was a heap of muck destined for the intellectual compost heap, and whose views were "dishonest," "obscene," "venomous," "uneducated," "indecent," "grotesque," and "laughable."[24]

Like much postmodernist writing, the defense of de Man by the deconstructionists was riddled with contradictions. On the one hand, Derrida and his supporters insisted theoretically on the infinite possibilities of textual interpretation; on the other, they argued in practice that to interpret de Man's early writings as collaborationist or antisemitic was just plain wrong. On the one hand, the author himself theoretically had no control over the meaning of what he wrote; on the other, Derrida denounced in the most polemical terms those he thought were willfully misunderstanding what he said in de Man's defense. On the one hand, everything, including antisemitism, was a text, and all texts were theoretically subject to the infinite play of significations; on the other, Derrida described antisemitism as "essentially vulgar." On the one hand, it was wrong to prioritize elite culture over popular culture, one kind of text over another; on the other, de Man's defenders bitterly resented the involvement of journalists in the debate and clearly loathed its escape from the elitist discourse of academia. Postmodernists seemed to want to have their cake and eat it. Behind postmodernism's claim, symbolized in its heavy use of jargon and specialized language, to be scientific, there is in the end a desire to prioritize a particular way of reading texts that runs completely counter to its own postulate of the essential arbitrariness and openness of textuality.

To equate criticism of a literary theorist with Nazi exterminism was an act of rhetorical hyperbole that went far beyond anything warranted by the evidence. It was, after all, de Man himself who had "censored" and figuratively "burned" his own early work. It was not the case that as Derrida argued, the circumstances in which de Man had written his articles "remain unclear to us." They were easily ascertainable. Nor did the dispute turn on a single article or passage, but on a very large collection of texts, written over two whole years, as well as, crucially, on the way de Man had suppressed all mention of them for decades after the war. To read them as an act of resistance to Nazism was completely implausible. If they had been intended as such, why did de Man suppress them? Most significant of all, perhaps, here was an example of new documents coming to light which materially altered people's perceptions of the past, irrespective of the views they held in the present. As Alan B. Spitzer has commented in his careful dissection of the controversy, "at a time when there has been considerable emphasis on the way historical writing 'constructs' the past, we have an example of the transformation of the present by the unanticipated evidence of past events."[25] The result was, as another historian commented: "Although deconstruction should survive the attack of de Man's critics, as a tool for historians it may not survive de Man's defense."[26] The real issue in the debate, still another commentator noted, was "not what 'resistance to theory' the attack on de Man evinces but what 'resistance to history' the defense of de Man entails."[27] Even Dominick LaCapra concluded that the debate indicated how "deconstruction can be used to justify or rewrite anything."[28] In the end, as Spitzer concluded, the real message of the debate was how both sides, including the postmodernists, appealed to common standards of factuality and evidence and occupied common ground over which they fought, the ground of what inferences or interpretations it was appropriate to derive from a set of documents. "The people who are indignant over what they take to be misrepresentations of de Man's past are not simply choosing one set of rhetorical conventions over another; they are saying what they think is true and doing what they think is right."[29]

III

EXTREME relativism leaves the door wide open, as Christopher Norris has warned, to far-right historians to create "a massively falsified consensus, brought about by the misreading or manipulative use of evidence, the suppression of crucial facts and the creation of a certain selective amnesia in those whose memory might otherwise go far back."[30] To be sure, because White accepts the possibility of proving historical truth at the level of the individual fact, he denies the validity of revisionist attempts to argue away Auschwitz as if it had never happened.[31] But in his view, this is below the real level of history as such, and here his approach makes it impossible for him (or anyone else, if he or she accepts it) to say that a Nazi or fascist interpretation of Hitler's "final solution" which accepted that it actually happened could be any less valid than any other interpretation. Total relativism provides objective criteria by which fascist or racist views of history can be falsified. Thus "Holocaust denial" literature, which declares that six million Jews were never murdered by the Nazis and that Auschwitz and similar extermination camps are fabrications of a postwar, anti-German, pro-Jewish political lobby, has been given respectability above all in the United States—in Germany it is illegal— by a widespread belief that "both sides of the picture should be heard," or in other words, that both have at least in principle equal validity. A leading authority on this literature, Professor Deborah E. Lipstadt of Emory University, Atlanta, Georgia, consistently refuses to take part in public debates with the deniers on the ground that "to do so would give them a legitimacy and a stature they in no way deserve. It would elevate their antisemitic ideology—which is what Holocaust denial is—to the level of responsible historiography—which it is not."[32] She reported that radio and television producers repeatedly registered their amazement at her stance, asking her every time why she did not think that their listeners or viewers should hear "both sides of the story." A similar attitude was evident on a number of campuses where there had been controversy about the activities of deniers. A commitment to freedom of speech enshrined in the Constitution of the United States led a number of universities protecting the right of "revisionists" to speak on their premises, but of course the First Amendment covers only the right of the government, not that of independent institutions like universities, to censor free speech. More serious, and more relevant, was the conviction of many that, as one campus newspaper put it, "Revisionists are ... reinterpreting history, a practice that occurs constantly, especially on a college campus."[33]

The History Department at the university where this claim was made in an advertisement in a campus newspaper unanimously rejected this argument. It noted:

That historians are constantly engaged in historical revision is certainly correct; however, what historians do is very different from this
advertisement. Historical revision of major events is not concerned
with the actuality of these events; rather it concerns their historical
interpretation—their causes and consequences generally.[34]

The Holocaust "revisionists" *appeared* to be scholarly, with an
"Institute for Historical Review" devoted to their activities, a journal with fully footnoted articles and many other adornments of academic style. In fact, they were not scholarly, although their style evidently deceived a number of campus newspaper editors into believing that they were. The issue, as Lipstadt puts it, is between prejudice
and propaganda, on the one hand, and rational arguments and scholarship, on the other. Students at one midwestern university, where a
history instructor was dismissed for arguing that the Nazi death
camps were an anti-German hoax (an argument he put forward, with
a dubious sense of relevance, during a class on the Napoleonic Wars),
protested that he had been unfairly treated and that his dismissal vio-
lated a basic principle of free speech. "These students," Lipstadt notes,
"seemed not to grasp that a teacher has a responsibility to maintain
some fidelity to the notion of truth."[35]

The increase in scope and intensity of the Holocaust deniers'
activities since the mid-1970s has among other things reflected the
postmodernist intellectual climate, above all in the United States, in
which scholars have increasingly denied that texts had any fixed
meaning, and have argued instead that meaning is supplied by the
reader, and in which attacks on the Western rationalist tradition have
become fashionable. Coupled with the denial that the notion of
truth has any validity at all, this has, in Lipstadt's view, "created an
atmosphere of permissiveness toward questioning the meaning of
historical events" and made it difficult "to assert that there was anything 'off limits.' ... A sentiment had been generated in society—not
just on campus—that made it difficult to say: 'This has nothing to do
with ideas. This is bigotry.' "This sentiment, argues Lipstadt, "fosters
deconstructionist history at its worst. No fact, no event, and no
aspect of history has any fixed meaning or content. Any truth can be

retold. Any fact can be recast. There is no ultimate historical reality." And, she warns,

> Holocaust denial is part of this phenomenon. It is not an assault on the history of one particular group. Though denial of the Holocaust may be an attack on the history of the annihilation of the Jews, at its core it poses a threat to all who believe that knowledge and memory are among the keystones of our civilization . . . [and] to all who believe in the ultimate power of reason.[36]

That this threat is real has been shown by the postmodernist historian Diane Purkiss, who has argued that "most neo-Nazi historians adopt the most conservative possible protocols of discovery, revelation and truth-telling" in their denial of the existence of the death camps. Their use of the scholarly apparatus of footnotes and references, and their insistence that they are telling the objective truth, demonstrate, in Purkiss's view, the "dire consequences" of such a scholarly apparatus, the bankruptcy of such a belief in objectivity and truth. But the point is, of course, that the pseudoscholarship of the Holocaust deniers is easily unmasked as a sham. If footnotes really were nothing more than a rhetorical device designed solely to produce a spurious "reality effect," then we really would not be able to tell the difference between genuine scholarship and pseudoscholarship. But they are not. Relativism and "the indeterminacy of truth" do not effectively undermine "the self-proclaimed certitude of deniers," as Purkiss claims; they simply put it on a par with real histories of Auschwitz, and support the claim (which Purkiss endorses) that we can never know the objective truth about either. Purkiss's solution is to tell stories about Auschwitz and not worry too much about whether or not they are based in fact. It certainly is the case that the stories told by Holocaust survivors, as Purkiss says, are "moving," but does it really not matter whether or not they are true?[37]

In the end, as this suggests, it trivializes Nazism and the Third Reich, as the German history specialist Jane Caplan has argued, to discuss them in terms of "theories that appear to discount rationality as a mode of explanation, that resist the claims of truth, relativize and disseminate power, cannot assign responsibility clearly, and do not privilege [one] truth or morality over [multiple] interpretation." She goes on:

> It is one thing to embrace poststructuralism and postmodernism, to disseminate power, to decenter subjects, and all in all let a hundred kinds of meaning contend, when *Bleak House* or philology or even the archaeology of knowledge are the issue. But should the rules of contention be different when it is a question, not simply of History, but of a recent history of lives, deaths, and suffering, and the concept of a justice that seeks to draw some meaningful relation between these?[38]

Like other new approaches to history, therefore, postmodernist theory would seem to be more applicable to some areas of history than to others. A recognition of this likelihood is the first step in the direction of harnessing its more positive ideas to the research and writing of history in the twenty-first century.

IV

"POSTMODERN history," a group of its critics has complained, "too often seems to consist of denunciations of history as it has been known rather than of new histories for present and hence future time."[39] The very nature of extreme postmodernism makes it difficult for anyone who subscribes to its doctrines to write history at all.[40] But there are plenty of real historical works in which the influence of postmodernist theory, to put it no more strongly, is clearly evident. Postmodernism comes in many guises. If some postmodernists, as we have seen, embrace an extreme skepticism which denies the possibility of historical knowledge altogether, others adopt a more moderate position in which the writing of history is still at least a possibility.[41] Here it has opened up possibilities of self-renewal for the historical discipline, suggesting a way out of the impasse into which social determinism, above all in its Marxist variants, had run by the beginning of the 1990s. That is not to say that postmodernist history is necessarily always as novel as it frequently takes itself to be, but it has both extended the range of historical writing and breathed new life into some old and rather tired subjects like the history of royalty and the elites, or the study of "big names" in the history of ideas. Historical writing on that great and problematic phenomenon of the nineteenth and twentieth centuries, nationalism, for example, can only benefit from a shift of focus from the social bases of nationalist movements to the sources and determinants of changing senses and meanings of national identity. A concern with gender and ethnicity, as aspects of social inequality which depend as least as much on discursive constructions of identity as they do on real and identifiable physical characteristics, can only enrich a social history impoverished by a restrictive concentration on class.

Postmodernist history, as one might expect, has rejected the faith in reason and progress which was so central to modernist historiography, and much of its attention has been directed toward the irrational in history, the extraordinary, the transgressive, and the magical. It has often thrown over the real for the symbolic. In refusing to prioritize one aspect of history over others, or to construct a central grand narrative and relegate everything else to the margins, it has also in many cases turned to subjects historians had previously thought trivial or without significance. It has frequently followed the belief that the most interesting animals and plants are to be found on the verges and ditches by the roadside, not on the highway itself. What, then, does the best postmodernist history look like? What are its advantages and its disadvantages?

One thing the postmodernist treatment of history as a form of literature has done is to reinstate good writing as legitimate historical practice. In place of the rebarbative social science jargon of the 1970s we can now turn to brilliantly written narratives such as Simon Schama's *Citizens*[42] or Orlando Figes's *A People's Tragedy*.[43] Both these books tackle big, "traditional" subjects, but both interweave small incidents and personal histories, of the famous and the obscure, into the broader narrative, with a constantly shifting focus which is a world away from the smooth factual recounting of more old-fashioned treatments of these themes. Neither pretends to be definitive, and by including detailed subplots and biographies whose selection is self-confessedly personal and—though illustrative of larger points—arbitrary, both implicitly admit that the same story could be told in other, equally valid ways. Both have an argument, in Schama's case heavily concealed beneath the surface detail; both emphasize, perhaps overemphasize, the bloody and violent nature of revolution. In *Citizens*, indeed, the French Revolution of 1789–94 becomes almost meaningless in the larger sense and is reduced to a kind of theater of the absurd; the social and economic misery of the masses, an essential driving force behind their involvement in the revolutionary events, is barely mentioned; and the lasting significance of the Revolution's many political theories and doctrines for modern European and world history more or less disappears. Both make utterly compelling reading, in which a major effort has gone into structuring the narrative and rather less into building an interpretation. Neither embodies the explicit use of poststructuralist theory, but it is surely legitimate to argue that it is the postmodernist climate of opinion among historians that has made possible such new approaches to big historical subjects as these.

At the opposite extreme in terms of scale of events are Natalie Zemon Davis's *The Return of Martin Guerre* and Robert Darnton's *The Great Cat Massacre*. These two are compellingly told narratives, but they build on the obscure and the unknown rather than on the great and the famous. Both books take very small incidents of everyday life and retell them as stories, analyzing them as metaphorical and symbolic clues to larger things. In doing so, they bring the reader into contact with the fabric and feel of everyday life in a distant and remote mental and physical world, in a manner which the generalizing social historical projects of the 1970s were quite incapable of doing. Both, however, have been sharply criticized by historians for their allegedly cavalier handling of the evidence, and it is possible that here the influence of postmodernist theory has played a somewhat questionable role.

Davis confesses in the preface to her book that "what I offer you is in part my invention." She wants to make room in the story, she says, for "perhapses" and "may-have-beens." The documents on which she bases her work tell the story of an impostor who fooled an innocent woman into believing that he was her husband, Martin Guerre, returning from the wars. The deception was revealed only when the real Martin Guerre turned up, and even so, the wife still defended the impostor at his subsequent trial. Davis reworks this into a narrative of a clever and sensual woman who colluded with the impostor when he was hauled up before the courts on the return of her real husband, because he was better in bed than the inadequate wretch who was the genuine Martin Guerre. In doing this, however, Davis, according to her critics, is indulging in pure speculation. There is nothing in the documents to support any of the major aspects of her reading of the story, not the alleged inadequacy of the real Martin Guerre, not the cleverness and sensuality of the wife, not the supposed virtues of the impostor. Davis's most severe critic, Robert Finlay, commented that

> Speculation, whether founded on intuition or on concepts drawn from anthropology and literary criticism, is supposed to give way before the sovereignty of the sources, the tribunal of the documents. The historian should not make the people of the past say or do things that run counter to the most scrupulous respect for the sources.[44]

On the other hand, Davis countered that her portrayal of Martin Guerre's wife, though not directly based on sources about her or documents from the case itself, was legitimated by everything that we knew about peasant women in that part of France at the time, who appear uniformly in other sources as shrewd, active, and enterprising. Indeed, indirect and inferential procedures such as these are frequently employed even in the most traditional kinds of history, where the direct source material is inadequate. The question of whether Davis was justified in her interpretation or whether, as Finlay implied, she was reading into the case of Martin Guerre her present-day feminist belief in the strength and ingenuity of women must remain open. In the end the element of doubt, and the critical reading it encourages, add to the book's importance and appeal rather than detract from it.

Robert Darnton, for his part, bases his entire narrative of the "great cat massacre" on a three-page pamphlet written in 1762, some thirty years after the incident it purported to describe. There is no other evidence to show that the apprentices whom he discusses ever massacred any cats at all. Still is there any justification for arguing, as Darnton does—and this is the central point of his argument—that the cat massacre was a symbolic prefiguration of the great massacres of the French Revolution, another thirty years on, in the 1790s. The symbolism of the cat massacre, if it ever happened, was directed at master artisans, not at the aristocrats or rural seigneurs who were the objects of popular fury in the Revolution, and in any case, the author of the account of 1762 wrote it partly to reassure the authorities that apprentices took out their fury on their employers symbolically rather than through the exercise of real violence. Darnton's essay on the cat massacre does not stand up to even the most cursory scrutiny on Rankean principles, according to his critics. It reveals itself to be a tissue of speculation from start to finish. Yet this is taking too austere a view. We need to understand the violence which accompanied and drove on the French Revolution of 1789, and Darnton's narrative helps us do just that. Full of fascinating detail, it follows the model of "thick description" pioneered by the anthropologist Clifford Geertz, with whom Darnton has taught at Princeton, and demonstrates many of the strengths of interweaving interpretation into the detail of a narrative.[45]

Postmodernism in its more constructive modes has encouraged historians to look more closely at documents, to take their surface patina more seriously, and to think about texts and narratives in new ways. It has been particularly influential among American historians of culture and ideas in early modern and, more recently, modern Britain, France, and Italy, and perhaps less so among the mainstream of writers and researchers on American history or on modern German history. It has had some influence on historians of Australia and the South Pacific, and produced major, if controversial, works such as Greg Dening's *Mr. Bligh's Bad Language*, a study of the mutiny on the *Bounty*, subject of a number of Hollywood films, which concentrates, as the title implies, on language and culture as keys to understanding the episode.[46] It has been particularly helpful in reorienting historical approaches to seemingly irrational phenomena, such as witchcraft and witchcraft accusations. It is instructive, for example, to contrast a social historical approach to this subject, like Paul Boyer and Stephen Nissenbaum's *Salem Possessed*, with a poststructuralist work, like Stuart Clark's *Thinking with Demons*. *Salem Possessed*, published in 1974, more or less ignored the content of the accusations brought against the alleged witches of Salem, Massachusetts, and treated them instead as tools used by various factions and families in the village in resolving long-term quarrels over more tangible things, such as power and land. *Thinking with Demons*, published in 1997, by contrast, dismisses the question of the rationality or otherwise of witchcraft beliefs in relation to the *reality* or otherwise of witchcraft as a phenomenon as an irrelevant question because it is ultimately an unanswerable one. Instead it concentrates on relating the language and concepts of witchcraft beliefs to the language and concepts used by those who held these beliefs when they wrote or talked about other things, such as religion or science. Although it is based on a self-contradiction (if you can't determine how witchcraft accusations related to behavioral reality, can you really determine how they related to linguistic reality?), this delivers a fruitful approach which results in a major remapping of early modern thought on a number of levels. In the end, both accounts are surely complementary rather than contradictory, however much their respective authors might like to think otherwise.[47]

Historians influenced by postmodernism have sometimes self-consciously departed from the historian's customary narrative technique of telling everything with a single voice and experimented with multiple voices. Thus David Farber, in his account of the street violence and other events which accompanied the Democratic National Convention in Chicago in 1968, uses different typefaces to accentuate the fact that he is presenting different narratives of the same events from different points of view: the radical Yippies, the anti–Vietnam War movement, and the police and city authorities. Only in the last sections of the book does he revert to the historian's voice and analyze these narratives by linking them to other contexts of which the participants in them may not have been aware. A "polyvocal" technique which some have advocated as the only possible way of presenting a truly multicultural history thus gives way in the end to a more conventional technique in which the voice of the historical narrator dominates, and rightly so, since in the end to abdicate the historian's responsibility to assess the issues at hand in the light of the wider perspectives provided by the passage of time would be irresponsible, and in any case, the very process of reconstructing the points of view of the participants demands an input from the historian which the more extreme postmodernists would claim ultimately, and inevitably, takes the dominant role. The difficulties of writing a truly multicultural history should not be underestimated, yet an awareness of different perspectives on the past will surely lead to new and challenging experiments in historical writing, and this can only be welcomed.[48]

Postmodernism in its more moderate guises has thus helped open up many new subjects and areas for research, while putting back on the agenda many topics which had previously seemed to be exhausted. It has forced historians to interrogate their own methods and procedures as never before, and in the process has made them more self-critical and self-reflexive, which is all to the good.[49] It has led to a greater emphasis on open acknowledgment of the historian's own subjectivity, which can only help the reader engaged in a critical assessment of historical work. It has shifted the emphasis in historical writing—though not in writing about history as a discipline—back from social-scientific to literary models and, in so doing, has begun to make it more accessible to the public outside the universities (and indeed to students within them). It has restored individual human beings to history, where social science approaches had more or less written them out. It has also inspired, or at least informed, many outstanding historical works in the last decade or more, works which have been none the worse for continuing in other respects to conform to many of the traditional canons of scholarship which postmodernism in its more radical moments affects to despise.

V

SIR Geoffrey Elton remarked acidly that to the "disciples of total relativism history matters only insofar as it contributes to their own lives, thoughts and experiences. . . . To me, I fear," he added, "this is the ultimate heresy. For the historian is in the first place concerned with the people of the past—with *their* experiences, thoughts and actions—and not with the people of the present, least of all with himself."[50] We rake over the ashes of the past, and only with difficulty can we make out what they once were; only now and then can we stir them into a flicker of life. Yet we should not despair at the difficulty of the goals we have set ourselves. Everyone, even the most diehard deconstructionist, concedes in practice that there is extratextual reality. History is an empirical discipline, and it is concerned with the content of knowledge rather than its nature. Through the sources we use, and the methods with which we handle them, we can, if we are very careful and thorough, approach to a reconstruction of past reality that may be partial and provisional, and certainly will not be totally neutral, but is nevertheless true. We know of course that we will be guided in selecting materials for the stories we tell, and in the way we put these materials together and interpret them, by literary models, by social science theories, by moral and political beliefs, by an aesthetic sense, even by our own unconscious assumptions and desires. It is an illusion to believe otherwise. But the stories we tell will be true stories, even if the truth they tell is our own, and even if other people can and will tell them differently, for the fact that no description of anything can be wholly independent of its author's point of view does not mean that no description of anything can be true.[51] Anyone who thinks that the truth about the past does not matter has not perhaps lived under a regime, like that of the Soviet or Eastern bloc Communists, where it is systematically distorted and suppressed. The feeling of liberation, the excitement, the consciousness that justice was at last being done to the victims of Stalin was palpable among Russian historians in the process of opening up begun by Mikhail Gorbachev.[52] It stood in an exaggerated way for the feelings all his-

torians have when beginning their journey into the past. For as G.
M. Trevelyan once wrote:

> The appeal of history to us all is in the last analysis poetic. But the
> poetry of history does not consist of imagination roaming at large,
> but of imagination pursuing the fact and fastening upon it. That
> which compels the historian to "scorn delights and live laborious
> days" is the ardour of his own curiosity to know what really hap-
> pened long ago in that land of mystery which we call the past. To
> peer into that magic mirror and see fresh figures there every day is
> a burning desire that consumes and satisfies him all his life, that car-
> ries him each morning, eager as a lover, to the library and the muni-
> ment room. It haunts him like a passion of terrible potency, because
> it is poetic. The dead were and are not. Their place knows them no
> more, and is ours today. Yet they were once as real as we, and we shall
> tomorrow be shadows like them. . . . The poetry of history lies in
> the quasi-miraculous fact that once, on this earth, once, on this
> familiar spot of ground, walked other men and women, as actual as
> we are today, thinking their own thoughts, swayed by their own pas-
> sions, but now all gone, one generation vanishing into another, gone
> as utterly as we ourselves shall shortly be gone, like ghosts at cock-
> crow.[53]

For a long time Trevelyan's views have seemed deeply unfashionable
and out-of-date. Yet an ironic consequence of the postmodernist
incursion into history is to make their emphasis on poetry and imagination seem contemporary once more.

The whole idea of objectivity, concludes Peter Novick in the
introduction to several hundred pages of his own writing on the subject, is "essentially confused."[54] Yet the book to which he prefaces this
remark is objective enough in most normal senses of the word. It
does not willfully distort or manipulate the evidence. It presents the
positions adopted by historians on their professional activities fully
and fairly. This does not mean that it has no argument or point of
view; far from it. But as Thomas L. Haskell has pointed out, it is
important not to confuse objectivity with neutrality, indifference, or
lack of passion, as Novick himself appears to do. The pursuit of history, Haskell argues,

requires of its practitioners that vital minimum of ascetic self-discipline that enables a person to do such things as abandon wishful thinking, assimilate bad news, discard pleasing interpretations that cannot pass elementary tests of evidence and logic, and, most important of all, suspend or bracket one's own perceptions long enough to enter sympathetically into the alien and possibly repugnant perspectives of rival thinkers.

All this needs "detachment," the ability not to put oneself at the center of a view of the world, as the most narcissistic of the postmodernists do, but to develop what Haskell calls "a view of the world in which one's own self . . . appears merely as one object among many." Otherwise, for example, how would we be able to understand phenomena like Nazism or individuals like Stalin and Pol Pot?

None of this means that historical judgment has to be neutral. But it does mean that the historian has to develop a detached mode of cognition, a faculty of self-criticism, and an ability to understand another person's point of view. This applies as much to politically committed history as it does to a history that believes itself to be politically neutral. Politically committed history only damages itself if it distorts, manipulates, or obscures historical fact in the interests of the cause it claims to represent.[55] When a postmodernist writer triumphantly proclaims that "objectivity, that dull-witted monarch who despotically ruled the discipline of history since the late nineteenth century, lies dethroned," the obvious retort is that there is nothing at all dull-witted about the notion of objectivity and its application. On the contrary it is far more difficult to apply the notion of objectivity in one's own historical work than it is simply to follow one's own prejudices and preferences.[56]

As Novick defines it, the idea of objectivity involves a belief in "the reality of the past, and to the truth as correspondence to that reality."[57] The truth about patterns and linkages of facts in history is in the end discovered, not invented, found, not made, though, as Haskell adds, "not without a process of imaginative construction that goes so far beyond the intrinsic properties of the raw materials employed that one can speak of their being 'made' as well"[58] Making such patterns and linkages, causal and otherwise, is by no means the only function of history, which also has a duty to establish the facts and re-create the past in the present, but it is in the end what distinguishes it from chronicle. Trevelyan was both right to point to the importance of the historical imagination in this process and to insist on the strict limits within which that imagination is bound. Objective history in the last analysis is history that is researched and written within the limits placed on the historical imagination by the facts of history and the sources which reveal them, and bound by the historian's desire to produce a true, fair, and adequate account of the subject under consideration.[59]

It is right and proper that postmodernist theorists and critics should force historians to rethink the categories and assumptions with which they work and to justify the manner in which they practice their discipline. But postmodernism is itself one theory, one approach among many, and as contestable as all the rest. For my own part, I remain optimistic that objective historical knowledge is both desirable and attainable. So when Patrick Joyce tells us that social history is dead, and Elizabeth Deeds Ermarth declares that time is a fictional construct, and Roland Barthes announces that all the world's a text, and Frank Ankersmit swears that we can never know anything at all about the past so we might as well confine ourselves to studying other historians, and Keith Jenkins proclaims that all history is just naked ideology designed to get historians power and money in big university institutions run by the bourgeoisie, I will look humbly at the past and say, despite them all: It really happened, and we really can, if we are very scrupulous and careful and self-critical, find out how it did and reach some tenable conclusions about what it all meant.

NOTES

INTRODUCTION

1. Keith Jenkins, *On "What Is History?": From Carr and Elton to Rorty and White* (London, 1995), pp. 2–3.

2. John Tosh, for example, in a widely used history primer, still thought in 1991 that the controversy between Carr and Elton was "the best starting point for the debate about the standing of historical knowledge" (John Tosh, *The Pursuit of History* [London, 1991], p. 236). Carr's book was quickly translated into other languages and went through many reprintings.

3. Dominick LaCapra, *History and Criticism* (Ithaca, 1985), p. 136. However, LaCapra goes on to contradict himself by saying that most introductory history courses in universities end up by providing students with a "more or less pragmatic and eclectic 'synthesis' of the two works" and indeed agrees implicitly with this by saying that "extreme documentary objectivism and relativistic subjectivism do not constitute genuine alternatives" (ibid., p. 137).

4. Jenkins, *On "What Is History?"* pp. 87–88. Arthur Marwick, *The Nature of History,* 3d ed. (London, 1989), p. 412, also describes G. R. Elton's *The Practice of History* (London, 1967), as a "clear statement of the mainstream professional position."

5. Alan Munslow, *Deconstructing History* (London, 1997), p. 46. However, at other places in the same book, Munslow seems to forget this observation and declares that virtually all historians believe in "moral detachment, disinterestedness, objectivity, authenticity . . . and . . . allowing the sources to speak for themselves" (p. 16), or in other words, the Eltonian ideal of "disinterested interpretations" of a "truthful past" (p. 59).

6. Some postmodernists have attempted to preempt criticism of their positions by denying that there is such a thing as postmodernism ("I for one have no idea what a post-modern position would look like," as one of them put it) or to label the term "largely unhelpful" because it conflates the views of a number of very different contemporary thinkers. But as others have pointed out, the fact that this label covers a variety of sometimes contradictory and conflicting ideas invites critical investigation rather than silent acceptance of such ideas. Postmodernism is a convenient label; it is not an organized movement, nor does it amount to a coherent ideology, and remarks in the present work about postmodernism should not be taken as generalizations applying to every variant and every practitioner. Another common term, poststructuralism, may be taken as a narrower term denoting certain methods of reading texts. For these claims and counterclaims, see James Vernon, "Who's afraid of the 'linguistic turn'? The politics of social history and its discontents," *Social History*, vol. 19 (1994), pp. 81–97, here pp. 96–97; and Neville Kirk, "History, language, ideas and post-modernism: a materialist view," *Social History*, vol. 20 (1995), pp. 222–40, here p. 222. For a useful survey, see David Harvey, *The Condition of Postmodernism: An Enquiry into the Origins of Cultural Change* (Oxford, 1991).

7. Roger Chartier, *On the Edge of the Cliff: History, Language and Practices* (Baltimore, 1997), p. 13.

8. David Harlan, "Intellectual History and the Return of Literature," *American Historical Review*, vol. 94 (1989), pp. 581–609, here p. 581.

9. Joyce Appleby, Lynn Hunt, and Margaret Jacob, *Telling the Truth about History* (New York, 1995), p. 1. See also Harvey J. Kaye, *The Powers of the Past: Reflections on the Crisis and the Promise of History* (Minneapolis, 1991).

10. Gabrielle Spiegel, "History and Post-Modernism," *Past and Present*, 135 (May 1992), pp. 194–208, here p. 195, referring to Nancy Partner, "Making Up Lost Time: Writing on the Writing of History," *Speculum*, vol. lxi (1986), p. 95.

11. Lawrence Stone, "History and Post-Modernism," *Past and Present*, 131 (1991), pp. 217–18.

12. See the diagnosis in Robert F. Berkhofer, Jr., *Beyond the Great Story: History as Text and Discourse* (Cambridge, Mass., 1995), p. 25.

13. Beverley Southgate, *History: What and Why? Ancient, Modern and Postmodern Perspectives* (London, 1996), p. 71. See also Munslow, *Deconstructing History*.

14. Diane Purkiss, *The Witch in History: Early Modern and Twentieth-Century Representations* (London, 1996), p. 69.

15. Keith Windschuttle, *The Killing of History: How a Discipline Is Being Murdered by Literary Critics and Social Theorists* (Paddington, New South Wales, 1994), p. 119.

16. David Harlan, *The Degradation of American History* (Chicago, 1997), p. xx.

17. Allan Megill, "Recounting the Past: 'Description,' Explanation, and Narrative in Historiography," *American Historical Review*, vol. 94 (1989), pp. 627–53, here p. 631.

18. Nancy F. Partner, "Historicity in an Age of Reality-Fictions," in Frank Ankersmit and Hans Kellner (eds.), *A New Philosophy of History* (London, 1995), pp. 21–39, here p. 22.

19. Vernon, "Who's afraid of the 'linguistic turn'?" p. 81.

20. Patrick Joyce, "History and Post-Modernism," *Past and Present,* 133 (November 1991), pp. 204–09, here pp. 204–05.

21. Idem, "The imaginary discontents of social history: a note of response to Mayfield and Thorne, and Lawrence and Taylor," *Social History*, vol. 18 (1993), pp. 81–85, here p. 83; a charge repeated in idem, "The end of social history?" *Social History*, vol. 20 (1995), pp. 73–91, here p. 73.

22. Idem, "The end of social history?" pp. 80–81.

23. David Mayfield and Susan Thorne, "Reply to 'The poverty of protest' and 'The imaginary discontents,'" *Social History*, vol. 18 (1993), pp. 219–33, here p. 221.

24. Geoff Eley and Keith Nield, "Starting over: the present, the post-modern and the moment of social history," *Social History*, vol. 20 (1995), pp. 355–64, here p. 364.

25. G. R. Elton, *Return to Essentials: Some Reflections on the Present State of Historical Study* (Cambridge, U.K., 1991), pp. 27, 34, 41, 43, 49.

26. Stone, "History and Post-Modernism," pp. 217–18.

27. Raphael Samuel, "Reading the Signs II," *History Workshop Journal,* 33 (1992), pp. 220–51, here pp. 220–21.

28. Arthur Marwick, "Two Approaches to Historical Study: The Metaphysical (Including 'Postmodernism') and the Historical," *Journal of Contemporary History*, vol. 30 (1995), pp. 5–35, here p. 5.

29. Ibid., p. 29.

30. Ellen Somekawa and Elizabeth A. Smith, "Theorizing the writing of history, or, 'I can't think why it should be so dull, for a great deal of it must be invention,'" *Journal of Social History*, vol. 22 (1988), pp. 149–61, here p. 150.

31. F. R. Ankersmit, "Historiography and Postmodernism," *History and Theory*, vol. 28 (1989), pp. 137–53, here p. 149.

32. Jenkins, *On "What Is History?"* p. 35. For a more wide-ranging account of

the postmodernist critique of history, see Pauline Marie Rosenau, *Post-Modernism and the Social Sciences: Insights, Inroads, and Intrusions* (Princeton, 1992), pp. 62–76.

33. Joyce, "The end of social history?" p. 73. He also says the same for sociology (ibid., p. 83). Add the Foucauldian critique of classificatory systems, such as psychology, psychiatry, demography, statistics, economics, and criminology, and there is not much left of contemporary systems of knowledge outside the natural sciences.

34. Eley and Nield, "Starting over," p. 364.

35. C. Behan McCullagh, *The Truth of History* (London, 1998), p. 4.

36. Appleby, Hunt, and Jacob, *Telling the Truth*, p. 9.

37. Christopher Lloyd, "For Realism and against the Inadequacies of Common Sense: A Response to Arthur Marwick," *Journal of Contemporary History*, vol. 31 (1996), pp. 191–207, here p. 192.

38. Theodore Zeldin, "Social History and Total History," *Journal of Social History*, vol. 10 (1976), pp. 237–45, here p. 237.

39. Norman Stone, "Grim Eminence," *London Review of Books* (January 20,1982), pp. 9–12.

40. For some considerations on this question, see J. H. Hexter, *Doing History* (London, 1971), pp. 67–71.

41. Ronald F. Atkinson, *Knowledge and Explanation in History: An Introduction to the Philosophy of History* (London, 1978), p. 8.

42. Elton, *Return*, p. 34.

43. Quoted in J. H. Hexter, *On Historians: Reappraisals of Some of the Makers of Modern History* (London, 1979), p. 145.

44. Hayden White, "Response to Arthur Marwick," *Journal of Contemporary History*, vol. 30 (1995), pp. 233–46, here p. 245.

45. Raymond Martin, "Objectivity and Meaning in Historical Studies: Toward a Post-Analytic View," *History and Theory*, vol. 32 (1993), pp. 25–50, here p. 31.

46. Robert William Fogel and G. R. Elton, *Which Road to the Past? Two Views of History* (London, 1983), p. 2.

47. Appleby, Hunt, and Jacob, *Telling the Truth*, p. 9.

48. Perez Zagorin, "Historiography and Postmodernism: Reconsiderations," *History and Theory*, vol. 29 (1990), pp. 263–74, here p. 264.

49. Joyce, "The imaginary discontents," p. 84.

50. Jenkins, *On "What Is History?"* p. 6.

51. Ibid., p. 92.

CHAPTER ONE: THE HISTORY OF HISTORY

1. For an elaboration of these brief introductory remarks, see Ernst Breisach, *Historiography: Ancient, Medieval and Modern,* 2d ed. (London, 1994). The quotation, often attributed to the eighteenth-century English philosopher Bolingbroke, in fact originated with the ancient rhetorician Dionysius of Halicarnassus (*Oxford Dictionary of Quotations,* 3d ed. [Oxford, 1979], p. 184).

2. Fritz Stern (ed.), *The Varieties of History: From Voltaire to the Present* (Cleveland, 1956), p. 57.

3. Peter Novick, *That Noble Dream: The "Objectivity Question" and the American Historical Profession* (Cambridge, U.K., 1988), pp. 27–29; Leopold von Ranke, *The Secret of World History: Selected Writings on the Art and Science of History,* ed. Roger Wines (New York, 1981), p. 21; see also the discussion in Stephen Bann, *The Clothing of Clio: A study of the representation of history in nineteenth-century Britain and France* (Cambridge, U.K., 1984), pp. 8–10.

4. Stern (ed.), *The Varieties of History,* p. 55.

5. Leopold von Ranke, *The Theory and Practice of History,* ed. Georg G. Iggers and Konrad von Moltke (Indianapolis, 1973), p. 119.

6. My account here follows Novick, esp. *That Noble Dream,* p. 36.

7. Robert Harris, *Selling Hitler: The Story of the Hitler Diaries* (London, 1986), pp. 23, 354. For forgeries and falsifications relating to the origins of the First World War, see, for example J. C. G. Röhl, "Admiral von Müller and the Approach of War," *Historical Journal,* vol. XII (1969), pp. 651–73; and Fritz Fischer, *Juli 1914: Wir sind nicht hineingeschlittert: Das Staatsgeheimnis um die Riezler-Tagebücher. Ein Streitschrift* (Reinbek, 1983), pp. 49–54, 75–82.

8. Novick, *That Noble Dream,* p. 33.

9. Stern (ed.), *The Varieties of History,* p. 179.

10. All quoted in Novick, *That Noble Dream.,* pp. 37–39, by far the best account of the "Rankean revolution" in American historical scholarship.

11. Lytton Strachey, *Eminent Victorians: Cardinal Manning—Florence Nightingale—Dr. Arnold—General Gordon* (London, 1925), p. vii.

12. John Kenyon, *The History Men: The Historical Profession in England since the Renaissance,* 2d ed. (London, 1993), p. 212.

13. Peter Gay, *Style in History* (London, 1975), ch. 2.

14. John Pemble, *Venice Rediscovered* (Oxford, 1995), pp. 82–83.

15. J. B. Bury, *An Inaugural Lecture, delivered in the Divinity School, Cambridge, on January 26, 1903* (Cambridge, U.K., 1903).

16. For other similar reactions to Bury's lecture, and other, similar echoes of Bury's argument among Edwardian historians, see Kenyon, *The History Men*, pp. 183–86.

17. Stern (ed.), *The Varieties of History*, pp. 227–45.

18. G. M. Trevelyan, *England under Queen Anne,* 3 vols. (London, 1930–34).

19. Stern (ed.), *The Varieties of History*, pp. 229–33.

20. Droysen quoted in Stern (ed.), *The Varieties of History*, p. 138. More generally, see Georg G. Iggers, *The German Conception of History: The National Tradition of Historical Thought from Herder to the Present* (Middletown, Conn., 1968).

21. Novick, *That Noble Dream*, pp. 86–108; Richard Hofstadter, *The Progressive Historians: Turner, Beard, Parrington* (New York, 1968); Charles Beard, *An Economic Interpretation of the Constitution of the United States* (New York, 1913). As late as 1998 a conservative historian such as Oscar Handlin could date the crisis of history in his own time to what he saw as the fateful introduction of the criterion of "relevance" by Beard and the Progressives over three quarters of a century before (Oscar Handin, *Truth in History,* 2d ed. [New Brunswick, 1998]).

22. Novick, *That Noble Dream*, pp. 116–32, 206–24; Christopher Parker, *The English Historical Tradition since 1850* (Edinburgh, 1990), pp. 104–17.

23. Klaus Schwabe, *Wissenschaft und Kriegsmoral* (Göttingen, 1969); Stuart Wallace, *War and the Image of Germany: British Academics 1914–1918* (Edinburgh, 1988), pp. 29–42, 58–73.

24. Quoted in Wallace, *War and the Image of Germany*, p. 37.

25. David Cannadine, *G. M. Trevelyan: A Life in History* (London, 1992), pp. 213–15.

26. Novick, *That Noble Dream*, pp. 131–32.

27. H. A. L. Fisher, *A History of Europe,* 3 vols. (London, 1935), p. vii. For a particularly savage attack on Fisher's views, see Christopher Hill, "A Whig Historian," *The Modern Quarterly*, vol. 3 (1938), pp. 276–84.

28. Benedetto Croce, *History as the Story of Liberty* (London, 1941), p. 19.

29. R. G. Collingwood, *The Idea of History* (Oxford, 1946), part V, sections 4–5.

30. E. H. Carr, *What Is History?* 2d ed. (London, 1987), p. 21.

31. All quotes on Namier in Ved Mehta, *Fly and the Fly-Bottle: Encounters with British Intellectuals* (London, 1963), pp. 179, 183.

32. Even in 1995, however, Professor John Vincent thought that "the great historians of the twentieth century in England were two: Namier and Butterfield. Both stood out the more," he adds, "because of the surrounding dullness." They were great, he says, not because they wrote great historical masterpieces, but because they destroyed the dominant "Whig Interpretation" of history based on the supposed rise of parliamentarism, and so affected the wider political culture of the country (John Vincent, *An Intelligent Person's Guide to History* [London, 1995], pp. 58–62).

33. Linda Colley, *Lewis Namier* (London, 1969), p. 63.

34. Anon., "The Namier View of History," *Times Literary Supplement*, August 28, 1953.

35. See L. B. Namier, *The Structure of Politics at the Accession of George III* (London, 1927; 2d ed., 1957); idem, *England in the Age of the American Revolution* (London, 1930). More generally, see Frank O'Gorman, *The Rise of Party in England: The Rockingham Whigs 1760–82* (London, 1975); John Cannon, *The Fox-North Coalition: Crisis of the Constitution 1782–4* (London, 1969); and John Brewer, *Party Ideology and Popular Politics at the Accession of George III* (London, 1976). Namier's obsession with the *History of Parliament* led to a critical comment from E. H. Carr: "Bricks are important, but a pile of bricks is not a house. And should the master-builder spend his time in a brick field?" (E. H. Carr, "English History's Towering Outsider," *Times Literary Supplement*, May 21, 1957).

36. Colley, *Lewis Namier*, pp. 91–3. The attacks mounted from the left on the Whig interpretation by Marxist historians such as Christopher Hill and E. P. Thompson, who argued that there was a good deal of self-interest behind the middle-class advocacy of parliamentarism on the seventeenth and eighteenth centuries, were just as effective as the assault launched by Namier from the right.

37. Karl Popper, *The Poverty of Historicism* (London, 1957).

38. For elaborations of these points, and numerous examples, see Richard J. Evans, *Rereading German History: From Unification to Reunification* (London, 1997).

39. Peter Burke, *Sociology and History* (London, 1980) is a good, if rather belated, example of this genre.

40. Lawrence Stone, "History and the Social Sciences in the Twentieth Century," idem, *The Past and the Present* (London, 1981).

41. Emmanuel Le Roy Ladurie, *The Territory of the Historian* (Chicago, 1979), pp. 15, 6.

42. Oscar Handlin et al., *Harvard Guide to American History* (Cambridge, Mass., 1954), pp. 24–25.

43. Fogel, " 'Scientific' and Traditional History," in Fogel and Elton, *Which Road?* pp. 7–70.

44. The ambitions of American quantifiers like J. Morgan Kousser can be traced in the early issues of the journal *Social Science History*. It is worth noting that in Britain, grants for postgraduate research in economic and social history are administered by the government-funded Economic and Social Research Council, which will not issue them for university institutions unless they have a training program in place that includes statistical and "cliometric" techniques. The bulk of the large-scale faculty research grants given to historians by the council now goes mainly to teams of researchers working on the computer-assisted compilation and analysis of serial quantitative data and publishing their results in specialized articles rather than general books. At the end of the line, historical epistemology thus translated into hard cash.

45. Georg Iggers, introduction to the *International Handbook of Historical Studies: Contemporary Research and Theory*, ed. idem and Harold Parker (Westport, Conn., 1979), pp. 1–22.

46. Elton, "Two Kinds of History," in Fogel and Elton, *Which Road?* pp. 71–122; also Stone, "History and the Social Sciences in the Twentieth Century," pp. 32–35.

47. Robert W. Fogel and Stanley L. Engerman, *Time on the Cross* (Boston, 1974).

48. Paul A. David et al., *Reckoning with Slavery: A Critical Study in the Quantitative History of American Negro Slavery* (New York, 1976), p. 339; for further critiques, see Herbert Gutman, *Slavery and the Numbers Game: A Critique of "Time on the Cross"* (Urbana, Ill., 1975) and Peter Kolchin, "Toward a Reinterpretation of Slavery," *Journal of Social History*, vol. 9 (1975), pp. 99–111.

49. Thomas Kuhn, *The Structure of Scientific Revolutions*, 2d ed. (Chicago, 1970), pp. 164–65.

50. For an overview, see Georg G. Iggers, *Historiography in the Twentieth Century: From Scientific Objectivity to the Postmodern Challenge* (Hanover, N.H., 1997).

CHAPTER TWO: HISTORY, SCIENCE, AND MORALITY

1. Carr, *What Is History?* p. 56.

2. However, in Britain at the beginning of the 1980s, the education secretary

in Mrs. Thatcher's Conservative government, Sir Keith Joseph, forced the government-funded Social Science Research Council to change its name to the Economic and Social Research Council because he did not believe that there was such a thing as social science.

3. See the sensible discussion in Novick, *That Noble Dream*, pp. 24–25.

4. Carr, *What Is History?* pp. 72–73.

5. Elton, *Return*, p. 51.

6. Ibid., pp. 62–63.

7. Quentin Skinner, "Sir Geoffrey Elton and the Practice of History," *Transactions of the Royal Historical Society*, 6th Series, vol. 7 (1997), pp. 301–16, here pp. 308–10, misunderstands Elton's argument on this point.

8. Ibid., pp. 49, 66.

9. Jenkins, *On "What Is History?"* p. 70.

10. Carr, *What Is History?* p. 162.

11. David Knowles, *The Historian and Character* (Cambridge, 1955), p. 19.

12. W. C. Sellar and R. J. Yeatman, *1066 and All That: a memorable history of England: comprising all the parts you can remember* . . . (London, 1930).

13. Carr, *What Is History?* pp. 78–79.

14. Ibid., pp. 80–86.

15. David Knowles, *The Religious Orders in England,* vol. III (Cambridge, U.K., 1959), p. 468.

16. Ibid., pp. 121, 126.

17. Elton, *Return*, pp. 62–63.

18. J. A. Froude, *Short Studies on Great Subjects* (London, 1963, first published 1867), p. 21.

19. Pieter Geyl, *Debates with Historians* (London, 1955), pp. 176–82, 201–03, 210. Geyl's comprehensive demolition of Toynbee stretches across several chapters of the book, from p. 112 to p. 210. See also idem, *Encounters in History* (London, 1963), pp. 276–306, for Geyl's riposte to Toynbee's answer to his critics, which occupied 674 pages of an additional volume of *A Study in History*.

20. H. T. Buckle, *History of Civilization in England,* 2 vols. (London, 1856 and 1861).

21. Carr, *What Is History?* p. 63.

22. Ibid., p. 69.

23. Vincent, *Intelligent Person's Guide*, p. 19.

24. Allan Megill, "Recounting the Past: 'Description,' Explanation, and Narrative in Historiography," *American Historical Review*, vol. 94 (1989), pp. 627–53, here p. 633. The German philosopher Wilhelm Windelband's distinction between "nomothetic" sciences concerned with general laws and "idiographic" sciences concerned with particular entities did not rule out the one or the other as a science. Both, as far as he was concerned, were sciences. But this of course meant the German term *Wissenschaft* (organized knowledge) and so had little relevance to the debate as it was proceeding in English-speaking lands. (Wilhelm Windelband, "History and Natural Science," *History and Theory*, vol. 19 [1980], pp. 169–85 [translation of work originally published in 1894, with an introduction by Guy Oakes].)

25. For a particularly striking example of this failure, see Richard J. Evans, *In Hitler's Shadow: West German Historians and the Attempt to Escape from the Nazi Past* (New York, 1989), pp. 105–06.

26. Paul M. Kennedy, *The Rise and Fall of the Great Powers: Economic Change and Military Conflict from 1500 to 2000* (London, 1987), p. 513.

27. Elton, *Return*, pp. 56–58.

28. Quoted in Kenyon, *The History Men*, p. 198.

29. Quoted in Stern (ed.), *The Varieties of History*, p. 193.

30. Somekawa and Smith, "Theorizing," p. 152.

31. Zeldin, "Social History and Total History," p. 237.

32. White, "Response," p. 243.

33. Elton, *Practice*, p. 148.

34. Stone, "History and Post-Modernism II," *Past and Present*, 135 (May 1992), pp. 189–94, here p. 189.

35. Ibid., p. 99.

36. LaCapra, *History and Criticism*, p. 36. LaCapra unfortunately fails to give any examples of this use of language. Russell Jacoby, "A New Intellectual History?" *American Historical Review*, vol. 97 (April 1992), pp. 405–24, here p. 416, similarly notes that LaCapra "rarely tells us which historians or what histories are guilty" of the "sins" he so trenchantly criticizes. See also Anthony Pagden, "Rethinking the Linguistic Turn: Current Anxieties in Intellectual History," *Journal of the History of Ideas*, vol. 49 (1988), pp. 519–29.

37. LaCapra, *History and Criticism*, p. 42.

38. McCullagh, *The Truth of History*, pp. 75–81, 90.

39. Alan Knight, reviewing Marjorie Becker, *Setting the Virgin on Fire: Lázaro Cárdenas, Michoacán peasants and the redemption of the Mexican revolution* (Berkeley, 1995) in *Times Literary Supplement*, no. 4864 (June 21, 1996), p. 31.

40 Note the wonderfully double-edged testimony on the cover of *Historical Culture* by Professor Mark Poster: "No historian who reads and comprehends this book will ever write in the same way again." See Sande Cohen, *Historical Culture: On the Recoding of an Academic Discipline* (Berkeley, 1988).

41 Jacoby, "A New Intellectual History?" pp. 413, 419.

42 Appleby, Hunt, and Jacob, *Telling the Truth*, p. 229. See also Zagorin, "Historiography and Postmodernism: Reconsiderations," p. 264, and the special *Beiheft*, vol. 19 (1980) of *History and Theory* devoted to White's *Metahistory: Six Critiques*.

43. Hayden White, *Metahistory: The Historical Imagination in Nineteenth-Century Europe* (Baltimore, 1973); White's subsequent work contains almost no references at all to history as it has been researched and written in the twentieth century. See also Stephen Bann, *The Clothing of Clio;* idem, *The Inventions of History: Essays on the Representations of the Past* (Manchester, U.K., 1990); Linda Orr, *Jules Michelet: Nature, History and Language* (Ithaca, 1990); Ann Rigney, *The Rhetoric of Historical Representation* (Cambridge, U.K., 1990), also on nineteenth-century histories of the Revolution; Frank Ankersmit, "Tocqueville and the Sublimity of Democracy," *Tocqueville Review,* vol. 14 (1993), pp. 173, and vol. 15 (1994), pp. 193–218; L. Shiner, *The Secret Mirror: Literary Form and History in Tocqueville's Recollections* (Ithaca, 1988).

44. Marwick, "Two Approaches," p. 29.

45. Arthur Marwick, *Culture in Britain since 1945* (Oxford, 1991), p. 5.

46. Arthur Marwick, *Beauty in History: Society, Politics and Personal Appearance c. 1500–the Present* (London, 1988), pp. 365, 47.

47. Arthur Marwick, *British Society since 1945* (London, 1982), pp. 63, 75.

48. Isaiah Berlin, *Historical Inevitability* (London, 1954), p. 5, n. 1. For a comparable view of the hybrid nature of history, see Michel de Certeau, *Heterologies: Discourse on the Other* (Manchester, U.K., 1980), pp. 199–224, and Bann, *The Clothing of Clio*, pp. 164–77.

49. Marc Bloch, *The Historian's Craft*, with an introduction by Peter Burke (Manchester, U.K., 1992).

CHAPTER THREE: HISTORIANS AND THEIR FACTS

1. Elton, *Return*, pp. 27, 65. For Elton, the historian was always a "he" or a "him."

2. Ibid., p. 68. These views are echoed by the senior American historian Oscar Handlin, who argued for the "rejection of theory as a guide" and saw its influence as deeply damaging to standards of historical scholarship (Oscar Handlin, *Truth in History,* 2d ed. [New Brunswick, 1998] p. x).

3. Carr, *What Is History?* p. 12, echoed by Gareth Stedman Jones, "History: the poverty of empiricism," in Robin Blackburn (ed.), *Ideology in Social Science* (London, 1972), p. 113.

4. See, for example, Anthony Easthope, "Romancing the Stone: history-writing and rhetoric," *Social History*, vol. 18 (1993), pp. 235–49, here p. 236; and Marwick, *The Nature of History*, pp. 194–96 (a useful, if rather intemperate, discussion).

5. George Kitson Clark, *The Making of Victorian England* (Cambridge, U.K., 1962), pp. 61–62, citing Lord George Sanger, *Seventy Years a Showman,* 2d ed. (London, 1926), pp. 188–89. Here the crowd is identified as a group of miners wearing iron-tipped clogs. For contemporary reports, see *Manchester Guardian*, July 17, 1850, p. 7, col. 3; July 27, 1850, p. 9, col. 6; *Manchester Examiner and Times,* July 17, 1850, p. 7, col. 6; July 20, 1850, p. 7, col. 3; *Manchester Courier and Lancashire General Advertiser,* July 20, 1850, p. 8, col. 1; July 27, 1850, p. 8, col. 2; *Manchester Spectator and Commercial Gazette,* July 20, 1850, p. 8, col. 3; July 27, 1850, p. 8, col. 4. In 1850 Stalybridge, which was in Lancashire (it is now in Cheshire), had no local newspaper of its own, nor did Ashton-under-Lyme, which was the nearest fair-sized town. The Manchester papers therefore carried Stalybridge news under the rubric "Stalybridge" or "Ashton-under-Lyme." There were no reports of disturbances at the wakes in 1851 or 1852 either, ruling out the possibility that Sanger has got the year wrong.

6. Nancy F. Partner, "Making Up Lost Time: Writing on the Writing of History," *Speculum*, vol. 61 (1986), p. 105.

7. Thomas A. Bailey and David M. Kennedy, *The American Pageant* (Lexington, Mass., 1994), p. 225.

8. Munslow, *Deconstructing*, pp. 1, 6–7. Berkhofer, *Beyond the Great Story* regards a historical fact as established only by the sources (for which he uses the term "evidence"); historical facts for which there is no warrant in the sources are not historical facts. My argument here is that their existence as facts does not depend on the availability of source material for them; that is why the discovery of new source material leads to the discovery of facts which had not been known about before. All that depends on the availability of source material is our ability to say that they existed.

9. White, "Response," pp. 233–46.

10. Skinner, "Sir Geoffrey Elton," pp. 301–03.

11. Ibid., p. 239.

12. Southgate, *History,* pp. 26–27.

13. Partner, "Historicity," p. 23.

14. Somekawa and Smith, "Theorizing," p. 151.

15. LaCapra, *History and Criticism*, p. 11.

16. Ibid., pp. 11, 17.

17. Ibid., p. 38.

18. Ibid., p. 47.

19. Partner, "Historicity," p. 21.

20. Catriona Kelly, "History and Post-Modernism," *Past and Present,* 133 (November 1991), pp. 209–13.

21. Stone, "History and Post-Modernism II," pp. 189–90.

22. Raphael Samuel, "Reading the Signs," *History Workshop Journal,* 32 (1991), pp. 88–109, and vol. 33 (1992), pp. 220–51; quote on p. 233.

23. Keith Thomas, *Religion and the Decline of Magic: Studies in Popular Beliefs in Sixteenth- and Seventeenth-Century England* (London, 1977).

24. E. P. Thompson, *The Making of the English Working Class* (London, 1963).

25. Emmanuel Le Roy Ladurie, *Montaillou. Village occitan de 1294 à 1324* (Paris, 1978).

26. Elton, *Return*, p. 55.

27. H. Stuart Hughes, "Contemporary Historiography: Progress, Paradigms, and the Regression toward Positivism," in Gabriel Almond, Marvin Chodorow, and Roy Harvey (eds.), *Progress and Its Discontents* (Berkeley, 1982), p. 245.

28. William H. McNeill, "Mythistory, or Truth, Myth, History, and Historians," *American Historical Review*, vol. 91 (1986), pp. 8–9.

29. Elton, Return, p. 53. But cf. Q. R. D. Skinner, *Reason and Rhetoric in the Philosophy of Hobbes* (Cambridge, U. K., 1996)

30. Alan B. Spitzer, *Historical Truth and Lies about the Past* (Chapel Hill, 1996), p. 61.

31. Richard J. Evans (ed.), *Kneipengespräche im Kaiserreich: Die Stimmungsberichte der Hamburger politischen Polizei 1892–1914* (Reinbek, 1989).

32. Otto Brunner et al. (eds.), *Geschichtliche Grundbegriffe: Historisches Lexicon zur politisch-sozialen Sprache in Deutschland* (Stuttgart, 1972–94).

33. Keith Jenkins, *Re-thinking History* (London, 1991), pp. 40–41, and George Steiner, *After Babel* (Oxford, 1975), p. 18.

34. McCullagh, *The Truth of History*, pp. 13–14, 22.

35. Carr, *What Is History?* p. 16.

36. Peter Burke, "Overture: The New History," in idem (ed.), *New Perspectives on Historical Writing* (Oxford, 1991), pp. 1–23, here p. 5.

37. Somekawa and Smith, "Theorizing," p. 153.

38. Carr, *What Is History?* p. 52.

39. Quoted in Kenyon, *The History Men*, pp. 8–9. See also Marwick, *The Nature of History*, pp. 198–200, including a discussion of the uncertain status of autobiography, which is an eyewitness account but not contemporary with the events it attests.

40. See the useful summary account in David Lehman, *Signs of the Times: Deconstruction and the Fall of Paul de Man* (London, 1991), pp. 28–37, 106–09. Among voluminous writings, see Roland Barthes, *Image, Music, Text* (New York, 1977) and Jacques Derrida, *Of Grammatology* (Baltimore, 1976), *Writing and Difference* (Chicago, 1978), *Positions* (Chicago, 1981), and *Dissemination* (Chicago, 1983).

41. Stone, "History and Post-Modernism," p. 218. See also the same author's "Dry Heat, Cool Reason: Historians under Siege in England and France," *Times Literary Supplement*, January 31, 1992.

42. Spiegel, "History and Post-Modernism," p. 197, and idem, "History, Historicism, and the Social Logic of the Text in the Middle Ages," *Speculum*, vol. 65 (1990), pp. 59–96.

43. Joyce, "History and Post-Modernism," p. 208.

44. Hans Kellner, "Introduction: Describing Redescriptions," in Ankersmit and Kellner (eds.), *New Philosophy of History*, p. 10.

45. Munslow, *Deconstructing*, pp. 2, 178.

46. Jenkins, *Re-thinking*, pp. 47–48.

47. Ibid., p. 47.

48. Ankersmit, "History and Postmodernism," pp. 152, 144.

49. Jenkins, *Re-thinking*, p. 34.

50. Munslow, *Deconstructing*, p. 2.

51. Purkiss, *The Witch in History*, pp. 2–4, 59–63.

52. White, *Metahistory*, pp. xi–xii, 5–7.

53. Somekawa and Smith, "Theorizing," p. 50.

54. Hayden White, *The Content of the Form* (Baltimore, 1987), pp. 44–47.

55. See the discussion in Berkhofer, *Beyond the Great Story*, pp. 45–75.

CHAPTER FOUR: SOURCES AND DISCOURSES

1. Harlan, "Intellectual History," p. 585.

2. Harlan, *Degradation*, pp. 92–94.

3. Paul Ricoeur, *Hermeneutics and the Human Sciences* (Cambridge, U.K., 1981), p. 146, quoted in Harlan, "Intellectual History," p. 587. For Ricoeur's critique of White, see his *The Reality of the Historical Past* (Milwaukee, 1984), pp. 33–34.

4. Dominick LaCapra, *Rethinking Intellectual History: Texts, Contexts, Language* (Ithaca, 1983), pp. 34–36, 40.

5. Quoted in Roy Porter, *Gibbon: Making History* (London, 1988), p. 163.

6. Appleby, Hunt, and Jacob, *Telling the Truth*, pp. 245–46.

7. Quoted in Porter, *Gibbon*, p. 163.

8. Southgate, *History*, p. 8.

9. Joyce, "History and Post-Modernism," p. 208.

10. Patrick Joyce, *Visions of the People: Industrial England and the Question of Class, 1848–1914* (Cambridge, U.K., 1991), pp. 17, 330, 338, quoted in Spiegel, "History and Post-Modernism," p. 202.

11. Joyce, *Visions*, p. 338, quoted in Joyce, "The Imaginary Discontents," p. 81. Joyce subsequently came to criticize his own book's "nostalgia for collective social subjects and bedrock 'experience' ": See, idem, *Democratic Subjects. The Self and the Social in Nineteenth-Century England* (Cambridge, U.K., 1994), pp. 11–12. See also Joan W. Scott, "The evidence of experience," *Critical Inquiry*, vol. 17 (1991), pp. 773–97, and Mayfield and Thorne, "Reply to 'The poverty of protest' " p. 221.

12. Jenkins, *Re-thinking*, p. 42. However, in recent years the use of original documents in transcript or excerpt has become more important in history teaching at all levels, a development that is very welcome.

13. McCullagh, *The Truth of History*, pp. 125–28.

14. Hayden White, "New Historicism: A Comment," in H. A. Veeser (ed.), *The New Historicism* (London, 1989), pp. 293–302, here p. 297. But when White describes the phrase "history is a text" as a metaphor here, he clearly means history as a written representation of the past, not the past itself; the issue of whether or not the representation can be true is entirely separate.

15. Chartier, *On the Edge*, p. 20.

16. Spiegel, "History, Historicism," p. 76.

17. Spiegel, "History and Post-Modernism," p. 207 n. 31.

18. Vincent, *Intelligent Person's Guide*, p. 8. Vincent has himself been critical of "documentary fetishism," however. He cites with approval A. J. P.

Taylor's belief that no new secrets were to be found in unpublished archival sources, while himself advocating paying greater attention than is customary to the newspapers, declaring that newsprint is "the Venetian archive of tomorrow." Yet Taylor's reluctance to use manuscript sources and his excessive reliance on printed material were in fact one of his greatest weaknesses as a historian, while Vincent's partiality to newpapers as unbiased sources of information may possibly be colored by the fact that he himself wrote a column in the *Sun* newspaper for a number of years, until student demonstrations at his own university forced him to abandon it, an event which, however deplorable in itself, would scarcely have taken place had the column been a model of impartiality (Vincent, *Intelligent Person's Guide,* pp. 9–10).

19. Mark Monmonier, *How to Lie with Maps* (Chicago, 1991).

20. Jenkins, *On "What Is History?"* p. 30.

21. Hayden White, "The Problem of Change in Literary History," *New Literary History,* vol. 7 (1975), p. 109.

22. Zagorin, "Historiography and Postmodernism: Reconsiderations," p. 171.

23. Henry VIII to Anne Boleyn, Letter No. 2, in C. H. Williams (ed.), *English Historical Documents 1785–1558* (London, 1971), p. 700.

24. Spiegel, "History and Post-Modernism," p. 195.

25. Jenkins, *Re-thinking,* p. 19.

26. Appleby, Hunt, and Jacob, *Telling the Truth,* pp. 254–56. For the same view, see Somekawa and Smith, "Theorizing," pp. 156–57.

27. Chartier, *On the Edge,* p. 26.

28. Henry Abelove et al. (eds.), *Visions of History* (New York, 1978), p. 14.

29. Richard J. Evans, "From Hitler to Bismarck: Third Reich and *Kaiserreich* in Recent Historiography," *Historical Journal,* Vol. 26 (1983), pp. 485–97 and 999–1020, reprinted in idem, *Rethinking German History: Nineteenth-Century Germany and the Origins of the Third Reich* (London, 1987), pp. 55–92, here pp. 77–79.

30. Henry Ashby Turner, review of Abraham in *Political Science Quarterly,* vol. 97 (1982–83), pp. 739–41, and letter in the *American Historical Review,* vol. 88 (1983), pp. 1143–49, with Abraham's response.

31. This mass of material finally emerged into print in a controversy between Feldman and Abraham in *Central European History,* vol. 17 (1984), pp. 159–293, where Abraham in particular paraded many of the behind-the-scenes maneuvers of the previous two years before the readership, somewhat to the embarrassment of the journal's editor.

32. White, *Metahistory*, p. 284.

33. Tim Mason, letter in the *American Historical Review*, vol. 88 (1983), p. 1146.

34. Gerald D. Feldman, "A Collapse in Weimar Scholarship," *Central European History*, vol. 17 (1984), pp. 159–77, here p. 176. See also Ulrich Nocken, "Weimarer Geschichte(n)," *Vierteljahrschrift für Sozial- und Wirtschaftsgeschichte*, vol. 71 (1984), pp. 505–27, which, however, lists a large number of trivial errors and fails to distinguish them satisfactorily from the major ones which caused the controversy.

35. David Abraham, *The Collapse of the Weimar Republic*, 2d ed. (New York, 1986). This edition still contains numerous errors, however, because Abraham was unable to go back to the archives in Communist East Germany where he had gathered a substantial amount of documents, and so it repeats the mistakes made in his original transcriptions and notes on them.

36. Feldman, "A Collapse," p. 165.

37. David Abraham, "A Reply to Gerald Feldman," *Central European History*, vol. 17 (1984), pp. 178–245, here p. 184.

38. Feldman, "A Collapse," p. 169.

39. Abraham, "A Reply," p. 186.

40. Hexter, *On Historians*, pp. 243, 250–51, quoting Christopher Hill, *Intellectual Origins of the English Revolution* (Oxford, 1965), p. vii. However, Hexter was arguably doing the same in combing Hill's work for evidence in favor of his own critique of it. Hexter criticized Hill for "lumping" diverse historical groups together into a small number of crudely oversimplified categories, but then "lumped" all historians into the two even cruder categories of "lumpers" supposedly like Hill and "splitters" like himself, who had an allegedly more differentiated and therefore more accurate view of the past. For these points, see William G. Palmer, "The Burden of Proof: J. H. Hexter and Christopher Hill," *Journal of British Studies*, vol. 19 (1979), pp. 121–29.

41. Novick, *That Noble Dream*, pp. 612–21; Novick was honest enough to admit that Abraham "was my student, and is my good friend" and that therefore, by implication, his own account of the affair was inevitably partisan.

42. Quoted in Novick, *That Noble Dream*, p. 620.

43. Lawrence Stone, "The Anatomy of the Elizabethan Aristocracy," *Economic History Review*, vol. 18 (1948), pp. 1–53; Hugh Trevor-Roper, "The Elizabethan Aristocracy: An Anatomy Anatomized," *Economic History Review*, 2d series, vol. 3 (1951), pp. 279–98; Lawrence Stone, "The

Elizabethan Aristocracy—A Restatement," *Economic History Review*, 2d series, vol. 4 (1952), pp. 302–21; J. P. Cooper, "The Counting of Manors," *Economic History Review*, 2d series, vol. 8 (1956), pp. 377–89; J. H. Hexter, *Reappraisals in History* (London, 1961), pp. 117–62 ("Storm over the Gentry"), esp. p. 138; Kenyon, *The History Men*, p. 258.

44. Hayden White, "Historical Emplotment and the Problem of Truth," in Saul Friedländer (ed.), *Probing the Limits of Representation: Nazism and the "Final Solution"* (Cambridge, Mass., 1992), pp. 37–53. White's citation of a comic book version of Auschwitz, Art Spiegelman's *Maus*, in which the characters are portrayed as various types of animal, does not amount to a statement that Auschwitz can be "emplotted" as a comedy. Spiegelman's comic strip is a moving double autobiography, undeniably cast in the tragic mode.

45. White, "Response," p. 241.

46. Jacoby, "A New Intellectual History?" p. 418.

47. Stone, "History and Post-Modernism," p. 190.

48. Jenkins, *Re-thinking*, p. 15.

49. Ibid., p. 32.

50. Somekawa and Smith, "Theorizing," p. 153.

CHAPTER FIVE: CAUSATION IN HISTORY

1. Carr, *What Is History?* p. 87.

2. Ibid., pp. 86–104.

3. Ibid., pp. 104–05.

4. Appleby, Hunt, and Jacob, *Telling the Truth*, p. 304.

5. A. J. P. Taylor, *War by Timetable* (London, 1976).

6. Idem, *A Personal History* (London, 1985).

7. Carr, *What Is History?* p. 108.

8. Ibid., p. 120.

9. Martin, "Objectivity and Meaning," pp. 48–49.

10. Megill, "Recounting the Past," p. 627.

11. Geoffrey Barraclough, *History and the Common Man* (London, 1967), pp. 3–15.

12. Vincent, *Intelligent Person's Guide*, pp. 45–49.

13. Zeldin, "Social History and Total History," p. 243. The word "links" is misquoted, amusingly, and no doubt because of mere carelessness, by Gertrude

Himmelfarb as "lines" in her book *On Looking into the Abyss: Untimely Thoughts on Culture and Society* (New York, 1995), p. 138.

14. Zeldin, "Social History and Total History," p. 243.

15. Theodore Zeldin, *France 1848–1945*, vol. I, *Ambition, Love and Politics* (Oxford, 1973), vol. II, *Intellect, Taste and Anxiety* (Oxford, 1977).

16. Geoffrey Roberts, "Narrative History as a Way of Life," *Journal of Contemporary History*, vol. 31 (1996), pp. 221–28, here p. 222.

17. M. C. Lemon, *The Discipline of History and the History of Thought* (London, 1995) develops a whole philosophy of history which rests on this misconception.

18. Herbert Butterfield, *The Whig Interpretation of History* (London, 1931).

19. Lloyd, "For Realism and against the Inadequacies of Common Sense," p. 192.

20. Skinner, "Sir Geoffrey Elton," p. 304.

21. Hayden White, "The Burden of History," in idem, *Tropics of Discourse* (Baltimore, 1978), pp. 27–50; see also Hans Kellner, "White's Linguistic Humanism," *History and Theory*, supplement 19 (1980), pp. 1–29.

22. White, "The Politics of Historical Interpretation: Discipline and Sublimation," in idem, *The Content of the Form*, pp. 58–82.

23. White, *Metahistory*, pp. xi–xii.

24. Jenkins, *Re-thinking*, pp. 32–33.

25. F. R. Ankersmit, *History and Tropology: The Rise and Fall of Metaphor* (Berkeley, 1994), pp. 33–34.

26. Rosenau, *Post-Modernism*, pp. 67–68.

27. Elizabeth Deeds Ermarth, *Sequel to History: Postmodernism and the Crisis of Historical Time* (Princeton, 1992), pp. 22, 212; Appleby, Hunt, and Jacob, *Telling the Truth*, pp. 205, 211, 235; see also Robert Young, *White Mythologies: Writing History and the West* (London, 1990), in which history *tout court* is seen as "colonialist."

28. David Carr, review of Ermarth, *Sequel to History*, in *History and Theory*, vol. 32 (1993), pp. 179–87, quoting pp. xi, 14, 29, 25,

29. Ibid., p. 184, quoting p. 191.

30. White, *The Content of the Form*, p. 27.

31. LaCapra, *History and Criticism*, p. 119.

32. Possibly LaCapra has only consulted the English abridgment of the book, from which most of the anthropological analysis of the original French edition has been omitted.

33. Richard J. Evans, *Death in Hamburg: Society and Politics in the Cholera Years 1830–1910* (Oxford, 1987).

34. Munslow, *Deconstructing*, p. 11.

35. White, *Tropics of Discourse*, p. 50.

36. Hofstadter, *The Progressive Historians*, pp. 463–66.

37. Cohen, *Historical Culture*, pp. 19–21, 171, 174, 228, 326.

38. Munslow, *Deconstructing*, p. 12.

39. See Geoff Bennington, *Lyotard: Writing the Event* (Manchester, U.K., 1988) and Jean-François Lyotard, *Dérive à partir de Marx et Freud* (Paris, 1973) and *Instructions païennes* (Paris, 1977).

40. Jean-François Lyotard, *The Postmodern Condition: A Report on Knowledge* (Minneapolis, 1984), pp. xxiii–xxiv.

41. Elton, *Return*, p. 44.

42. Ibid., p. 45.

43. Zeldin, "Social History and Total History," p. 245.

44. Namier, *Structure*; Fernand Braudel, *The Mediterranean and the Mediterranean World in the Age of Philip II*, 2 vols. (London, 1972–73); Eugene D. Genovese, *Roll, Jordan, Roll: The World the Slaves Made* (New York, 1974); Hans-Ulrich Wehler, *Das Deutsche Kaiserreich 1871–1918* (Göttingen, 1973). The fact that narrative is not central to history undermines the theories of those philosophers, such as Arthur C. Danto, who suppose that it is. See Arthur C. Danto, *Narration and Knowledge* (New York, 1985) and, for this point, Martin Bunzl, *Real History: Reflections on Historical Practice* (New York, 1997), pp. 32–33. Narrative is nothing if not chronological, and theories which attempt to expand its definition beyond this empty it of all meaning (for example, Paul Ricoeur, *Time and Narrative*, 3 vols. [Chicago, 1984–85]), Paul Veyne, *Writing History: Essay on Epistemology* [Baltimore, 1987], and Michel de Certeau, *The Writing of History* [New York, 1988]).

45. F. W. Maitland, *Domesday Book and Beyond: Three Essays in the Early History of England* (Cambridge, 1897); Hellmut Diwald, *Geschichte der Deutschen* (Frankfurt am Main, 1978).

46. Quoted in Peter Burke, "Preface" to Bloch, *The Historian's Craft,* p. xvi.

47. For an example of this ignorance, see Somekawa and Smith, "Theorizing," pp. 155–56.

48. Southgate, *History*, p. 114.

49. Quoted in Peter Burke, *The French Historical Revolution: The Annales School 1929–1989* (Oxford, 1990), p. 39.

50. Ibid., p. 35.

51 Skeptically inclined postmodernist critics have labeled Braudel's *Mediterranean* as "narrative history" anyway because the view that it is not depends on a simplistic understanding of narrative as a description of events sequential in time, whereas a more sophisticated view would have it combining action, happening, character, and setting, and of the last named, there certainly is plenty in Braudel's great work. But while it is at least welcome that someone has actually sought to define narrative instead of simply assuming we all know what it is, this definition is really far too all-encompassing to be really useful, and flies in the face not only of common usage among historians but also of the concept employed by Braudel himself—namely, "*histoire évenementielle*," an event-based history.

52. Jean Delumeau, *La peur en Occident (XIVe—XVIIIe siècles), une cité assiegée* (Paris, 1978); *La péché et la peur: la culpabilisation en Occident (XIIIe—XVIIIe siècles)* (Paris, 1983).

53. Confusingly, perhaps, Ermarth dates the beginnings of postmodernism to the beginning of the twentieth century, thus excluding modernist art, music, and architecture from the modern.

54. Kenyon, *The History Men*, pp. 195–96.

55. Berkhofer, *Beyond the Great Story*, pp. 106–37, has a useful discussion of historical time, and its final chapter enters a strong plea for historians to be more experimental in the methods they adopt to present their findings.

56. Zagorin, "Historiography and Postmodernism: Reconsiderations," pp. 269–70.

57. McCullagh, *The Truth of History*, pp. 172–208.

58. Elton, *Practice*, p. 100. Skinner's objections to this point ("Sir Geoffrey Elton," p. 303) seem to be based on a misunderstanding of what Elton was trying to say.

59. Kirk, "History, language, ideas," p. 227.

60. Harlan, *Degradation*, p. xxii.

61. Appleby, Hunt, and Jacob, *Telling the Truth*, pp. 223–25.

CHAPTER SIX: SOCIETY AND THE INDIVIDUAL

1. Joan W. Scott criticizes unnamed American colleagues for ascribing this famous saying to Herbert Baxter Adams, only to misattribute it herself to Edward Freeman (Joan Wallach Scott, "History in Crisis? The Other Side of the Story," *American Historical Review*, vol. 94 [1989], pp. 680–92, here p. 680). For the correct attribution, in Seeley's *The Growth of British Policy*

(1895), see the *Oxford Dictionary of Quotations,* 3d ed. (Oxford, 1979), p. 419.

2. Gertrude Himmelfarb, "Some Reflections on the New History," *American Historical Review,* vol. 94 (1989), pp. 661–70, here p. 663.

3. Quoted in Richard Cobb, *The Police and the People* (Oxford, 1970), p. 81.

4. Mehta, *Fly and the Fly-Bottle,* pp. 187–89.

5. Cannadine, *Trevelyan.*

6. See Lawrence W. Levine, "The Unpredictable Past: Reflections on Recent American Historiography," *American Historical Review,* vol. 94 (1989), pp. 671–79, here p. 674.

7. Skinner, "Sir Geoffrey Elton," pp. 306, 315–16.

8. He subsequently brought it out with another publisher, defiantly retitled *An Intelligent Person's Guide to History.*

9. Carr, *What Is History?* p. 149.

10. Vincent, *Intelligent Person's Guide,* pp. 1–8.

11. Thompson, *The Making of the English Working Class,* p. 12.

12. G. M. Trevelyan, *English Social History,* rev. ed. (London, 1978).

13. Quoted in Kenyon, *The History Men,* p. 167.

14. Eric Hobsbawm, "From Social History to the History of Society," *Daedalus,* no. 100 (1971), pp. 20–45.

15. Geoff Eley and Keith Nield, "Why Does Social History Ignore Politics?," *Social History,* vol. 5 (1980), pp. 249–71; Tony Judt, "A Clown in Regal Purple: Social History and the Historians," *History Workshop Journal,* 7 (1979) pp. 66–94.

16. Appleby, Hunt, and Jacob, *Telling the Truth,* pp. 202, 216.

17. Peter N. Stearns, "Coming of Age," *Journal of Social History,* vol. 10 (1976), pp. 246–55. This article is notable for the unintentionally hilarious consequences of the author's confusion of Lord Acton the historian with Dr. William Acton the Victorian expert on prostitution and female sexuality (p. 249).

18. John Breuilly, "What Is Social History?" in Juliet Gardiner (ed.), *What Is History Today?* (London, 1988), pp. 49–51, here p. 51.

19. Geoff Eley, "Some Recent Tendencies in Social History," in Iggers and Parker, eds., *International Handbook of Historical Studies,* pp. 55–70.

20. Ankersmit, *History and Tropology,* p. 175.

21. Zeldin, "Social History and Total History," pp. 240, 242.

22. Jon Lawrence and Miles Taylor, "The poverty of protest: Gareth Stedman Jones and the politics of language—a reply," *Social History*, vol. 18 (1993), pp. 1–15, here p. 12.

23. Gardiner (ed.), *What is History Today?* pp. 1–2.

24. Laurence Veysey, quoted in Novick, *That Noble Dream, p. 592;* Carr, *What Is History?* p. 15.

25. See Jim Sharpe, "History from Below," in Burke (ed.), *New Perspectives on Historical Writing,* p. 37.

26. Thomas Nipperdey, *Deutsche Geschichte 1800–1866: Bürgerwelt und starker Staat* (Munich, 1983); *Deutsche Geschichte 1866–1918*, vol. I, *Arbeitswelt und Bürgergeist* (Munich, 1990), vol. II, *Machtstaat vor der Demokratie* (Munich, 1992). Hans-Ulrich Wehler, *Deutsche Gesellschaftsgeschichte*, vol. I, *Vom Feudalismus des Alten Reiches bis zur Defensiven Modernisierung der Reformära 1700–1815* (Munich, 1987), vol. II, *Von der Reformära bis zur industriellen und politischen "Deutschen Doppelrevolution" 1815–1845/49* (Munich, 1987), vol. III, *Von der "Deutschen Doppelrevolution" bis zum Beginn des Ersten Weltkrieges 1849–1914* (Munich, 1995).

27. Philippe Ariès and Georges Duby (eds.), *A History of Private Life,* 5 vols. (Cambridge, Mass., 1989–92); Georges Duby and Michelle Perrot (eds.), *A History of Women in the West,* 5 vols. (Cambridge, Mass., 1993–95).

28. Mark Kishlansky, *A Monarchy Transformed: Britain 1603–1714* (London, 1996); Peter Clarke, *Hope and Glory: Britain 1900–1990* (London, 1996), both volumes in the *Penguin History of Britain,* edited by David Cannadine; the publisher's claim is taken from the dust jacket.

29. Norman Davies, *Europe: A History* (Oxford, 1996), a book whose imaginative sweep is seriously compromised by its factual inaccuracy. The second (paperback) edition, published in 1997, should be consulted in preference to the first; it includes a large number of corrections.

30. Novick, *That Noble Dream,* p. 628.

31. Vincent, *Intelligent Person's Guide,* p. 103.

32. Ibid., p. 107.

33. Hugh Trevor-Roper, *The Rise of Christian Europe* (London, 1965), p. 9.

34. Ibid., p. 104. "We" presumably means the British historians and history students to whom Vincent is addressing his book.

35. Kenyon, *The History Men,* pp. 297, viii.

36. Carr, *What Is History?* pp. 150–52.

37. Elton, *Return,* pp. 101–26.

38. Juliet Gardiner (ed.), *The History Debate* (London, 1990).

39. Élie Halévy, *A History of the English People in the Nineteenth Century,* 5 vols. (London, 1924–32); François Bédarida, *A Social History of England, 1851–1975* (London, 1979).

40. See, for example, note 27 above; or Philippe Ariès, *The Hour of Our Death* (London, 1971).

41. Jonathan D. Spence, *The Search for Modern China* (New York, 1990).

42. See Levine, "The Unpredictable Past," p. 674.

43. David Mayfield and Susan Thorne, "Social history and its disconcents: Gareth Stedman Jones and the politics of language," *Social History*, vol. 17 (1992), pp. 165–88, here pp. 165–67.

44. Ibid, p. 179.

45. Eley and Nield, "Starting Over."

46. David Carr, review of Ermarth, *Sequel to History,* p. 185, quoting pp. 56, 60, 62, 147, 177.

47. Wendy Lesser, *Pictures at an Execution: An Enquiry into the Subject of Murder* (Cambridge, Mass., 1994).

48. Lest this be thought unfair, it may be noted that Joyce, *Democratic Subjects,* pp. 12–15, explicitly embraces a linguistic determinism in which society, poverty, and so on are determined by language, culture, and imagination, not by experience, or in other words, people aren't really poor, they only imagine they are.

49. Carr, *What Is History?* p. 34.

50. J. Arch Getty, *Origins of the Great Purges: The Soviet Communist Party Reconsidered, 1933–1938* (Cambridge, U.K., 1985).

51. E. H. Carr, *Socialism in One Country*, vol. I (London, 1958), p. 151.

52. Carr, *What Is History?* pp. 169–70.

53. Carlo Ginzburg, *The Cheese and the Worms: The Cosmos of a Sixteenth-Century Miller* (Baltimore, 1980). More generally, see Edward Muir and Guido Ruggiero (eds.), *Microhistory and the Lost Peoples of Europe* (Baltimore, 1991).

54. For a particularly crass example of this kind of approach, see Robert Conquest, *Stalin: Breaker of Nations* (London, 1991).

CHAPTER SEVEN: KNOWLEDGE AND POWER

1. Brenda Marshall, *Teaching the Postmodern* (London, 1992), p. 4.

2. Carr, *What Is History?* p. 26.

3. Elton, *Return,* p. 8.

4. See also Handlin, *Truth in History,* for the rejection of relevance to the present as significant for historical scholarship.

5. Braudel, *The Mediterranean,* vol. I, pp. 19–21, and vol. II, pp. 32, 67, 71.

6. Pierre Chaunu, "Le fils de la morte," in Pierre Nora (ed.), *Essais d'égo-histoire* (Paris, 1987), pp. 61–107, here p. 93.

7. Skinner, "Sir Geoffrey Elton," p. 316.

8. Quoted in Kenyon, *The History Men,* p. 223.

9. Stone, *The Past and the Present,* pp. 109–11.

10. Sheila Rowbotham, *Hidden from History: 300 Years of Women's Oppression and the Fight against It* (London 1973); Renate Bridenthal and Claudia Koonz (eds.), *Becoming Visible: Women in European History* (Boston, 1977).

11. Kaye, *The Powers of the Past,* p. 13.

12. For this general point, see Vernon, "Who's afraid of the 'linguistic turn'?," p. 83 n. 8.

13. For this argument, see Mayfield and Thorne, "Social History," p. 173.

14. Michel Foucault, *Language, Counter-Memory, Practice: Selected Essays and Interviews,* trans. Donald F. Bouchard and Sherry Simon (Ithaca, 1977), p. 153.

15. Purkiss, *The Witch,* pp. 1–4, 59.

16. Rudy Koshar, "Playing the Cerebral Savage: Notes on Writing German History before the Linguistic Turn," *Central European History,* vol. 22 (1989), pp. 343–59.

17. Newton to Robert Hooke, February 5, 1675/6 (*Oxford Dictionary of Quotations,* 3d ed. [Oxford, 1979], p. 362).

18. See the note on "post-modernism's replication of the eternally recurring pretension of absolute originality characteristic of intellectual debate since the Enlightenment" in William Reddy, "Postmodernism and the public sphere: implications for an historical ethnography," *Cultural Anthropology,* vol. 7 (1992), pp. 135–68.

19. Peter N. Stearns, "Some Comments on Social History," *Journal of Social History,* vol. 1 (1967), pp. 3–6.

20. Stearns, "Coming of Age," pp. 246–55. What can happen to a newly created subdiscipline over the long term is shown by the case of economic history, which emerged in the 1880s. The first university chair in the subject

was created in 1892, at Harvard. In Britain, the Economic History Society was founded in 1926, and by 1975 its membership had reached 2,500. But in the mid-1980s the economic historian Martin Daunton declared that while separate departments of economic history had originally emerged in order to escape from the narrow concentration on high political and diplomatic history which had characterized mainstream history departments in the earlier part of the century, "a separate identity is no longer required to protect a neglected area of enquiry and, on the contrary, it is now Departments of Economic History which have become introverted and narrow." By 1993 the membership of the British Economic History Society had declined to 1,750. The next year the Economic History Section of the British Academy was abolished, and its members migrated either to the Economics Section or to one or other of the various History sections. In their 1996 Research Assessment Exercise, the Higher Education Funding Councils rolled up History and Economic History into a single unit of assessment, in contrast with their previous practice. All these were signs of the demise of economic history as a separate discipline a mere century or so after its original emergence. See M. J. Daunton, "What Is Economic History?" in Gardiner (ed.), *What Is History Today?* pp. 37–38, and Vincent, *Intelligent Person's Guide*, p. 97.

21. George Melly, *Revolt into Style: The Pop Arts in Britain* (London, 1970).

22. Jenkins, *Re-thinking*, p. 19.

23. Ibid., pp. 20–21.

24. Southgate, *History*, p. 24.

25. Ibid., p. 8.

26. Somekawa and Smith, "Theorizing," p. 157.

27. Tony Bennett, *Outside Literature* (London, 1991), pp. 16–30.

28. Munslow, *Deconstructing*, p. 13.

29. Wulf Kansteiner, "Searching for an Audience: The Historical Profession in the Media Age—A Comment on Arthur Marwick and Hayden White," *Journal of Contemporary History*, vol. 31 (1996), pp. 215–19. For a similar argument, see Theodore S. Hamerow, *Reflections on History and Historians* (Madison, Wis., 1987).

30. Jenkins, *On "What Is History?"* p. 22.

31. Munslow, *Deconstructing*, p. 39.

32. E. P. Thompson, *Warwick University Limited: Industry, Management and the Universities* (Harmondsworth, U.K., 1970); idem, *The Making of the English Working Class*. Thompson was elected a fellow of the British Academy, an

accolade accorded to many historians much his junior in age and reputation, only near the end of his life.

33. Penry Williams and G. L. Harriss, "A Revolution in Tudor History?" *Past and Present,* 25 (1963), pp. 3–58.

34. G. R. Elton, *The Tudor Revolution in Government: Administrative Changes in the Reign of Henry VII* (Cambridge, U.K., 1953); Stone, *The Past and the Present,* p. 107. Elton's pupils and admirers sometimes take a different view; see the largely uncritical account by Kenyon, *The History Men,* pp. 219–24.

35. Vincent, *Intelligent Person's Guide,* p. 53.

36. Ibid., pp. 52, 54.

37. John Vincent, *The Formation of the Victorian Liberal Party 1857–1868* (London, 1966).

38. Laura Lee Downs, "If 'Woman' Is Just an Empty Category, Then Why Am I Afraid to Walk Alone at Night? Identity Politics Meets the Postmodern Subject," *Comparative Studies in Society and History,* vol. 35 (1993), pp. 414–37, here p. 416.

39. Vincent, *Intelligent Person's Guide,* pp. 12, 15.

40. Ibid., pp. 40–42.

41. Southgate, *History,* p. 116.

42. Carl Bridenbaugh, "The Great Mutation," *American Historical Review,* vol. 68 (1963), pp 322–23.

43. Fernand Braudel, *The Identity of France,* vol. I (London, 1988), pp. 15, 19–21.

44. J. F. C. Fuller, *The Decisive Battles of the Western World, and Their Influence upon History,* 3 vols. (London, 1954–56); idem, *The Conduct of War, 1789–1961: A Study of the Impact of the French, Industrial and Russian Revolutions on War and Its Conduct* (London, 1961); Edward Gibbon, *Autobiography* (London, 1907 ed.), p. 106.

45. Paul Boghossian, "What the Sokal hoax ought to teach us: the pernicious consequences and internal contradictions of 'postmodernist' relativism," *Times Literary Supplement,* December 13, 1996, pp. 14–15.

46. Joanna Bourke, *Dismembering the Male: Men's Bodies, Britain and the Great War* (London, 1996); Ute Frevert, *Ehrenmänner. Das Duell in der bürgerlichen Gesellschaft* (Munich, 1991).

47. Andreas Hillgruber, *Zweierlei Untergang: Die Zerschlagung des Deutschen Reiches und das Ende des europäischen Judentums* (Berlin, 1986).

48. Downs, "If 'Woman,' ", pp. 414–15.

49. Ibid., pp. 423–24.

50. Joan Scott, " 'The Tip of the Volcano,' " *Comparative Studies in Society and History*, vol. 35 (1993), pp. 438–43; see also Laura Lee Downs, "Reply to Joan Scott," *Comparative Studies in Society and History*, vol. 35 (1993), pp. 444–51.

51. Ragnhild Hatton, *George I, Elector and King* (London, 1978); Olive Anderson, *Suicide in Victorian and Edwardian England* (Oxford, 1987); Annie Kriegel, *Aux Origines du communisme français 1914–1920,* 2 vols. (Paris, 1964). These are three more or less arbitrarily chosen examples from a list that could be extended almost indefinitely.

52. Purkiss, *The Witch*, pp. 66–68.

53. Southgate, *History*, p. 9.

54. Ann Wordsworth, "Derrida and Foucault: Writing the History of Historicity," in D. Attridge et al. (eds.), *Post-structuralism and the Question of History* (Cambridge, U.K., 1987), p. 116.

55. Harlan, *Degradation*, pp. 96, xxiii, xxx, 93, 54, 188–94.

56. Somekawa and Smith, "Theorizing," p. 154.

57. Ibid., p. 153.

58. Boghossian, "What the Sokal hoax ought to teach us," p. 15.

59. Martin Bernal, *Black Athena,* 2 vols. (London, 1987 and 1991); Mary R. Lefkowitz and Guy Mclean Rogers (eds.), *Black Athena Revisited* (Chapel Hill, 1996); and Mary R. Lefkowitz, *Not Out of Africa* (New York, 1996).

60. John Boswell, *Christianity, Social Tolerance, and Homosexuality: Gay People in Western Europe from the Beginning of the Christian Era to the 19th Century* (Chicago, 1980); idem, *The Marriage of Likeness: Same-Sex Unions in Pre-Modern Europe* (New York, 1994); Jeffrey Weeks, *Sex, Politics and Society: The Regulation of Sexuality since 1800* (London, 1981), esp. ch. 6; Richard Davenport-Hines, *Sex, Death and Punishment: Attitudes to Sex and Sexuality in Britain since the Renaissance* (London, 1990).

61. Chartier, *On the Edge*, pp. 26–27.

CHAPTER EIGHT: OBJECTIVITY AND ITS LIMITS

1. Carr, *What Is History?* p. 30. H. Carr, *The Bolshevik Revolution*, vol. I (London, 1950), pp. 5–6.

5. Quoted in Mehta, *Fly and the Fly-Bottle*, p. 117.

6. H. R. Trevor-Roper, reviewing *What Is History?* in *Encounter*, quoted in Mehta, *Fly and the Fly-Bottle*, p. 117.

7. E. H. Carr, *Michael Bakunin* (London, 1937); idem, *The Romantic Exiles: A Nineteenth-Century Portrait Gallery* (London, 1933).

8. Francis Fukuyama, *The End of History and the Last Man* (London, 1992).

9. It is on grounds such as these that Carr's work on Soviet history can legitimately be criticized, rather than on the supposed personal failings cataloged in Norman Stone's vitriolic attack on Carr in 1983 ("Grim Eminence," pp. 9–12).

10. Elton, *Practice*, pp. 4–7.

11. Berkhofer, *Beyond the Great Story*, p 19.

12. Thus Appleby, Hunt, and Jacob, *Telling the Truth*; Jenkins, *Re-thinking History*; Southgate, *History*, and many others.

13. Munslow, *Deconstructing*, p. 70.

14. Harlan, *Degradation*, pp. xvi, 33, 52, 54, 66, and ch. 2 in general.

15. Bill Readings, *Introducing Lyotard: Art and Politics* (London, 1991), p. 61.

16. McCullagh, *The Truth of History*, pp. 41–42.

17. Zagorin, "Historiography and Postmodernism: Reconsiderations," p. 273.

18. McCullagh, *The Truth of History*, p. 11.

19. For a readable and intelligent account of de Man's career, see Lehman, *Signs of the Times*. The documents are usefully collected in Werner Hamacher, Neil Hertz, and Thomas Keenan (ed.), *Responses: On Paul de Man's Wartime Journalism* (Lincoln, Neb., 1989) and the same editors' *Wartime Journalism 1939–1943, by Paul de Man* (Lincoln, Neb., 1988).

20. Cited in Lehman, *Signs of the Times*, p. 209.

21. Richard Rorty, "Taking Philosophy Seriously," *New Republic* (April 14, 1988), quoted in Lehman, *Signs of the Times*, p. 229.

22. J. Hillis Miller, "An Open Letter to Professor Jon Wiener," in Hamacher et al. (eds.), *Responses*, p. 342.

23. As pointed out by Spitzer, *Historical Truth*, pp. 68–71, here quoting Hillis Miller, who elsewhere had stated that every interpretation of everything was always necessarily false (see Rosenau, *Post-Modernism*, p. 119).

24. All cited in Lehman, *Signs of the Times*, pp. 214, 216, 323–29.

25. Spitzer, *Historical Truth*, p. 11.

26. James T. Kloppenberg, "Objectivity and Historicism: A Century of American Historical Writing," *American Historical Review*, vol. 94 (1989), p. 1030.

27. Paul Morrison, "Paul de Man: Resistance and Collaboration," *Representations*, vol. 32 (1990), p. 71, quoted in Spitzer, *Historical Truth*, p. 94.

28. Dominick LaCapra, "The Personal, the Political and the Textual: Paul de Man as Object of Transference," *History and Memory*, vol. 4 (1992), p. 30, in an article devoted mainly to an utterly implausible psychoanalytical account of the behavior of Derrida and other defenders of de Man.

29. Spitzer, *Historical Truth*, pp. 95–96.

30. Christopher Norris, *Deconstruction and the Interests of Theory* (Norman, Okla., 1989), p. 16.

31. White, *The Content of the Form*, pp. 78–80.

32. Deborah E. Lipstadt, *Denying the Holocaust: The Growing Assault on Truth and Memory* (New York, 1993), p. 1.

33. The *Duke Chronicle*, justifying a decision to print an advertisement by Holocaust deniers, quoted in Lipstadt, *Denying the Holocaust*, p. 198.

34. Cited in Lipstadt, *Denying the Holocaust*, p. 198.

35. Ibid., pp. 3, 137–56, 183–208.

36. Ibid., pp. 19–20.

37. Purkiss, *The Witch*, pp. 164–66. Purkiss argues in ch. 1 of her book, however, that it is wrong of extreme radical feminists to argue that the persecution of witches was comparable to the Holocaust, a view that implies the possibility of objective knowledge of the latter.

38. Jane Caplan, "Postmodernism, Poststructuralism, and Deconstruction: Notes for Historians," *Central European History*, vol. 22 (1989), pp. 274, 278. In quoting these passages, Himmelfarb, *On Looking into the Abyss*, p. 143, convicts Caplan of being unable to decide these issues. But the questions are clearly rhetorical.

39. Appleby, Hunt, and Jacob, *Telling the Truth*, p. 236.

40. Berkhofer, *Beyond the Great Story*, p. 25.

41. See the useful distinctions made in Rosenau, *Post-Modernism*.

42. Simon Schama, *Citizens: A Chronicle of the French Revolution* (New York, 1989).

43. Orlando Figes, *A People's Tragedy: The Russian Revolution 1891–1921* (London, 1996).

44. Robert Finlay, "The Refashioning of Martin Guerre," *American Historical Review*, vol. 93 (1988), pp. 553–71; see also Natalie Zemon Davis, "On the Lame," ibid., pp. 572–603.

45. Harold Mah, "Suppressing the Text: The Metaphysics of Ethnographic History in Darnton's Great Cat Massacre," *History Workshop Journal*, vol. 31 (1991), pp. 1–20; McCullagh, *The Truth of History*, pp. 158–59.

46. Greg Dening, *Mr Bligh's Bad Language: Passion, Power and Theatre on the Bounty* (Cambridge, U.K., 1992), but see also Gannath Obeyesekere, *The Apotheosis of Captain Cook: European Mythmaking in the Pacific* (Princeton, 1992), and Windschuttle, *The Killing of History*, pp. 69–92.

47. Paul Boyer and Stephen Nissenbaum, *Salem Possessed: The Social Origins of Witchcraft* (Cambridge, Mass., 1974); Stuart Clark, *Thinking with Demons: The Idea of Witchcraft in Early Modern Europe* (Oxford, 1997).

48. Berkhofer, *Beyond the Great Story*, pp. 197–201; David Farber, *Chicago '68* (Chicago, 1988).

49. Berkhofer, *Beyond the Great Story*, pp. 281–83.

50. Elton, *Return*, p. 43.

51. McCullagh, *The Truth of History*, pp. 14, 23–25.

52. R. W. Davies, *Soviet History in the Gorbachev Revolution* (London, 1989); Gerd Meyer (ed.), *Wir brauchen die Wahrheit: Geschichtsdiskussion in der Sowjetunion*, 2d ed. (Cologne, 1989).

53. Quoted in Cannadine, *Trevelyan*, pp. 75, 196.

54. Novick, *That Noble Dream*, p. 6.

55. Thomas L. Haskell, "Objectivity Is not Neutrality: Rhetoric and Practice in Peter Novick's *That Noble Dream*," *History and Theory*, vol. 29 (1990), pp. 129–57; quotations on p. 132.

56. Kenneth Cmiel, "After Objectivity: What Comes Next in History?" *American Literary History*, vol. 2 (1990), p. 170, quoted in Harlan, *Degradation*, p. xx.

57. Novick, *That Noble Dream*, pp. 1–2.

58. Haskell, "Objectivity," p. 141. Harlan, *Degradation*, pp. 88–94, attempts to counter Haskell's arguments by asserting that the central criteria they use are moral rather than intellectual. Not only is this not true, but it also sits rather oddly beside the central argument of Harlan's own book, which is precisely that history should be a moral rather than an intellectual enterprise.

59. For this last point, see McCullagh, *The Truth of History*, p. 10.

FURTHER READING

THE classic starting point for thinking about problems such as objectivity, causation, and the role of the individual in history, E. H. Carr's *What Is History?* (London, 1961), was reprinted posthumously in 1987 with a new chapter added on by his collaborator the Soviet specialist R. W. Davies, giving some of Carr's reconsiderations based on notes for a second, revised edition. Carr completed the preface to this planned second edition before he died in 1982, and it is also reprinted by Professor Davies, along with Davies's commentary on Carr's notes. The new material makes interesting reading. Carr evidently intended, for example, to deal with the challenge to history posed by structuralist linguistics; it is a pity that death prevented him from grappling with this problem. Carr's own historical work *A History of Soviet Russia,* 14 vols. (London, 1950–78), is worth consulting to see how he put his views into practice; his book *The Russian Revolution from Lenin to Stalin 1917–1929* (London, 1979) is a handy one-volume summary. Norman Stone, "Grim Eminence," *London Review of Books*, January 20, 1983, pp. 9–12,, is a notorious demolition job on Carr the man as well as Carr the historian.

Carr's principal conservative critic, G. R. Elton, put his views most cogently in *The Practice of History* (Sydney, 1967). This not only offers a trenchant defense of the neo-Rankean view of history as grounded essentially in the sources rather than in the theories and ideas of the historian, but also provides many hints on the practicalities of researching, writing, and teaching. A second book, *Political History: Principles and Practice* (Cambridge, U.K., 1970), adds detail but little else to the argument. Elton's *Return to Essentials: Some Reflections on the Present State of Historical Study* (Cambridge, U.K., 1991), which contains three lectures on postmodernism and history, delivered in Michigan in 1990, is a late exposition of his views in the face of new postmodernist approaches to history. The product of Elton's dotage, they mix prejudice and pomposity in equal measure and are useful mainly as a quarry for alarmist quotes; only the last of the three lectures is really worth reading. The two earlier lectures which make up the rest of this rather thin volume are not much better.

Elton's own qualities as a practicing historian are still best sampled through his first book, *The Tudor Revolution in Government: Administrative Changes in the Reign of Henry VIII* (Cambridge, U.K., 1953). His argument was cogently criticized both in Lawrence Stone, *The Past and the Present* (London, 1981; subsequently republished with new material as *The Past and the Present Revisited* and containing a splendidly readable collection of review essays mostly on major works of social history) and in Penry Williams and G. L. Harriss, "A Revolution in Tudor History?" *Past and Present,* 25 (1963), pp. 3–58. Quentin Skinner, "Sir Geoffrey Elton and the Practice of History," *Transactions of the Royal Historical Society,* 6th series, vol. 7 (1997), pp. 301–16, is a savage and sarcastic critique of Elton's views.

For those who wish to know more about the history of history as a discipline, which features (mostly in passing) in both Carr's and Elton's work, the best introduction is the collection of extracts from historians' manifestos through the ages published by Fritz Stern, *The Varieties of History: From Voltaire to the Present* (Cleveland, 1956). For those seeking an outline history of history, Ernst Breisach, *Historiography: Ancient, Medieval and Modern,* 2d ed. (Chicago, 1994) provides a serviceable, if inevitably brief and selective, introduction. Georg G. Iggers, *New Directions in European Historiography* (Middletown, Conn., 1984) and the same author's updated account, *Historiography in the Twentieth Century: From Scientific Objectivity to the Postmodern Challenge* (Hanover, N.H., 1997), are balanced, lucid, and perceptive. The coverage of German social history is particularly useful. For critical accounts of recent German historiography, see Richard J. Evans, *Rereading German History* (London, 1997) and Stefan Berger, *National Identity and Historical Consciousness in Germany since 1800* (Providence, 1997). The Italian "microhistorians" are best approached through Edward Muir and Guido Ruggiero (eds.), *Microhistory and the Lost Peoples of Europe* (Baltimore, 1991).

Peter Novick, *That Noble Dream: The "Objectivity Question" and the American Historical Profession* (Cambridge, U.K., 1988) is a major historical survey of the American scene, far wider in scope than its title implies. Brilliantly written and profoundly researched, it is full of fascinating material and acutely perceptive analysis; not only essential reading but enjoyable, too. Novick's strongly relativist position has attracted a predictable chorus of criticism. The lengthiest and most persuasive is perhaps by Thomas L. Haskell, "Objectivity Is Not Neutrality: Rhetoric vs. Practice in Peter Novick's *That Noble Dream,*" *History and Theory*, vol. 29 (1990), pp. 129–59; another perceptive critique is James T. Kloppenberg, "Objectivity and Historicism: A Century of American Historical Writing," *American Historical Review*, vol. 94 (1989), pp. 1011–30.

Theodore Hamerow, *Reflections on History and Historians* (Madison, Wis., 1987) offers an alternative, often rather gloomy view of the American historical profession from a conservative point of view, arguing that historians need to reconnect with the popular demand for knowledge about the past, which social science–oriented history has failed to satisfy. Oscar Handlin, *Truth in History,* 2d ed. (New Brunswick, 1998) is a collection of splenetic essays by a curmudgeonly historian of the older generation, lamenting what he sees as a comprehensive decline in standards of historical scholarship in the course of the twentieth century.

Although he wrote little original history himself, the Yale historian J. H. Hexter published a considerable quantity of well-informed, perceptive, and often entertaining analyses of other historians' work. Some of these were collected in his *Reappraisals in History* (London, 1961). See also his *Doing History* (London, 1971), with a useful chapter on E. H. Carr. Hexter's book *On Historians* (London, 1979) contains the famous attack on Christopher Hill, worth looking at as basis for a discussion of perils of some historical methods led by ideology and for the question of whether similar things can be said about all methods. William G. Palmer, "The Burden of Proof: J. H. Hexter and Christopher Hill," *Journal of British Studies*, vol. 19 (1979), pp. 121–29, is a rather self-consciously literary account of the debate that nevertheless manages to make some good critical points. Hexter's attack originally appeared under the title "The Burden of Proof" in the *Times Literary Supplement*, October 24, 1975; for Hill's "Reply to Hexter," see the issue of November 7, 1975; Hexter wrote a "Reply to Hill" in the issue of November 28, 1975.

The changing aspirations and fortunes of social history in America can be traced in three editorials by Peter N. Stearns: "Some Comments on Social History," *Journal of Social History*, vol. 1 (1966–67), pp. 3–6; "Coming of Age," *Journal of Social History*, vol. 10 (1976–77), pp. 246–55; and "Social History Update: Encountering Postmodernism," *Journal of Social History*, vol. 23 (1989–90), pp. 176–87. Ernst Breisach, *American Progressive History: An Experiment in Modernization* (Chicago, 1993) chronicles an important forerunner. Michael Kammen, *The Past before Us: Contemporary Historical Writing in the United States* (Ithaca, 1980) gives an account of the era of social-science domination in the profession.

The conservative American historian Gertrude Himmelfarb, a specialist in the history of Victorian England, has been one of the most trenchant and articulate critics of all forms of historical scholarship which displace politics and events from the center of the picture. Her two collections of essays, *The New History and the Old: Critical Essays and Reappraisals* (Cambridge, Mass., 1987) and *On Looking into the Abyss* (New York, 1994), are essential: highly readable and thought-provoking, but marred by a polemical technique which simply states her own position without arguing it and tries to dispose of alternatives mainly by innuendo about the motives of those who advocate them. Himmelfarb invents something called "the new history" out of very diverse forms of historical scholarship and then castigates it for failing to achieve unity or synthesis, as the (equally imaginary) "old history" of politics supposedly did. Nevertheless, while her overall argument does not really convince, she manages to make a number of important points along the way.

Harvey J. Kaye, *The British Marxist Historians* (Cambridge, U.K., 1984) is a useful and sympathetic introduction to a notable group of practitioners including E. P. Thompson, Eric Hobsbawm, and Christopher Hill. It can be supplemented by Kaye's collection of essays *The Education of Desire: Marxists and the Writing of History* (New York, 1992). There is also an illuminating collection of interviews with these historians and others from the United States edited by Henry Abelove and others, *Visions of History* (New York, 1978), made by the quaintly named Mid-Atlantic Radical Historians' Organization and originally published in its journal, *Radical History*. Georg G. Iggers, *Marxist Historiography in Transformation: East German Social History in the 1980s* (New York, 1991) gives an account of another, more orthodox Marxist tradition, with a number of samples.

The coming of modern, largely non-Marxist social history in Britain was heralded by a special issue of the *Times Literary Supplement* on April 7, 1966, in which the contribution by Keith Thomas is perhaps the most notable. Eric Hobsbawm, "From Social History to the History of Society," *Daedalus*, no. 100 (1971), pp. 20–45, is a classic statement of the optimism social historians felt around this time. Theodore Zeldin, "Social History and Total History," *Journal of Social History*, vol. 10 (1976), pp. 237–45, was an early expression of skepticism by a historian more influenced, perhaps, by the *Annales* school.

On the *Annales* school itself, Peter Burke, *The French Historical Revolution: The Annales School 1929–89* (Oxford, 1990) is disappointingly basic and descriptive and written in almost complete ignorance of the wider intellectual history of France in the period it covers. Peter Burke (ed.), *New Perspectives on Historical Writing* (Oxford, 1991) is also disappointing, arbitrarily thrown together, with contributions of very variable quality, some of them extremely obscurely written; Jim Sharpe's chapter "History from Below," pp. 24–41, is perhaps the most perceptive. The best approach to the *Annales* school is still the wonderful essay by J. H. Hexter in his *On Historians*, written as a parody of the style of Fernand Braudel. Braudel's own musings can be found in his *On History* (Chicago, 1980); those of a leading figure in the third generation of *Annalistes* in Emmanuel Le Roy Ladurie, *The Territory of the Historian* (Brighton, U.K., 1979). Philippe Carrard, *Poetics of the New History: French Historical Discourse from Braudel to Chartier* (Baltimore, 1992) is a recent, critical account of the broader context, approaching this most scientistic of schools through the characteristic postmodernist concept of poetry.

On French thinking about history in a wider sense, Roger Chartier, *On the Edge of the Cliff: History, Language and Practices* (Baltimore, 1997) is a collection of essays, mostly biographical, about historians, mostly French. The first three chapters are by far the most important, steering a middle course between postmodernist skepticism and traditional respect for archivally based facts. Michel de Certeau, *The Writing of History* (New York, 1988) takes a similar line; Paul Ricoeur, *Time and Narrative,* 3 vols. (Chicago, 1984–85), and Paul Veyne, *Writing History: Essay on Epistemology* (Baltimore, 1987) lean more toward the postmodernist side.

John Kenyon, *The History Men: The Historical Profession in England since the Renaissance,* 2d ed. (London, 1993) is an entertaining and well-informed survey of its chosen subject, full of excellent detail; on the other hand, it is also a monument to the inveterate parochialism and conservatism of so many native specialists on English history. This applies even more to John Vincent, *An Intelligent Person's Guide to History* (London, 1995), a brief and sometimes thought-provoking introduction to the discipline which takes much the same point of view as Kenyon, but narrows it down still further, and has some remarkably blinkered and prejudiced passages that demonstrate considerable ignorance about the world of historical scholarship outside the narrow confines of the history of Victorian high politics. As an antidote to Kenyon, Christopher Parker, *The English Historical Tradition since 1850* (Edinburgh, 1990) launches a sustained attack on the traditional empiricism of the profession.

Ved Mehta, *Fly and the Fly-Bottle: Encounters with British Intellectuals* (London, 1963) reprints a series of four lengthy articles originally published in the *New Yorker* magazine. The first two deal with philosophers; the third and fourth are about historians. They include a number of revealing and often hilarious interviews with notable scholars of the day, such as Hugh Trevor-Roper, A. J. P. Taylor, and the eccentric Namierite John Brooke, and offer an entertaining, intelligent, and highly enjoyable introduction to some of the major historical controversies of the 1950s and early 1960s, including the row caused by E. H. Carr's *What Is History?* The fragmentation of the discipline a quarter of a century later can be observed in Juliet Gardiner (ed.), *What Is History Today?* (London, 1988), which brings together a large number of very brief essays on the nature of political history, religious history, military history, and so on by British practitioners of these various genres, some of whom pursue their own hobbyhorses, others of whom occasionally have something of wider interest to say.

Among older works, Pieter Geyl, *Debates with Historians* (London, 1955) is still worth reading for its discussions of historians from Macaulay and Michelet onward and, above all, for its demolition of Arnold Toynbee's *Study of History* in chapters 5 to 8. Geyl's *Napoleon: For and Against* (London, 1954) is a classic study of how historians' judgments have varied and clashed over time, according to the context in which the historians have written; the book concludes with Geyl's famous statement that history is "argument without end."

Writings by philosophers on the nature of history are generally concerned with a narrow range of questions which are approached at a high level of abstraction, far above the level of real works of history. One of the most highly praised of such works, W. H. Walsh, *An Introduction to Philosophy of History*, 3d ed. (London, 1967), is disappointingly labored and now seems seriously out-of-date. Michael Stanford, *The Nature of Historical Knowledge* (Oxford, 1986) is even more labored and mainly tries to develop a systematic description of what historians do, in terms acceptable to a reader trained in philosophy. Stanford's *Companion to the Study of History* (Oxford, 1994) is a disappointingly pedestrian survey of some of the major theoretical problems, relentlessly didactic in tone. R. G. Collingwood, *The Idea of History* (Oxford, 1946) is a difficult but rewarding classic. M. C. Lemon, *The Discipline of History and the History of Thought* (London, 1995) is dense to the point of unreadability and shows little awareness of the real nature of history as it is written and researched today. Martin Bunzl, *Real History: Reflections on Historical Practice* (New York, 1997) seeks to bridge the gap between the philosophy and the practice of history but remains resolutely imprisoned within the former, despite allusions to real historical practice.

The best starting point for postmodernist theories of history is probably the work of the Dutch philosopher Frank Ankersmit, *Narrative Logic: A Semantic Analysis of the Historian's Language* (The Hague, 1983); "Historiography and Post-modernism," *History and Theory*, vol. 28 (1989), pp. 137–53; and *History and Tropology: The Rise and Fall of Metaphor* (Berkeley, 1994). Ankersmit and his American colleague Hans Kellner have edited a varied collection of essays on *A New Philosophy of History* (London, 1995), of which the contribution by the medievalist Nancy F. Partner is the most intelligible. The nature of the turn to postmodernism of radical American historians is clearly expressed by Ellen Somekawa and Elizabeth A. Smith, "Theorizing the Writing of History, or 'I can't think why it should be so dull, for a great deal of it must be invention,' " *Journal of Social History*, vol. 22 (1988), pp. 149–61. David Attridge et al. (eds.), *Poststructuralism and the Question of History* (Cambridge, U.K., 1987) is another collection of essays championing the "linguistic turn."

The most influential single figure in all this has probably been Hayden White, whose much-discussed but little-imitated *Metahistory: The Historical Imagination in Nineteenth-Century Europe* (Baltimore, 1987) was followed by a string of essays, collected in *Tropics of Discourse* (Baltimore, 1978), and *The Content of the Form* (Baltimore, 1987). These texts, for those who care about such things, were structuralist rather than poststructuralist in inspiration, but their use of literary theory to study historical works, and their relativistic relegation of the empirical content of history writing to a side issue or an irrelevancy, opened the way to more radical postmodernist attacks on the ideas of truth and objectivity in historical research in texts such as Linda Hutcheon's *A Poetics of Postmodernism: History, Theory, Fiction* (London, 1988).

David Harlan, *The Degradation of American History* (Chicago, 1997) argues in favor of a "prescientific" idea of history as a form of moral education and includes lengthy accounts of the ideas of White, Rorty, and Foucault. While Harlan still believes in the possibility of writing some kind of history, Elizabeth Deeds Ermarth, *Sequel to History: Postmodernism and the Crisis of Representational Time* (Princeton, 1992), one of the most radical of postmodernist texts on history, argues for the abolition of historical concepts of time and the abandonment of any attempt to write coherently about the past. For an acute critique, see the review by David Carr in *History and Theory*, vol. 32 (1993), pp. 179–87. Sande Cohen, *Historical Culture: On the Recoding of an Academic Discipline* (Berkeley, 1986) is perhaps the most extreme text of all, worth looking at mainly to get an idea of the extent to which an author will go to invent jargon in order to advertise his scientific approach to the subject.

A more moderate and thoughtful survey of postmodernist challenges to historical theory and practice is provided by Robert F. Berkhofer, Jr., *Beyond the Great Story: History as Text and Discourse* (Cambridge, Mass., 1995). Although written in a prose that is dense to the point of sometimes being clogged, Berkhofer's account of the various postmodernist positions is cool and judicious and linked to a real knowledge of how historians actually go about their business. He deals at length with such problems as fact and fiction and the nature of historical time, and puts the characteristic postmodernist plea for reflexive and experimental historical practice in a way that probably comes closer than anybody else's to being acceptable to historians.

For those seeking shortcuts through this thicket of often difficult and demanding literature, two useful anthologies of postmodernist writings on history are: Keith Jenkins (ed.), *The Postmodernist History Reader* (London, 1997) and Joyce Appleby et al. (eds.), *Knowledge and Postmodernism in Historical Perspective* (London, 1996). An early classic is Roland Barthes, "Discourse of History," *Comparative Criticism—A Yearbook,* vol. 3 (Philadelphia, 1991), pp. 3–20; see also the article by Barthes's translator Stephen Bann, "Analysing the Discourse of History," *Renaissance and Modern Studies,* vol. 27 (1983), pp. 61–84.

There have been some notable attempts recently to popularize postmodernist ideas of history. One of the more accessible is Beverley Southgate, *History: What and Why? Ancient, Modern and*

Postmodern Perspectives (London, 1996). The heavy weighting given to the discussion of ancient historians does not help the book's championing of the postmodernist approach. Alun Munslow, *Deconstructing History* (London, 1996) is another postmodernist history primer arguing along broadly similar lines; repetitive and jargon-ridden, it does not make easy reading, and its confused exposition makes it difficult to extract a coherent argument. Keith Jenkins, *Re-thinking History* (London, 1991), an irritating mixture of condescending didacticism and willful obscurity, is still a useful summary—and sometimes vulgarization—of some of the main postmodernist positions. The same author's *On "What Is History"? From Carr and Elton to Rorty and White* (London, 1995) goes over the same ground at greater length and takes up some of the points made by both sides in the growing controversy over postmodernist approaches to history since the beginning of the 1990; nearly half the book is taken up with a labored exposition of the ideas of Richard Rorty and Hayden White. Geoff Eley, "Is all the world a text? From social history to the history of society two decades later," in T. McDonald (ed.), *The Historical Turn in the Human Sciences* (Ann Arbor, 1992), is a largely uncritical account of the "linguistic turn," whose precepts Eley has so far done little to incorporate into his own historical writing.

Among the many replies to and criticisms of the postmodernist attack on history and the "linguistic turn" in historical studies, some of the best have so far appeared in article form. Perez Zagorin, "Historiography and Postmodernism: Reconsiderations," *History and Theory*, vol. 29 (1990), pp. 263–74, is a good place to start, offering a point–by–point reply from an American specialist in seventeenth–century English history to the earlier article in the same journal by Frank Ankersmit in the same journal referred to above; Ankersmit's "Reply to Professor Zagorin," *History and Theory*, vol. 29 (1990), pp. 275–96, is characteristically arrogant and unconvincing. Hayden White's *Metahistory* was the subject of the *Beiheft* No. 19 of *History and Theory*, issued in 1980 under the title *Metahistory: Six Critiques*. Among the most cogent critiques of White's work is an essay by the great historian of ancient Rome Arnaldo Momigliano in his paper "The Rhetoric of History and the History of Rhetoric:

On Hayden White's Tropes," *Comparative Criticism: A Yearbook,* ed. Elinor Shaffer (Cambridge, U.K., 1981), pp. 259–68. White's ideas have also been taken up, and intelligently criticized, in a number of articles by the American intellectual historian Dominick LaCapra. His *History and Criticism* (Ithaca, 1985) is a brief collection of essays, of which the first, "Rhetoric and History," is particularly relevant. Lloyd S. Kramer, "Literature, Criticism, and Historical Imagination: The Literary Challenge of Hayden White and Dominick LaCapra," in Lynn Hunt (ed.), *The New Cultural History* (Berkeley, 1989), pp. 97–128, offers a critical perspective on both writers.

Among recent book-length defenses of history against extreme postmodernist critiques, the most cogent and comprehensive is probably the densely argued but rewarding treatise by the Australian philosopher C. Behan McCullagh, *The Truth of History* (New York, 1998). McCullagh puts forward a reasoned defense of weak but meaningful concepts of truth and objectivity and illustrates his argument with numerous examples from real historical practice. He takes on the whole range of postmodernist writing on history, from White to Jenkins, and deals carefully with all the principal arguments, though sometimes at what may seem excessive length to the more impatient reader.

The well-known essay by Joyce Appleby, Lynn Hunt, and Margaret Jacob *Telling the Truth about History* (New York, 1994), by contrast, is disappointing. Mainly devoted to the specialist field of the history of science, it fails to come up with a convincing refutation of cultural relativism; the last three chapters, however, are worth reading as an attempt to refute the more subversive implications of the postmodernist critique of historical scholarship. A shorter and less pretentious book, by Alan B. Spitzer, *Historical Truth and Lies about the Past* (Chapel Hill, 1996), argues that all political debates about the past, including those in which postmodernists are involved, ultimately appeal to criteria of objective truth and historical accuracy. His account of the de Man affair is particularly illuminating in this respect.

The most vigorous of the book-length critiques, Keith Windschuttle, *The Killing of History: How a Discipline Is being Murdered by Literary Critics and Social Theorists* (Paddington, New South Wales, 1994) is a collection of critical studies on postmodernist historians and their work rather than a general engagement with postmodernist historical theory. As for the author's general argument, the title says it all: This is an alarmist polemic that trashes postmodernist history so comprehensively that the reader is left puzzled as to why anybody should bother with it at all. Where Windschuttle knows his subject, he sometimes hits his target (as in the interesting chapter on *Mutiny on the Bounty*); where he does not, he often misses (as in the chapter on Foucault, where he is let down by his lack of knowledge of European history).

David Lehman, *Signs of the Times. Deconstruction and the Fall of Paul de Man* (London, 1991) is a lucid, witty, and persuasive account of the furor surrounding the discovery of de Man's wartime activities and its implications for some aspects of postmodernist theory. Two volumes edited by Werner Hamacher, Neil Hertz, and Thomas Keenan, *Wartime Journalism 1939–1943, by Paul de Man* (Lincoln, Neb., 1988) and *Responses: On Paul de Man's Wartime Journalism* (Lincoln, Neb., 1989), conveniently present virtually all the relevant material. Taking its cue from another, far less weighty scandal, Paul Boghossian, "What the Sokal hoax ought to teach us," *Times Literary Supplement*, December 13, 1996, pp. 14–15, is a cogent and forceful attack on key postmodernist positions, taking as its starting point the uproar occasioned by the acceptance of the postmodernist magazine *Social Text* of an article its author subsequently admitted was a parody of postmodernism, signaling its identity as a spoof by including numerous deliberate mistakes.

The most balanced and informed critique from the left came from Raphael Samuel, in his two-part article "Reading the Signs," *History Workshop Journal,* 32 and 33 (1992), pp. 220–51. Like much of Samuel's work, it remained unfinished, and the promised third part, containing a direct critique of postmodernist hyperrelativism, never appeared. Bryan D. Palmer, *Descent into Discourse: The Reification of Language and the Writing of History* (Philadelphia, 1990) is a disappointingly crude attack on the "linguistic turn," reflecting the vulgar-Marxist position of its author. Another Marxist attack, on a more general front, Terry Eagleton's self-indulgent and overwritten tract *The Illusions of Postmodernism* (Oxford, 1996), does not even begin to address the challenge postmodernism poses to history. Much better is Eric Hobsbawm's *On History* (London, 1997), a collection of essays which includes a perceptive critique of postmodernist anthropology and some trenchant defenses of Hobsbawm's own brand of Marxism. Another Marxist text, Alex Callinicos, *Theories and Narratives: Reflections on the Philosophy of History* (Cambridge, U.K., 1995), argues a similar position based on a belief that the truth in history can be found and Marxism is the best way to find it. Harvey J. Kaye, *The Powers of the Past: Reflections on the Crisis and the Promise of History* (Madison, Wis., 1991) urges the restoration of "grand narratives" written from a self-consciously left-wing point of view. Christopher Norris, *Deconstruction and the Interests of Theory* (Norman, Okla., 1989) is another, rather less lucid attack from the left.

Pauline Marie Rosenau, *Post-Modernism and the Social Sciences: Insights, Inroads, and Intrusions* (Princeton, 1992) is a levelheaded and wide-ranging survey of the state of play at the beginning of the 1990s. It usefully distinguishes between ultraskeptical variants of postmodernism, which are deeply subversive of the social sciences, including history, and more constructive ones, which can be helpful and stimulating to self-reflection and disciplinary renewal. Another useful survey is provided by David Harvey, *The Condition of Postmodernism: An Enquiry into the Origins of Cultural Change* (Oxford, 1991).

Joan W. Scott, *Gender and the Politics of History* (New York, 1988) offers some postmodernist arguments in favor of the "linguistic turn" from a feminist perspective. Catherine Hall, "Politics, Post-structuralism and Feminist History," *Gender and History*, vol. 3 (1991), pp. 204–10, voices some mild doubts. The Michigan-based historical anthropology journal *Comparative Studies in Society and History* ran an interesting and important exchange at the feminist end of the postmodernist spectrum in 1993. Laura Lee Downs, "If 'Woman' Is Just an Empty Category, Then Why Am I Afraid to Walk Alone at Night? Identity Politics Meets the Postmodern Subject," *Comparative Studies in Society and History*, vol. 35 (1993), pp. 414–37, begins with a perceptive critique of Scott's approach, but follows it up by a lengthy and not very plausible account of some psychohistorical work as a possible alternative. Scott's angry and dismissive reply, accusing Downs of "ignorance and misrepresentation," a "glib . . . superficial . . . and schematic" approach, and "an abdication of professional responsibility," concluded that the article "cannot be the basis for a serious discussion of the issues raised by post-structuralist and psychoanalytic theories for history." It appeared as " 'The Tip of the Volcano,' " *Comparative Studies in Society and History*, vol. 35 (1993), pp. 438–43, and seems to me to be itself largely a tissue of misunderstandings and misrepresentations and indeed in part sheer invention; it was followed by Downs's "Reply to Joan Scott," *Comparative Studies in Society and History*, vol. 35 (1993), pp. 444-51, which does not add much, mainly because of its understandable refusal to pay back Scott in the same linguistic coinage.

Outside the specialized pages of *History and Theory*, the debate about history and postmodernism in the journals was slow to get started. The *American Historical Review* was first in the field, with an article by John E. Toews, "Intellectual History after the Linguistic Turn," *American Historical Review*, vol. 92 (1987), pp. 879–908, followed by a double symposium on postmodernism in its 1989 issue. The opening article, by David Harlan, "Intellectual History and the Return of Literature," *American Historical Review*, vol. 94 (1989), pp. 581–609, puts the postmodernist case that intellectual history which tried to recover the meanings intended by authors like Thomas Hobbes or John Locke by relating them to their historical context was simply a "trick"; the response by David Hollinger, "The Return of the Prodigal? The Persistence of Historical Knowing," *American Historical Review*, vol. 94 (1989), pp. 610–21, is disappointingly self-indulgent and fails to grapple with the central theoretical points at issue. David Harlan's "Reply to David Hollinger," *American Historical Review*, vol. 94 (1989), pp. 622–26, repays him in the same coin. A second piece, by Allan Megill, "Recounting the Past: 'Description,' Explanation, and Narrative in Historiography," *American Historical Review*, vol. 94 (1989), pp. 627–53, says little of interest beyond attempting to rehabilitate description and narrative in the face of criticisms by *Annales* and other "structural" historians who dismissed them as mere fact grubbing. It was followed by a diverse set of articles in a forum on "The Old History and the New": Theodore S. Hamerow, "The Bureaucratization of History," *American Historical Review*, vol. 94 (1989), pp. 654–60; Gertrude Himmelfarb, "Some Reflections on the New History," *American Historical Review*, vol. 94 (1989), pp. 655–70; Lawrence W. Levine, "The Unpredictable Past: Reflections on Recent American Historiography," *American Historical Review*, vol. 94 (1989), pp. 671–79; Joan Wallach Scott, "History in Crisis? The Others' Side of the Story," *American Historical Review*, vol. 94 (1989), pp. 680–92; and a judicious summing-up by John E. Toews, "Perspectives on 'The Old History and the New': A Comment," *American Historical Review*, vol. 94 (1989), pp. 693–98, which managed to place Hamerow and Scott in one camp and Himmelfarb and Levine in the other, thus neatly reversing the polarities intended by the other four contributors. The forum spawned a further set of contributions, including Joyce Appleby, "One Good Turn Deserves Another: Moving Beyond the Linguistic: A Response to David Harlan," *American Historical Review*, vol. 94 (1989), pp. 1326–32. It continued in the *American Historical Review*, vol. 97 (April 1992), in the form of an entertainingly critical article by Russell Jacoby, "A New Intellectual History?" pp. 405–24, and a rather pompous and vapid reply by Dominick LaCapra, "Intellectual History and Its Ways," pp. 425–39.

The debate in *Central European History*, though focusing on the implications of postmodernism and the "linguistic turn" specifically for historians of Germany, was also wide-ranging. A number of articles were published in a special double issue of vol. 22 (1989), nos. 53–54, on "German Histories: Challenges in Theory, Practice, Technique," resulting from a conference held in October 1989 on postmodern challenges to German history. The seeming promptness of publication was deceptive. At that time the journal, produced in Atlanta, Georgia, was running years behind schedule. Hence the seemingly incongruous remark of the editors of the special 1989 issue that the conference was held "ages ago" (p. 229), when the volume would actually seem to the uninitiated to have been published

actually before the conference had taken place. Among the most rel-
evant contributions are Michael Geyer and Konrad H. Jarausch, "The
Future of the German Past: Transatlantic Reflections for the 1990s,"
pp. 229–59; Isabel V. Hull, "Feminist and Gender History through the
Literary Looking Glass: German Historiography in Postmodern
Times," pp. 279–300; Rudy Koshar, "Playing the Cerebral Savage:
Notes on Writing German History before the Linguistic Turn," pp.
343–59; and Konrad H. Jarausch, "Towards a Social History of
Experience: Postmodern Predicaments in Theory and Interdisciplin-
arity," pp. 427–43, all of which are written from an explicitly postmodernist perspective. Jane Caplan, "Postmodernism, Poststructuralism, and Deconstruction: Notes for Historians," pp. 260–78,
offers an intelligently argued corrective. It is worth noting that while
the actual historical work of one of the two editors, Michael Geyer,
never easy to understand at the best of times, has now descended into
complete incomprehensibility, the work of the other, Konrad H.
Jarausch, remains resolutely empirical and has been seemingly completely uninfluenced by the postmodernist principles he appeared to
embrace in 1989 (see, for example, Konrad H. Jarausch, *The Rush to
German Unity* [New York, 1994]).

The debate in the British journals was generally less illuminating.
The controversy in *Social History* centered on a book of (mostly previously published essays) by the Cambridge historian Gareth
Stedman Jones, *Languages of Class: Studies in English Working Class
History 1832–1982* (New York, 1983), which registered its author's
early enthusiasm for the "linguistic turn." Reflecting Stedman Jones's
position as an influential figure in the rather restricted field of the
left-wing, broadly Marxist historiography of the nineteenth-century
British labor movement, the controversy had a decidedly parochial
feel to it, which became stronger as it developed. It began with an
article by David Mayfield, "Language and Social History," in *Social
History*, vol. 16 (1991), pp. 353–58, and followed up by David Mayfield
and Susan Thorne, "Social history and its discontents: Gareth
Stedman Jones and the politics of language," *Social History*, vol. 17
(1992), pp. 165–88. This was followed by an angry and rather opaque
riposte from two of Stedman Jones's Cambridge pupils, Jon

Lawrence and Miles Taylor, "The Poverty of Protest: Gareth Stedman Jones and the Politics of Language—a Reply," *Social History*, vol. 18 (1993), pp. 1–15, and another, even more irritated reply from the ubiquitous Patrick Joyce, "The imaginary discontents of social history: a note of response to Mayfield and Thorne, and Lawrence and Taylor," *Social History*, vol. 18 (1993), pp. 81–85. The controversy rumbled on, with an increasing tendency to generate more heat than light, and accusations of "reductionism" flying around on all sides, in David Mayfield and Susan Thorne, "Reply to 'The poverty of protest' and 'The imaginary discontents,' " *Social History*, vol. 18 (1993), pp. 219–33; James Vernon, "Who's afraid of the 'linguistic turn'? The politics of social history and its discontents," *Social History*, vol. 19 (1994), pp. 81–97; Neville Kirk, "History, Language, Ideas and Post-modernism: A Materialist View," *Social History*, vol. 19 (1994), pp. 221–40; Patrick Joyce, "The end of social history?" *Social History*, vol. 20 (1995), pp. 73–91; and Geoff Eley and Keith Nield, "Starting over: the present, the post-modern and the moment of social history," *Social History*, vol. 20 (1995), pp. 355–64, the last named being confined mainly to an attempt to rescue the concept of "class" in a Marxist sense, misreading Patrick Joyce's position and largely avoiding the substantive issues, as Joyce points out in his rejoinder, "The end of social history? A brief reply to Eley and Nield," *Social History*, vol. 21 (1996), pp. 96–98. The whole debate is predicated on a narrow understanding of social history as a fundamentally Marxist project; it is of course far wider, and more diverse, than that.

Somewhat tangential to this debate, but well worth reading, is Anthony Easthope, "Romancing the Stone: history-writing and Rhetoric," *Social History*, vol. 18 (1993), pp. 235–49, combining a brief exposition of some postmodernist ideas on history with an interesting analysis of the rather tired metaphors used by Professor Lawrence Stone in an article of 1958; the theoretical consequences of the not altogether new discovery that Professor Stone is prone to use cliché-ridden language are not immediately clear. Easthope does establish that the article in question assumes people bought titles for material rather than cultural reasons, but this is only an article, after all, and a familiarity with *The Crisis of the Aristocracy* would have shown Dr.

Easthope that Professor Stone was aware of other aspects of the aspirations of the upper classes in sixteenth- and seventeenth-century England as well. Nevertheless, this is one of a relatively small number of texts based on a linguistic analysis of a practicing historian's published work, and important for that reason if for no other.

Easthope's analysis was a discussion point when the debate exploded in the *Journal of Contemporary History* with an article by one of the journal's editorial board, Arthur Marwick, "Two Approaches to Historical Study: The Metaphysical (Including 'Postmodernism') and the Historical," *Journal of Contemporary History*, vol. 30 (1995), pp. 5–35, an intemperate and sometimes ill-informed attack on a variety of targets, first delivered as Professor Marwick's inaugural lecture (after decades of occupation of the chair of History at the Open University) under the title "Metahistory Is Bunk—History Is Essential." It should be read in conjunction with the measured and surprisingly readable "Response to Arthur Marwick" by Hayden White in the same journal, vol. 30 (1995), pp. 233–46. The exchange prompted a series of articles in the *Journal of Contemporary History*, vol. 31 (1996), in which the noise of grinding axes is sometimes difficult to ignore. They included Christopher Lloyd, "For Realism and against the Inadequacies of Common Sense: A Response to Arthur Marwick," pp. 191–207; Beverley Southgate, "History and Metahistory: Marwick versus White," pp. 209–14; Wulf Kansteiner, "Searching for an Audience: The Historical Profession in the Media Age—A Comment on Arthur Marwick and Hayden White," pp. 215–19; and Geoffrey Roberts, "Narrative History as a Way of Life," pp. 221–28.

Briefer, but more to the point than much of this, was the exchange in *Past and Present* sparked by Lawrence Stone's opening warning shot, "History and Post-Modernism," *Past and Present*, 131 (1991), pp. 217–18, and followed by Patrick Joyce, "History and Post-Modernism," *Past and Present*, 133 (1991), pp. 204–09, Gabrielle Spiegel, "History and Post-Modernism," *Past and Present*, 135 (1992), pp. 194–208, Catriona Kelly, "History and Post-Modernism," *Past and Present*, 133 (1991), pp. 209–13, and a further exchange between Stone and Joyce under the same title in issue 133, pp. 204–11, and 135, pp.

189–94. Gabrielle Spiegel, "History, Historicism, and the Social Logic of the Text in the Middle Ages," *Speculum*, vol. 65 (1990), pp. 59–96, is also relevant here.

What a postmodernist history might look like can be sampled in Patrick Joyce, *Democratic Subjects: The Self and the Social in Nineteenth-Century England* (London, 1994), Diane Purkiss, *The Witch in History: Early Modern and Twentieth-Century Representations* (London, 1996), Stuart Clark, *Thinking with Demons: The Idea of Witchcraft in Early Modern Europe* (Oxford, 1997), Natalie Zemon Davis, *The Return of Martin Guerre* (Cambridge, Mass., 1983), and Robert Darnton, *The Great Cat Massacre* (London, 1983). Two important critiques of the two last-named books, raising many wider issues, are Robert Finlay, "The Refashioning of Martin Guerre," *American Historical Review*, vol. 93 (1988), pp. 55–71, with a reply from Davis ("On the Lame"), ibid., pp. 572–603; and Harold Mah, "Suppressing the Text: The Metaphysics of Ethnographic History in Darnon's Great Cat Massacre," *History Workshop Journal*, 31 (1991), pp. 1–20. Simon Schama, *Citizens: A Chronicle of the French Revolution* (New York, 1989) and Orlando Figes, *A People's Tragedy: The Russian Revolution 1891–1921* (London, 1996) exemplify the best aspects of postmodernism's influence, conscious or otherwise, on mainstream history, Simon Schama, *Dead Certainties* (London, 1991), the worst (see the review by Gordon S. Wood in *New York Review of Books*, no. 38 [June 22, 1991], pp. 12–16).

Some of the most problematical aspects of postmodernist hyper-relativism are laid bare in Deborah E. Lipstadt, *Denying the Holocaust: The Growing Assault on Truth and Memory* (New York, 1993), a sober and well-informed account of the history of attempts, now effectively organized into a movement, to deny the reality of Hitler's death camps and the policies that led to them. Saul Friedländer (ed.), *Probing the Limits of Representation: Nazism and the "Final Solution"* (Cambridge, Mass., 1992) provides a crucial collection of conference papers, including a rethinking by Hayden White of his earlier positions ("Historical Emplotment and the Problem of Truth," pp. 37–53).

Finally, the "Abraham controversy," in which issues central to the debate over objectivity and partisanship in historical research were raised, is best approached through the special issue of the journal *Central European History* devoted to it, vol. 17 (1984), beginning with a lengthy critique of Abraham's work by Gerald D. Feldman, "A Collapse in Weimar Scholarship," on pp. 159–77.

INDEX